ORESTES AND OTHER PLAYS

EURIPIDES was born in Attica (the country whose main city was Athens) about 485 BCE. By the time of his death in 406 BCE he had written at least eighty plays, which were performed at the Great Dionysia, the Athenians' major drama festival. Seventeen of these survive complete. The universality of the conflicts he explores, and the startling realism of his characterization, ensure that he has also been by far the most often adapted, staged, and filmed of the ancient dramatists from the Renaissance to the present day. The four plays in this volume are all informed by implicit messages for the Athens of Euripides' own day. In them he explores ethical and political themes, contrasting the claims of patriotism with family loyalty, pragmatism, and expediency with justice, and the idea that 'might is right' with the ideal of clemency. *Ion* is a vivid portrait of the role of chance in human life and an exploration of family relationships, which combines a sympathetic portrait of a rape victim with remarks on Athenian xenophobia. In *Orestes*, the most popular of the tragedian's plays in the ancient world, Euripides explores the emotional consequences of Orestes' murder of his mother on the individuals concerned, and makes the tale resonate with advice to Athens about the threat to democracy posed by political pressure groups. *Suppliant Women* is a commentary on the politics of empire, as the Athenian king Theseus decides to use force of arms rather than persuasion against Thebes. *Phoenician Women* transforms the terrible conflict between Oedipus' sons into one of the most savage indictments of civil war in Western literature by highlighting the personal tragedy it brings.

ROBIN WATERFIELD is a full-time writer and translator whose work includes a biography of Kahlil Gibran and translations, for Oxford World's Classics, of Plato's *Republic*, *Symposium*, and *Gorgias*, Aristotle's *Physics*, Herodotus' *Histories*, Plutarch's *Greek Lives* and *Roman Lives*, and *The First Philosophers: The Presocratics and the Sophists*.

EDITH HALL is Leverhulme Professor of Greek Cultural History at the University of Durham, and co-director of the Archive of Performances of Greek and Roman Drama at the University of Oxford. She wrote introductions for the Oxford World's Classics editions of Euripides' *Medea and Other Plays*, *Bacchae and Other Plays*, and *The Trojan Women and Other Plays*.

JAMES MORWOOD is Grocyn Lecturer in Classics and Fellow of Wadham College at Oxford University where he teaches Latin and Greek. He has translated Euripides' *Medea and Other Plays*, *Bacchae and Other Plays*, and *The Trojan Women and Other Plays* for Oxford World's Classics, and his other books include *A Dictionary of Latin Words and Phrases* and works on Sheridan.

OXFORD WORLD'S CLASSICS

For over 100 years Oxford World's Classics have brought readers closer to the world's great literature. Now with over 700 titles—from the 4,000-year-old myths of Mesopotamia to the twentieth century's greatest novels—the series makes available lesser-known as well as celebrated writing.

The pocket-sized hardbacks of the early years contained introductions by Virginia Woolf, T. S. Eliot, Graham Greene, and other literary figures which enriched the experience of reading. Today the series is recognized for its fine scholarship and reliability in texts that span world literature, drama and poetry, religion, philosophy and politics. Each edition includes perceptive commentary and essential background information to meet the changing needs of readers.

OXFORD WORLD'S CLASSICS

EURIPIDES

Ion · Orestes
Phoenician Women
Suppliant Women

Translated by
ROBIN WATERFIELD

Introduction by
EDITH HALL

Notes by
JAMES MORWOOD

OXFORD
UNIVERSITY PRESS

Great Clarendon Street, Oxford OX2 6DP

Oxford University Press is a department of the University of Oxford.
It furthers the University's objective of excellence in research, scholarship,
and education by publishing worldwide in

Oxford New York

Athens Auckland Bangkok Bogotá Buenos Aires Cape Town
Chennai Dar es Salaam Delhi Florence Hong Kong Istanbul Karachi
Kolkata Kuala Lumpur Madrid Melbourne Mexico City Mumbai Nairobi
Paris São Paulo Shanghai Singapore Taipei Tokyo Toronto Warsaw

with associated companies in Berlin Ibadan

Oxford is a registered trade mark of Oxford University Press
in the UK and in certain other countries

Published in the United States
by Oxford University Press Inc., New York

First published as an Oxford World's Classics paperback 2001

British Library Cataloguing in Publication Data

Data available

Library of Congress Cataloging in Publication Data

Data available

ISBN-13: 978-0-19-283260-3

3

Typeset by RefineCatch Limited, Bungay, Suffolk
Printed in Great Britain by
Clays Ltd, St Ives plc

CONTENTS

ABBREVIATIONS

A&A	*Antike und Abendland*
AJP	*American Journal of Philology*
ASNP	*Annali della Scuola Normale di Pisa, Classe di Lettere e Filosofia*
BICS	*Bulletin of the Institute of Classical Studies*
CJ	*Classical Journal*
CP	*Classical Philology*
CQ	*Classical Quarterly*
CR	*Classical Review*
CSCA	*California Studies in Classical Antiquity*
G&R	*Greece & Rome*
GRBS	*Greek, Roman, and Byzantine Studies*
HSCP	*Harvard Studies in Classical Philology*
JHS	*Journal of Hellenic Studies*
PCPS	*Proceedings of the Cambridge Philological Society*
REA	*Revue des Études Anciennes*
REG	*Revue des Études Grecques*
SO	*Symbolae Osloenses*
TAPA	*Transactions and Proceedings of the American Philological Association*
WS	*Wiener Studien*
YCS	*Yale Classical Studies*
s.d.	*stage direction*

INTRODUCTION

EURIPIDES AND HIS TRADITION

The earliest surviving work of sustained theatrical criticism, Aristophanes' comedy *Frogs*, was first produced in 405 BCE, just three years after the premiere of Euripides' *Orestes* and one year after Euripides' death. The comic poet stages a contest in Hades for the throne of tragic poetry; the two contenders are the deceased tragedians Aeschylus and Euripides. One of Euripides' claims to supremacy is that his tragedy was 'democratic' in that it allowed women and slaves to talk as freely as male masters of households (948–50). The response of the 'umpire' Dionysus, the god of drama, is informative: 'Leave that issue alone, my friend. That is not a direction in which I would take the discussion, if I were you' (953).

Dionysus responds in this way because by the end of his life Euripides, far from being perceived as a democrat, was suspected of harbouring sympathy with the oligarchic faction in Athens. But, more importantly, this little interchange demonstrates that contemporary discussion about Euripides already acknowledged that his drama was politically charged. One of the reasons for grouping together the four plays included in this volume is that they are amongst the most political he composed. And they are political in a different way from the tragedies on the theme of international war between Greeks and Trojans in the volume *The Trojan Women and Other Plays*. Each one thinks about political discord as it affects individual Greek city-states, whether it is the Athenian obsession with the exclusion of aliens (*Ion*), imminent revolution in Argos (*Orestes*), civil war in Thebes (*Phoenician Women*), or the impact of Theban civil war on the politics of the Athenian empire (*Suppliant Women*).

Phoenician Women has always been seen as a play about statecraft. It was apparently much studied by Roman leaders. Julius Caesar enjoyed quoting the lines of Eteocles in which he argues that wrongdoing may be justifiable for the sake of winning a crown (524–5, Suetonius, *Caesar* 30); Augustus' favourite line from the play praises prudence in a soldier above courage (599, Suetonius, *Augustus* 25), while Tiberius had a playwright executed for embedding a line (393) in a new play of his own (Cassius Dio 58.24). *Suppliant Women*, similarly, was regarded by later antiquity as a theatrical exploration of the responsibilities inherent in the military dimension of government. These two plays' reputations gave rise to a fascinating story reported by the historian Diodorus Siculus (13.97) concerning the sea-battle of Arginusae in the eastern Aegean (406 BCE), the Athenians' last, tainted victory in the Peloponnesian war.

The Athenian commander Thrasyllus had a dream that he and six of the other Athenian generals were back at home, performing *Phoenician Women* in a theatrical competition. Opposing them were the commanders on the enemy side, acting in *Suppliant Women*. Although the Athenian acting team was victorious, they subsequently died, just like the seven besiegers of Thebes, whose deaths are central to both tragedies. Thrasyllus' dream proved prophetic, for the Athenian generals were indeed put to death by their own fellow citizens for failing to pick up and bring to safety large numbers of the shipwrecked crews. Euripides' late, political war tragedies have thus, by the time Diodorus was writing in the late first century BCE, already become embedded in the narrative of democratic Athens' own tragedy during the last years of the Peloponnesian war.

Yet however important the political dimension of these four tragedies, they are also connected by certain more psychological concerns, for example by their distinctive studies of old people. This feature of Euripidean tragedy used to inspire derision: critics throughout the nineteenth and early twentieth century recycled the influential A. W. Schlegel's complaint that Euripides' 'aged persons are always complaining of the wants and helplessness of age, and crawl with trembling joints up the ascent from the orchestra to the stage . . . sighing over the misery of their situation.'[1] But this is to misunderstand Euripides' senior citizens, whose age compounds their tragic situations, especially in the cases of the doubly bereaved Iphis of *Suppliant Women* or the suicidal Oedipus of *Phoenician Women*. Euripides was himself in his sixties and seventies when all these plays were first produced, and they emphasize that old people do not lose their capacity for destructive moral agency; both Creusa's ferocious slave in *Ion* and the vindictive Tyndareus of *Orestes* exert a malign influence on younger people for whom they have a responsibility of care.

[1] A. W. Schlegel, *A Course of Lectures on Dramatic Art and Literature*, second edn. trans. John Black (London, 1840), i. 149.

The plays are also profoundly theatrical texts, showing Euripides experimenting with the effect of crowding the stage with large numbers of people (all except *Ion* have a big cast and plethora of mute 'extras'), with the adventurous use of the physical theatre, with suspense, surprise, humour, and with pushing his audience's emotional responses to their limits. The innovative plot of *Orestes*, for example, takes its audience on a continuously accelerating roller-coaster from the pathos of the opening 'sickbed' scene through the shocking brutality of the plot to murder Helen, the overt comedy of Orestes' encounter with Helen's Asiatic slave, the tense denouement and unprecedentedly spectacular conclusion. Said by an ancient commentator to be one of the plays that 'works best in the theatre', *Orestes* achieved its success through serial laughter, tears, pity, fear, astonishment, and overwhelming excitement. It is little wonder that it was perhaps the most popular of all Euripides' plays in antiquity.

The Greeks and Romans were passionate about the innovative and emotive Euripides. A character in a comedy announced that he would be prepared to hang himself for the sake of seeing this (by then dead) tragedian (Philemon fr. 118).[2] Aristotle's formalist discussion of tragedy complains about Euripides' use of the *deus ex machina*, his unintegrated choruses, and the 'unnecessary' villainy of some of his characters, including the odiously two-faced Menelaus of *Orestes*. Yet even Aristotle conceded that Euripides was 'the most tragic of the poets', meaning that he was the best at eliciting fear and pity in his spectators (*Poetics* 56^{a}25–7, 54^{b}1, 61^{b}21, 53^{a}20).

In his *Rhetoric*, Aristotle also revealingly states that Euripides was the first tragic poet to make his characters speak naturally in everyday vocabulary (Aristotle *Rhet.* 3.1404^{b}18–25). For the single most significant reason underlying Euripides' remarkable ancient popularity was probably the accessible, fluent, and memorable poetry in which his characters expressed themselves: even Alexander the Great, no professional actor, is supposed to have been able to perform a whole episode of a Euripidean tragedy off by heart as a party trick (Athenaeus, *Deipnosophists* 12.537d–e). The audiences adored the accessibility and psychological immediacy not only of the diction but of the *sentiments* Euripides attributed to his Bronze Age heroes: a good example is Electra's irritated command to the chorus of *Orestes*,

[2] Fragments of comedy are cited throughout from R. Kassel and C. Austin (eds.), *Poetae Comici Graeci* (Berlin, 1983–95).

who enter dancing and singing enthusiastically, to be quiet lest they disturb her ailing brother (136–7).[3] Thus Argive princesses and Spartan heroes, slaves and high priestesses, practitioners of human sacrifice, incest, and kin-killing: Euripides made them all 'speak like human beings' (see Aristophanes, *Frogs* 1058).

Euripidean tragedy became 'classic' almost immediately after his death, and was consistently revived across the entire Greek-speaking world and the Roman empire into the Christian era. It was imitated by Roman tragedians—a version of *Phoenician Women* is attributed to Seneca—and made a huge impact on the non-tragic literature of succeeding generations, especially Menander, Virgil, Ovid, and the orators of both Greece and Rome. Both *Orestes* and *Phoenician Women* survived because they were regarded as sufficiently important in the first or second century CE to be chosen among the ten Euripidean tragedies selected for study in the schools of the ancient world; the reason was probably that they contain some of his most spectacularly rhetorical speeches, which made good models for an education centred on oratory. These two plays, along with *Hecuba*, were actually the Byzantines' favourite tragedies. Moreover, Euripides' plays are everywhere apparent in the *visual* culture of the Mediterranean. Homer apart, no author stimulated the arts more. The Romans painted Euripides' scenes on their walls and carved them on their sarcophagi; a painting of the late second century CE depicting actors performing the opening scene of *Orestes* has recently been discovered on the wall of a house in Ephesus in Asia Minor;[4] the Byzantines commissioned elaborate mosaics keeping his pagan myths alive in the visual imagination of Christendom.

The nineteenth-century scholar Benjamin Jowett said this tragedian was 'no Greek in the better sense of the term',[5] for after his revivification in the Renaissance Euripides often suffered by comparison with the structural perfection, 'purity', and 'Hellenic' spirit perceived in his rival Sophocles. This is, however, to simplify the complex and largely unwritten story of Euripidean reception and performance. *Ion*, although rarely performed in translation until

[3] All references to Euripides' plays refer to the standard numeration of the Oxford Classical Text of James Diggle.

[4] Reproduced in Richard Green and Eric Handley, *Images of the Greek Theatre* (Austin, Tex., 1995), 97.

[5] See A. N. Michelini, *Euripides and the Tragic Tradition* (Madison, 1987), 11 n. 40.

recently,[6] has been the source of several operas since Louis Lacoste's *Créuse l'Athénienne* was performed at the Paris Opéra in 1712. Its adaptations as a stage play include William Whitehead's *Creusa* (a star vehicle for David Garrick at Drury Lane in 1754), A. W. von Schlegel's *Ion*, performed at Weimar in 1803 under the direction of Goethe, a radical republican *Ion* by an advocate of universal suffrage, Thomas Talfourd, staged at Covent Garden in 1836, and even T. S. Eliot's verse drama *The Confidential Clerk*, which premiered at the Edinburgh festival in 1953. *Ion*'s famous recognition scene, with its basketwork crib, also lies behind the famous 'handbag' episode in Oscar Wilde's *The Importance of Being Earnest* (first performed in 1895).

Phoenician Women was a popular play in the Renaissance, adapted in an Italian version called *Giocasta* by Ludovico Dolce (1554); Dolce's play, freely adapted in English as *Jocasta* by George Gascoigne and F. Kinwelmershe, was, when performed at Gray's Inn in 1566, one of the earliest versions of a Greek tragedy to be seen on an English stage. The most important neoclassical adaptations were Racine's *Les Frères ennemis* (1664) and Alfieri's not dissimilar *Polinice* (1783), but Schiller translated part of *Phoenician Women*, and the tragedy's fratricidal theme underlies his *The Bride of Messina* (1803). In unadapted form, moreover, this tragedy has lately been revived in some important professional productions;[7] one reason is certainly that the recent dissolution of the former Eastern bloc has created profound contemporary resonances for the play's depiction of civil war.

In comparison, *Orestes* has been rarely performed or adapted, remaining in the shadow of the treatments of Orestes' story in Aeschylus' *Oresteia* and the *Electra* plays of Euripides and Sophocles; *Suppliant Women* is now one of the least read or acted of all Greek tragedies. Yet in general the last hundred years have smiled on Euripides more than any era since antiquity. One reason is his approach to myth, which has been characterized as subversive, experimental, playful, and eccentric in an identifiably modern way. Although he has occasionally been seen as a formalist or mannerist,

[6] In 1994 there were *two* important productions in London, one by the RSC (starring Jude Law) and the other by Actors' Touring Company at the Lyric, Hammersmith. See *TLS*, 28 Oct. 1994, 21; Ruth Padel, '*Ion*: Lost and Found', *Arion*, 4 (1996), 216–24; Edith Hall, 'Greek Tragedy and the British Stage', *Cahiers du GITA*, 12 (1999), 113–34, at p. 133.

[7] e.g. Katie Mitchell's stunning RSC production at The Other Place, Stratford-upon-Avon, in 1995. See *TLS* for 10 Nov 1995, 35.

the term 'irony' dominates criticism. 'Irony' is taken to describe Euripides' polytonality—his ability to write in two simultaneous keys. This 'irony', however, is conceived in more than one way: sometimes it describes the hypocritical gap between the rhetorical postures which Euripidean characters adopt and their true motives: an outstanding examples in *Orestes* is Menelaus, a smooth-talking liar and opportunist. Alternatively, 'irony' defines the confrontation of archaic myths with the values of democratic Athens, a process which deglamorizes violence, casting heroic stories of bloodshed and conflict—for example, the vindictive attempt made by Orestes and Pylades to murder Helen in *Orestes*—as sordid 'gangland killings'.[8]

Another reason for Euripides' modern popularity is that his supple and multi-faceted works easily adapt to the agendas of different interpreters. Euripides has been an existentialist, a psychoanalyst, a proto-Christian with a passionate hunger for 'righteousness', an idealist and humanist, a mystic, a rationalist, an irrationalist, and an absurdist nihilist. But perhaps the most tenacious Euripides has been the pacifist feminist.

'Radical' Euripides was born in the first decade of this century with Gilbert Murray as midwife. This famous liberal scholar, later Chairman of the League of Nations, was himself a radical, and found his own restless intellect and interests mirrored in Euripides. The ancient dramatist, wrote the young Murray, was 'a man of extraordinary brain-power, dramatic craft, subtlety, sympathy, courage, imagination; he pried too close into the world and took things too rebelliously to produce calm and successful poetry.'[9] A few years later Murray initiated in Edwardian London a series of performances of Euripides in his own English translations. *Trojan Women* (1905) was interpreted by many as a retrospective indictment of the concentration camps in which the British had interned and starved Boer women and children during the Boer War; as a result of *Medea* (1907) the heroine's monologue on the plight of women (see below, 'Athenian Society') was recited at suffragette meetings.[10] Murray's

[8] This phrase is borrowed from W. G. Arnott's excellent article, 'Double the Vision: A Reading of Euripides' *Electra*', *G&R* 28 (1981), 179–92.

[9] Gilbert Murray, *A History of Ancient Greek Literature* (London, 1897), 274. See Pat Easterling, 'Gilbert Murray's Readings of Euripides', *Colby Quarterly*, 33 (1997), 113–27.

[10] See further Edith Hall, 'Medea and British Legislation before the First World War', *G&R* 46 (1999), 42–77.

political interpretations of Euripides, developed in performance, found academic expression in *Euripides and his Age* (1913). This book has fundamentally conditioned all subsequent interpretation, whether by imitation or reaction. A decade later Euripides' radicalism had become apocalyptic: 'not Ibsen, not Voltaire, not Tolstoi ever forged a keener weapon in defence of womanhood, in defiance of superstition, in denunciation of war, than the *Medea*, the *Ion*, the *Trojan Women*'.[11]

EURIPIDES THE ATHENIAN

What would Euripides have made of his modern incarnations? The reliable external biographical information amounts to practically nothing. No dependable account of Euripides' own views on politics, women, or war survives, unless we are arbitrarily to select speeches by characters in his plays as the cryptic 'voice of Euripides'. Aristophanes and the other contemporary Athenian comic poets, who wrote what is now known as 'Old Comedy', caricatured Euripides as a cuckold and a greengrocer's son, but their portrait offers little more truth value than a scurrilous cartoon.

The problem is not any dearth of evidence but a dearth of factual veracity. For the student of Euripides has access to a late antique 'Life' (*Vita*) and a fragmentary third-century biography by Satyrus. There are also the so-called 'Letters of Euripides', a collection of five dull epistles purporting to be addressed to individuals such as Archelaus (King of Macedon) and Sophocles, but actually written in the first or second century CE. Collectively these documents provide the first example in the European tradition of the portrait of an alienated artist seeking solace in solitude. This Euripides is a misogynist loner with facial blemishes who worked in a seaside cave on the island of Salamis, and retired to voluntary exile in Macedon as a result of his unpopularity. Unfortunately, however, this poignant portrait is demonstrably a fiction created out of simplistic inferences from Euripides' own works or from the jokes in Athenian comedy. Beyond what is briefly detailed below, the only aspect of the 'Euripides myth' almost certain to be true is that he possessed a large personal library (see Aristophanes, *Frogs* 943, 1049).

Euripides' lifespan was almost exactly commensurate with that of

[11] F. L. Lucas, *Euripides and his Influence* (London, 1924), 15.

democratic Athens' greatness. He was born in about 485 BCE, and was therefore a small boy when the city was evacuated and his compatriots thwarted the second Persian invasion in 480 BCE. He spent his youth and physical prime in the thriving atmosphere of the 460s and 450s, a period which saw the consolidation of Athens' empire and position as cultural centre of the Greek-speaking world. He was witness in 431 BCE to the outbreak of the Peloponnesian war, fought between Athens and her rival Sparta over hegemony in the Aegean. He lived through the turbulent 420s, having opportunity to observe at first hand the ambition and brilliant oratory of Athenian leaders such as Pericles and Cleon; he lived through the Athenians' worst catastrophe ever, when in 413 the fleet and many thousands of men were lost at Syracuse in Sicily after an attempt to extend Athenian imperial influence westward. He witnessed the oligarchic coup of 411, which overturned the democracy for the first time in nearly a century; this was soon followed by the reinstatement of the democracy, marred by terrible factional struggles. But by dying in 406, Euripides did narrowly avoid the humiliating events of 404, when his city lost the war, her empire, and (briefly) her democracy and her pride.

All the plays in this volume date from the last two decades of Euripides' life, from about 423 to 408 BCE, a period during which conflict with Sparta or her allies was a semi-continuous fact of Athenian life. *Suppliant Women* was first performed in about 423, eight years after the outbreak of the Peloponnesian war. *Ion* is usually dated to about 414, before the Sicilian disaster. But the darker *Phoenician Women* was certainly produced after this pivotal moment, between 411 and 408 (probably in 409), and *Orestes* is firmly dated to 408.

It is tempting to speculate on Euripides' own reaction to the unfolding story of the Peloponnesian war, and to ask whether it affected the evolution of his dramatic technique. It could be argued that the authoritative Theseus of *Suppliant Women*, and the upbeat picture of Athenian foreign policy painted by that play, gave way to more pessimistic dramas such as *Phoenician Women*, which stress that amorality and atrocity are unavoidable by all warring nations and individuals. Yet such a notion of linear artistic and intellectual development is compromised by the survival of only nineteen plays attributed to Euripides, out of a total of at least eighty, and possibly ninety-two. The evolutionary model is also demonstrably inconsistent with the production of *Hecuba*, one of the bleakest war dramas ever written, in the 420s. Euripides' own plays cannot be made to lend any substantial support to the widely held view that after initially supporting Athenian expansionism the poet despaired and retreated from the contemporary scene as the promoters of war became more powerful. It may be that truth lies behind the biographical tradition that he spent his last two years at the Macedonian court of Pella, supposedly writing plays including *Bacchae* and *Iphigenia at Aulis*; it may be that the very existence of the 'Macedonian exile' tradition reveals Euripides' anti-democratic (and therefore anti-imperialist) sympathies. On the other hand the lack of evidence for a political career, in contrast with Sophocles' attested appointments to high office, may suggest a neutral emotional detachment from public affairs.

Yet Euripides was profoundly engaged with the intellectual and ethical questions which the war had asked and which underlay the policy debates in the Athenian assembly. For these appear in thin disguise in his tragedies, which repeatedly confront notions of patriotism, pragmatism, expediency, and *force majeure* with the ideals of loyalty, equity, justice, and clemency. Such ethical disputes echo closely the agonizing debates in Thucydides which decided the fates—usually death or slavery—of the citizens of rebel states on both sides in the Peloponnesian war, including Mytilene, Plataea, and Melos. Euripides was thought to have studied moral philosophy with Socrates, but the same source says that he also studied physics with Anaxagoras and rhetoric with Prodicus (Aulus Gellius, *Noctes Atticae* 15.20.4); his tragedies reveal interest not only in ethics and political theory, but in every other significant field studied by the professional intellectuals ('sophists') in contemporary Athens: ontology, epistemology, philosophy of language, medicine, psychology, and cosmology. Euripidean characters certainly adopt the new philosophical and rhetorical *methods*: they subtly argue from probability and relativism, and formulate their points as antilogy, proof, and refutation. In this they are patently influenced by the developing sophistic 'science' of rhetoric, or 'persuasion'. Euripides' flashiest orators appear in plays composed after the arrival in Athens in 427 BCE of the great Sicilian sophist and rhetorician Gorgias, famous for his verbal pyrotechnics and ability to make a tenuous argument appear overwhelmingly convincing, 'to make the weaker argument appear the stronger'. The plays in this volume contain some ostentatious verbal displays, especially in the so-called debate scenes (see below, 'Speech').

EURIPIDES IN PERFORMANCE

Most Euripidean tragedies were first performed at an annual festival in honour of Dionysus, the Greek god of wine, dancing, and theatrical illusion, who is the protagonist of Euripides' most obviously 'Dionysiac' tragedy, *Bacchae*. The Great Dionysia was held in the spring when sailing became feasible. It was opened by a religious procession in which a statue of Dionysus was installed in the theatre, along with sacrifices and libations. Yet the Dionysia was also a political event. It affirmed the Athenian citizenry's collective identity as a democratic body with imperial supremacy: front seats were reserved for distinguished citizens, and only Athenians could perform the prestigious benefaction of sponsorship (*chorēgia*). The spectators included representatives from Athens' allied states. The allies displayed their tribute in the theatre, where they also witnessed a 'patriotic' display by the city's war orphans—an aspect of the performance context which must be borne in mind when considering how the original audience might have reacted to 'war plays' such as *Suppliant Women* and *Phoenician Women*. The plays were expected to suit this audience: insulting Athens at the Dionysia may have been a prosecutable offence (Aristophanes, *Acharnians* 501–6). It is not certain whether women attended the drama competitions, although most scholars assume that if women were present at all it was in small numbers, perhaps consisting only of important priestesses.

The tragedies were performed over three successive days in groups by three poets: each poet offered three tragedies plus one satyr play. In 431, for example, Euripides took third place with three tragedies (*Medea*, *Philoctetes*, and *Dictys*), followed by a satyr play called *Theristai*, 'Reapers': the other two competitors were Euphorion (Aeschylus' son), who won first prize, and Sophocles, the runner-up. Euripides, indeed, only won in 441, in 428 with the group including *Hippolytus*, and posthumously (in ?405) with *Bacchae* and *Iphigenia in Aulis*. The plays were judged by a panel of democratically selected citizens, and care was taken to avoid juror corruption, but the audience's noisy applause and heckling influenced the outcome (Plato, *Republic* 6.492b5–c1).

The performances took place in the theatre of Dionysus on the south slope of the Athenian Acropolis. Individual actors probably performed their speeches and songs most of the time on the stage (*skēnē*), while the chorus of twelve sang and danced to forgotten steps and gestures in the dancing arena (*orchēstra*). All the performers were male, and all were masked; little is known about the degree to which actors in female roles attempted to disguise their true gender. For performance conventions we have to rely on the characters' words, since the Greeks did not use stage directions. The last three decades have produced important work on the visual dimension and its contribution to the meaning of tragedy: scholarship has focused on physical contact, and on entrances and exits. The evidence for the material resources of the theatre as early as the fifth century is slight, although the poets had access to a machine which permitted the airborne epiphanies *ex machina*, such as Athena at the end of *Ion* and *Suppliant Women*. There was also the *ekkuklēma*, a contraption allowing bodies to be wheeled out of the doors of the palace or tent forming the 'backdrop' to most surviving tragedies (two of the plays in this volume, more unusually, are set in religious sanctuaries): vase-paintings offer a stylized reflection of the costumes, masks, and scenery, and some are directly inspired by individual tragedies.[12]

ION

Antiquity believed that Euripides was an artist as well as a tragic poet, and that paintings of his were on display in the city of Megara (*Life of Euripides*, 5). This tradition was probably an invention inspired by the frequency of the references in his plays to the visual arts.[13] In no play is this interest more apparent than in *Ion*, from the moment when the entering chorus of Athenian women admiringly describe the mythical scenes sculpted on to the façades of the temple of Apollo, including an awesome image of Athena (184–218). When Ion and Creusa are discussing her grandfather Erichthonius, an important figure in Athenian foundation mythology, Ion comments that the moment when Athena gave Erichthonius as a baby to the daughters of Cecrops was a scene beloved of artists (271). When Ion erects his ceremonial tent, he uses tapestries adorned with a series of

[12] See A. D. Trendall and T. B. L. Webster, *Illustrations of Greek Drama* (London, 1971).

[13] See Froma Zeitlin, 'The Artful Eye: Vision, Ecphrasis and Spectacle in Euripidean Theatre', in S. Goldhill and R. Osborne (eds.), *Art and Text in Ancient Greek Culture* (Cambridge, 1994), 138–305.

mostly patriotic scenes (1141–52); at the tent's entrance Ion positions a statue of Cecrops, the snake-man who had sprung from the Athenian soil to become the original ancestor of the 'autochthonous', earthborn Athenians (1141–66). These passages draw attention to the status of theatre, by making the audience contemplate the visual dimension of the dramatic poem they are experiencing, but the myths chosen for visualization also situate the play's master narrative—the reunion of Ion and his mother Creusa, Queen of Athens—within the tradition of local mythology celebrated in every art form in the Athenians' city. Creusa's determination that the monarchy must be inherited by a true son of the Athenian royal family may result in what strikes the modern audience as a thought-provoking exploration of xenophobia, yet it is consonant with the pleasure Euripides' countrymen felt in believing that their ancestors were no immigrants, but born from the soil of their own city.

Paradoxically, *Ion* is a deeply private, personal drama. The setting is indeed the public shrine of the pan-Hellenic Delphic oracle, where Creusa and her husband have come to enquire about their (apparent) childlessness, and the play concludes with Athena uttering grand prophecies of importance to the whole Greek world (1575–94). But at the play's emotional centre is the evolving relationship between Creusa and her long-lost baby, a son conceived after Apollo had raped her. Most of the play consists of intimate dialogue between Creusa and people related to her by blood or close to her heart; even the chorus are her loyal servants. Much of the action involves sexual secrets, including Xuthus' secret that before marrying Creusa he had once slept with a girl at an all-night festival. Even the happy ending is compromised by the audience's collusion in the dangerous secret that Creusa and Ion are biological mother and son, knowledge which is never to be shared by Xuthus, the other member of their little nuclear family (1601–3).

In *Ion* Euripides experimented with plot devices which were to be of incalculable importance in later European theatre. Mistaken identity, for example, is shown to have both comic and tragic potential. Xuthus' assumption that Ion is his biological son produces a moment of pure farce; Xuthus tries to hug the astonished youth, who understandably enquires whether he has lost his mind (517–30). But when Creusa makes the same mistake, the result is reciprocal attempted murder. Euripides also explores the way random coincidence or chance (*tychē*) influences events; although the discovery of Ion's true identity, and his return to Athens, are part of a divine plan prepared by Apollo, chance events create dramatic tension, and almost sabotage the divine programme.

There is little evidence for attempts to revive this enchanting, atmospheric drama in later antiquity. But it exerted an incalculable subterranean influence as one of several Euripidean dramatic precursors of the Greek 'New Comedy' of Menander and his contemporaries, the Roman comedies of Terence and Plautus, and consequently of the ancient romantic prose fiction written by the novelists Heliodorus, Achilles Tatius, and Longus. Chance not only became one of the most important dramaturgical principles of New Comedy; it sometimes even made an appearance in the form of the goddess *Tychē* as prologist. Like *Ion*, New Comedy is driven by a fascination with foundlings, with family psychology, with servants, secrets, recognition, (mistaken) identity, paternity, and maternity; the difference is that these fascinations are explored in the context of contemporary everyday life, rather than a Bronze Age royal family. The theme of the foundling child was of course far more ancient than Euripides: it has an Old Testament parallel in the story of Moses, an Asiatic one in Herodotus' version of the infancy of Cyrus the Great, king of Persia (1.108–22), and a sombre Greek tragic counterpart in Sophocles' account of the life of Oedipus, tyrant of Thebes.[14] But it was Euripides more than any other writer whose fresh spin on this particular story pattern informed the incipient transformation of Greek comedy from the political and social satire of Aristophanes into middle-class domestic fiction.

Euripides' most important innovation was to focus on Creusa's sensibility. Although not as well known as Medea, Phaedra, or Hecuba, in Creusa Euripides painted his most elaborate—and arguably his most sympathetic—portrait of female psychology. Few rape victims in Western literature have until recently been offered such a full hearing, and Creusa's reaction to the assault is informed by a realistic, malignant anger against her rapist. Her anguish explodes in a heart-rending scene during which she divulges to the audience suppressed memories of the traumas she suffered as a teenager. While Apollo raped her she called ineffectually for her mother (893); she endured labour alone, without a midwife (948–9); she was in

[14] See M. Huys, *The Tale of the Hero who was Exposed at Birth in Euripidean Tragedy: A Study of Motifs* (Leuven, 1995).

psychological agony as she tried to ignore her infant's arms stretched out towards her (958–61). It is the intimacy of the exploration of Creusa's pain that makes the eventual recognition scene so affecting; its emotional force upstages the public significance of the tokens left in the crib, miniature artworks depicting scenes from Athenian mythology appropriate for Athens' future king.

In *Ion* Euripides shows how the blood of the autochthonous Athenians was infused with the divine blood of Apollo, lord of the Delphic oracle. But the divine paternity of Ion, in the end, seems far less significant than the revelation of how catastrophic an unwanted pregnancy can be for an unmarried girl. Euripides even underlines his unusual angle on Creusa's pregnancy by pointing out that the other (male) poets who have narrated myths involving scandalous sexual unions have routinely blamed the women involved. The angry chorus suggest that it is time for some poetry which tells how women have suffered at the hands of men (1096–8): 'May a song and a raucous Muse with the opposite theme | be let loose against men, to sing of their unions!'

ORESTES

This breathtakingly lively drama was probably the most famous of all Euripides' tragedies in antiquity: it was certainly more quoted than any play by Aeschylus or Sophocles. Virgil takes from it Aeneas' impulse to kill Helen (*Aeneid* 2.567–76), and the only simile in the whole *Aeneid* using the figure of a theatrical actor likens the raving Dido to 'Orestes, the son of Agamemnon' as he is pursued over the stage by visions of his mother's ghost and avenging Furies (4.471–3). *Orestes* was certainly still read and enjoyed in the Byzantine era—the trial scene informs the trial of Jesus Christ in the *Christus Patiens*, an 'imitation' classical tragedy on the theme of Christ's passion, composed as late as the twelfth century CE. After Euripides' revivification in the Renaissance, however, the play was poorly regarded until the last two decades of the twentieth century, largely because it was considered episodic and marred by inappropriate levity.

Yet the postmodern critical climate of recent times has rehabilitated the play's roller-coaster plot and distinctively self-parodying tone, together with the self-conscious—even arch—awareness of the literary legacy which underlies it. It is probably no accident that *Orestes* was first produced exactly fifty years after Aeschylus' *Oresteia*;

in providing an entirely original and outrageous version of the events which occurred after Clytemnestra's death but before Orestes went to Athens—that is, in 'filling in' the time between the plots of Aeschylus' *Choephori* and *Eumenides*—it may well be consciously written against its seminal Aeschylean forerunner. Yet despite all the frenetic stage activity, the plot is simple: Orestes is condemned to death by the citizens of Argos for murdering his mother, and retaliates by attempting to kill her sister Helen. Argos descends into anarchic civil conflict, whipped up by Orestes' ambitious uncle Menelaus, and a catastrophic ending (entailing Orestes' murder of his cousin Hermione and the burning down of the royal palace) is only averted in the very nick of time by Apollo.

An ancient scholar commented on *Orestes* that, besides Pylades, everyone in this play is bad. (He apparently had not noticed that the plan to murder Helen is Pylades' idea.) Part of the play's distinctive tone indeed results from the poor moral calibre of nearly everyone involved, from the vain and silly Helen, to the duplicitous Menelaus, to the horrifically bloodthirsty Electra. Orestes, in particular, has been transformed from Aeschylus' tortured but dignified Argive prince into an anarchic and cocky youth, whose appalling rudeness to his old grandfather Tyndareus both shocks and amuses. Indeed, the vicious argument between Orestes and Tyndareus sets the scene for one of the most important issues in the play: its emphasis on inter-generational conflict.

The age gap theme is connected with the immediate historical background in 408 BCE, when Athens was blighted by the trials of those suspected of involvement in the short-lived oligarchic coup of 411. Reprisals and a mentality of vendetta dominated both public and private life. One of the most important social developments had been the important role which 'clubs' of upper-class young people, called *hetairoi* ('comrades'), had played in working against the democracy; the 'clubs' swore oaths of undying loyalty and engaged in illicit and violent revolutionary activities. Thucydides says that in these groups 'reckless daring was held to be loyal courage ... the man who took counsel beforehand to have nothing to do with plots was considered a breaker of the bond ... the club bond was stronger than blood relationship, because the comrade was ready to dare without asking why' (3.82.4–6). The unholy alliance of the renegade Orestes, Pylades, and Electra, founded on the murder of Clytemnestra and now taking indiscriminate decisions to commit suicide, arson, and further murders, evokes the dangerous new political phenomenon of upper-class youthful conspirators.[15]

It is a paradox, therefore, that the play's most touching moments arise out of the obsessive emotional tie binding these three disaffected adolescents. Their scenes are full of embraces and kisses, affirmations of love, saccharine tenderness, and an informality of diction unheard of elsewhere in tragedy. The colloquialism suggests that the chaos articulated in ethical terms extends to the play's genre orientation. Indeed, two alternative denouements are offered, both belonging more to the realm of comedy than to tragedy: the burning down of the palace (reminiscent of the end of Aristophanes' comedy *Clouds*), or a triple wedding. The superficially happy ending is of exactly the type deemed appropriate to *comedy* by Aristotle, the conclusion of *Orestes* being one in which 'those who are the bitterest enemies in the story . . . go off at the end, having made friends, and nobody kills anybody' (*Poetics* 1453[a] 35–9). Even one ancient scholar notes that the denouement is 'more of the comic type'. The play itself is therefore locked in a battle between tragedy and comedy; it not only fragments the Athenian democratic charter-myth enacted in Aeschylus' *Oresteia*; it also threatens to dissolve the very genre, tragedy, which had always been the most important example of Athenian democratic cultural prestige. It seems entirely appropriate that during the original production of *Orestes* the entire theatre cracked up in laughter, because Hegelochus, the actor playing Orestes, mispronounced what is translated as 'calm waters', saying, with horrific bathos, the word for 'weasel' instead (so says the scholiast on line 279).

Numerous Euripidean plays end with the sudden intervention of a divinity, but *Orestes* is the only play where the conflict requiring resolution is patently political. Orestes is in conflict not only with Menelaus, but with the democratic citizens of Argos, who have voted that he must suffer capital punishment for the murder of his mother. Apollo suddenly appears to resolve the situation: he will, he claims, set the situation right as regards the Argive citizenry, and Orestes will rule over them happily henceforward. The play thus offers a fantastic ideological settlement, which enforces harmony between the criminalized young royals and the Argive democracy—a political

[15] See Elizabeth Rawson, 'Aspects of Euripides' *Orestes*', *Arethusa*, 5 (1972), 155–67, at p. 160.

compromise which the events of the last few years at Athens had shown was, in reality, quite impossible. Real life cannot be controlled like a literary narrative. While social and factional divisions of the type that afflicted Athens in 408 still existed, the class conflicts could never evanesce, as they do in Euripides' mythical Argos, at the wave of an omnipotent authorial wand.[16]

Many great dramas have been born out of moments of political conflict, but thereafter transcend the historical circumstances of their original composition to become 'classics' in the repertoire. It is possible to enjoy Euripides' Argive soap opera, in the way that most of later antiquity did, as an exceptionally fine piece of theatrical writing and an exceptionally funny tragedy. But the levity of tone and happy outcome never quite manage to obscure its bleak pessimism about human nature, a pessimism directly related to the dark days when it was first written and acted.

PHOENICIAN WOMEN

The size of the cast of *Orestes* sometimes makes it feel dangerously like an ancient Argive soap opera; *Phoenician Women*, though grimmer in tone, also presents its audience with several generations of a famous tragic household. The Thebans in *Phoenician Women* had long been famous stage characters from Aeschylus' 'Theban' trilogy, which had included the enactment of the death of the brothers Eteocles and Polynices in the extant *Seven against Thebes*. Euripides, however, decided to crowd his version of this myth with members of their profoundly dysfunctional Labdacid family; the incestuous spouses Jocasta and Oedipus are still alive, although Oedipus is now mad as well as blind and has already cursed his sons.

In reality Thebes was a bitter and longstanding enemy of Athens, and in tragedy it is often treated as the Athenian democracy's mirror opposite, a closed-in, suffocating, xenophobic tyranny whose royalty specialized in making both love and war within their immediate family. In this play Euripides has gone out of his way to emphasize the close but confused physical relationships in the royal family (Jocasta, we learn, even suckled her motherless nephew Menoeceus (987)). Euripides concentrates attention on his stifling picture of Thebes

[16] See Edith Hall, 'Political and Cosmic Turbulence in Euripides' *Orestes*', in Alan Sommerstein *et al.* (eds.), *Tragedy, Comedy and the Polis* (Bari, 1993), 263–85.

by choosing to add the perspective of a chorus of visitors from unusually far away, Phoenician devotees of Apollo, who are understandably shocked by the goings-on they discover in this incestuous Greek city.

Brothers in conflict are staples of world mythology. The Old Testament offers Cain and Abel; Roman prehistory tells of Romulus and Remus; the Greek imagination produced other fratricides such as the twins Phanoteus and Crisus, who were already fighting in their mother's womb. But for Euripides it is the political dimension of the fratricide story which is of particular interest. At the climax of the play the messenger reports that as he died Polynices expressed pity for his brother, 'a kinsman who became my enemy, but remained my own dear brother' (1446). The play places under a theatrical microscope the contradictions in group identity created when nation-states are so sundered that members of the same family take up arms against one another. Euripides' contemporaries had in recent decades acquired experience of these contradictions: Thucydides, describing the effects of civil war in Corfu in 427, bleakly describes the breakdown of familial loyalties while partisan politics tore this city and subsequently the rest of the Greek world apart: 'People went to every extreme and beyond it. There were fathers who killed their sons; men were dragged from the temples or butchered on the very altars ... family relations were a weaker tie than family membership ... revenge was more important than self-preservation' (3.81–3).

Although its picture of civil war is firmly rooted in contemporary experience, *Phoenician Women*, like most late Euripidean drama, is also acutely conscious of the literary legacy which lies beneath it.[17] Besides ironic allusions to its Aeschylean prototype, it examines many of the conventions of Homeric epic war poetry. Antigone excitedly views the heroes marshalled beneath the city walls; this scene (a *teichoscopia*) has a famous prototype in the third book of the *Iliad*, and treats war, in epic mode, as a glorious spectacle. In contrast, the most innovative sequence is the story of Creon's son Menoeceus' self-immolation, an episode whose impact lies in its very brevity and absence of sentiment. Menoeceus takes only a few unemotive lines to state his reasons for dying (997–1012). His dreadful leap from the walls is subsequently reported in a handful of words (1090–2), and

[17] See Helene Foley, *Ritual Irony: Poetry and Sacrifice in Euripides* (Ithaca, NY, 1985), 106–46.

Jocasta's response is callously epigrammatic: Creon, she says, has suffered a personal calamity which is nevertheless 'fortunate for the city' (1206–7). The Menoeceus episode not only underlines the tension between familial love and patriotic duty: it stresses that most people who die in war do not have the opportunity to deliver elaborate speeches and are not memorialized in poetry. Very few are publicly lamented like the royal princes Eteocles and Polynices.

Jocasta may not be emotionally overwhelmed by the death of her nephew, but this eloquent, ageing queen certainly provides the central focus of the tragedy. Her physical body is the key symbol of the drama, uniting in one form the maternal body which physically bore the family at war, and symbolizing the very earth of Thebes and its body politic which that family is tearing asunder. As mother/wife to Oedipus and sister to Creon she binds two ancient Theban households; it was from her womb that the two warriors sprang whose fraternal violence tears her city apart. The poetry returns repeatedly to the imagery of childbirth and lactation; it also construes the relationship of a citizen to the country 'which bore him' as that of a child to its mother. Jocasta's prologue draws curious attention to the moment she became pregnant with Oedipus, and the later birth of her four children by him (22, 55–7); she is conspicuously physical with Polynices, embracing and caressing him tenderly (303–9); when she appears, too late, on the battlefield, she remembers suckling the boys long ago (1434–5). In killing herself by a stab wound she tears the flesh of her own body as the war has torn the flesh of the Thebans, and she dies entwined with both sons' mutilated corpses (1458–9). At the play's heartbreaking climax the gory body of this incestuous mother, grandmother, sister, and aunt, this ageing symbol of the once proud kingdom of Thebes, returns to the stage to be displayed alongside those of her fratricidal offspring.

While the 'classic' repertoire of Greek tragedies was being consolidated in the fourth century BCE its texts were vulnerable to interpolation, especially by actors. *Phoenician Women* has been suspected of including many spurious lines. Although it is unlikely that the text we possess is the exact version composed by Euripides, it is important to remember that the play, more or less as we have it, is a written record of performances enjoyed by thousands of ancient spectators. But the modern reader should be aware that many editors and theatrical directors choose to conclude the play at line 1581 of the Greek text (see headnote to this play in Textual Notes, p. 217). This translation omits some of the final scene transmitted in the manuscripts; in this Oedipus prepares to depart for the exile and death enacted in Sophocles' *Oedipus at Colonus*, while Antigone defies Creon's refusal of burial to Polynices in a sequence reminiscent of Sophocles' *Antigone*. Although it is possible to make a good case for the dramatic coherence of this conclusion, many scholars, from antiquity onwards, have doubted its authenticity and deemed that the play packs a more powerful punch if it concludes with the laments for Jocasta at 1581.

The tragedies comprising the group of plays in which *Phoenissae* was performed were *Hypsipyle*, *Phoenissae*, and *Antiope*, apparently in that order. The fragments of the two lost plays suggest that all three depicted a relationship between a middle-aged mother and her two adult sons. *Hypsipyle* was popular (it was still being performed in Mauretania (Morocco) in the first century CE (Athenaeus, *Deipnosophists* 8.343 e–f)). Since it included references to the story of the Seven against Thebes, it is possible that there are aspects of *Phoenician Women* which the loss of its companion tragedies have rendered unrecoverable.[18] But most of antiquity enjoyed the tragedy, much as we do today, in the form of an independent artwork.

SUPPLIANT WOMEN

This stately, sombre tragedy, the extended mass funeral of the Argives who died besieging Thebes, provides some of the most impressive spectacles in Euripidean drama. Set in Athenian territory at the sacred sanctuary at Eleusis, outside the temple of Demeter, it opens as a group of black-robed women with shorn grey hair supplicate the Queen Mother of Athens. The Argive King Adrastus lies prostrate at the gate, surrounded by several boys. The air is filled with lamentation, but there are no corpses to grieve over. It is not until the climax that the funeral cortege appears (778–94)—another striking spectacle, since it is rare for more than two or three corpses to be seen in the Attic theatre. There is no parallel in Greek tragedy for the scene in which one crazed widow, Evadne, flings herself on to her husband Capaneus' pyre, nor for the choral re-entry of the bereaved boys, tearfully bearing in the bones of their cremated fathers.

Every year Euripides' fellow Athenians gathered to hold a public

[18] See G. W. Bond (ed.), *Euripides' Hypsipyle* (Oxford, 1963), 87–90, 144.

funeral for the citizens who had died in combat. The bones were gathered in a special tent; this was followed by a procession in which coffins—including an empty one for those missing in action—were borne on wagons to the cemetery. A prominent citizen delivered an oration to the assembled families (Thucydides 2.34), a unique occasion in the city's calendar, for women never normally heard political speeches. According to Thucydides, the oration Pericles delivered at the funeral in 431 BCE included extensive praise of Athens, but also a recommendation that the bereaved women bear up and aspire to their greatest glory—to be spoken of as little as possible.

Suppliant Women enacts the same concerns as this solemn event in the Athenian civic calendar. Its patriotic bent has been a critical commonplace since an ancient scholar baldly stated: 'This drama is an encomium of Athens'. It does indeed invite its audience to reflect on the ideals their democracy championed. It is also possible that the play displaces on to the mythical Argives an important sequence of events in very recent Athenian history, for it may be informed by a traumatic defeat suffered by the Athenians at Delium in 424.

The Thebans had refused to hand over the thousand Athenian dead for burial on the ground that the Athenians had fortified a temple of Apollo. The bodies were eventually recovered, but the Athenians had been severely shaken by the incident: Thucydides' account relates an unpleasant diplomatic exchange which counterposes the 'Hellenic law' proscribing the military occupation of temples and that which enforced the handing back of war dead (4.89–101). The details of the narrative's relationship with *Suppliant Women* are complicated,[19] but some members of the original audience would clearly have been reminded of Delium. The mythical Theseus, in front of an internal audience including representatives from several Greek city-states, and an equally pan-Hellenic external audience sitting in the Athenian theatre, shows the 'right' way to talk and act on behalf of the dead in the aftermath of battle. In no Greek tragedy are the Athenians more clearly portrayed as the 'moral policemen' of Greece.

Yet the immediate topicality can be stressed too much. The play is a rare surviving example of a whole sub-genre of Athenian tragedy which enacted important moments in Athenian mythical prehistory. According to Plutarch's *Life of Theseus* (29), *Suppliant Women* dealt

[19] For a discussion of *Suppliant Women*'s connection with the Delium campaign see A. M. Bowie, 'Tragic Filters for History: Euripides' *Supplices* and Sophocles' *Philoctetes*', in Christopher Pelling (ed.), *Greek Tragedy and the Historian* (Oxford, 1997), 39–62.

with the same episode as Aeschylus' lost *Eleusinians*. For Euripides' contemporary Athenians, Theseus was their most important mythical ancestor. By the late sixth century his myths had been elaborated into a cycle of exploits to rival those of Heracles. As a local hero he was honoured in festivals, poetry, and the visual arts. By the middle of the fifth century he was regarded as the founding father of Athenian democracy (Thucydides 2.15).[20] It is therefore to Theseus that Euripides gives some of his finest poetic monologues, exploring important human concerns in a distinctively philosophical register—an exposition of humanity's rise from the animal level by the acquisition of language, agriculture, shelter, sailing, trade, and augury (201–13), and meditations, informed by political theory, on the virtues of democracy (238–47, 433–56).

Yet the action and the poetry of the play undermine its superficial status as Athenian panegyric. Euripides juxtaposes the 'rational' rhetoric of Theseus the statesman with a series of heartrending laments. Theseus can recover the bodies of the dead, but he can never restore their lives. The bereaved women of Argos are permitted, by the multivocal form of tragedy, to express the very type of sentiment that Pericles tried to stop women expressing at the Athenian state funeral. The play's message is further complicated by visual pictures of wild beasts; the bereaved fear that the bodies of their dead will be mutilated by animals, Adrastus had a dream likening his future sons-in-law to a lion and a boar (140), the chorus compare a suppliant with a wild beast taking refuge in a cave (267), and Evadne sees herself as a bird hovering above a cliff (1046). Such images focus the audience's mind on the inadequacy of those social institutions and conventions—forums of debate, the rights of the suppliant, and international diplomacy—that supposedly distinguish humans from beasts by regulating passions and resolving conflicts.

The intervention of the Theban herald further complicates the play's ethical dimension. However unlikeable, he makes cogent points: sophisticated political oratory can do great harm (412–16); love for one's children should be stronger than respect for one's fatherland or parents; peace, under which children and the arts flourish, must always be the priority (486–91). Moreover, Theseus' own order to the Athenians to go into battle is just a little too enthusiastic

[20] See W. R. Connor, 'Theseus in Classical Athens', in A. G. Ward (ed.), *The Quest for Theseus* (London, 1970), 143–74.

(587, 593). The price paid by warring states is expressed by the traumatized messenger—men dragged bouncing in the reins, rivers of red blood, charioteers hurled headlong from their shattered vehicles (689–93). Finally, Evadne's shocking leap to her death not only demonstrates that war ruins lives, but in an inspired piece of writing Euripides makes Evadne herself echo the competitive, masculine ethos which started the war in the first place. Like a Homeric hero, she has come 'to claim a glorious victory' and to win eternal renown by dying gloriously (1059–61, 1067).

Thucydides' Pericles told the bereaved women of Athens that their greatest glory was to be spoken of as little as possible. He would not have approved of Evadne, who ensures that the grief of her widowhood is remembered for all time, nor of the chorus of Argive mothers, who lament insatiably. This tragedy may not contain the intense familial conflict or psychological intimacy of some other Euripidean dramas. But as an exercise in the subtle subversion of a patriotic story it is—intellectually and emotionally—one of his finer achievements.

ATHENIAN SOCIETY

Euripides' plays were first performed in Athens at a festival celebrating Athenian group identity, and consequently often reveal an 'Athenocentrism' manifested, for example, in the famous praise in *Medea* of the beauty of Athens' environment, the grace of its citizens, and its cultural distinction (824–45). In this volume the whole of *Suppliant Women*, including the suppliants' ode in praise of Athenian justice (365–80), is (at least superficially) a panegyric to the imperial city where the play were composed and acted; *Ion* is an extended exploration of an important episode in the Athenian mythical past, stressing the purity of its ancestral bloodline.

Yet the social fabric of Euripides' Athens was colourfully heterogeneous. In 431 BCE an estimated three hundred thousand human beings lived in the city-state of Attica. But at least twenty-five thousand were resident non-Athenians ('metics'), including businessmen and professionals; a third were slaves, the majority of whom came from beyond Hellenic lands—from the Balkans, the Black Sea, Asia, or Africa. This ethnic pluralism perhaps finds expression in the 'multi-ethnic' casts of tragedy. The characters in these plays, with their settings in the cities and shrines of central Greece, are ethnically less varied than the Egyptians, Colchians, Thracians, and Crimeans who appear in some other works by Euripides, but even so *Orestes* introduces the audience to an extraordinary eunuch from Phrygia in Asia Minor, and the chorus of *Phoenician Women* consists of a group of barbarian women on their way to the Delphic oracle.[21]

Slavery was fundamental to Athenian economy and society, and tragedy reminds us of this unfortunate portion of the population. In *Acharnians* Aristophanes comments on the intelligence Euripides imputed to his slaves (400–1), and his plays include slaves with important roles as well as mute attendants: in *Ion* the intimacy of the relationship between Creusa and her old male slave, once tutor to her father, is not only demonstrated on stage in a long, emotional scene, but is crucial to the plot's development (735–1047). The institution of slavery is itself much discussed: Creusa's slave is convinced that 'a slave is no worse than a free man, as long as he is good' (855–6), and a character in a lost play affirmed that a noble slave is not dishonoured by the title, because 'many slaves are superior to the free' (fr. 511).[22]

The ethical dilemmas and emotional traumas in Euripides are never wholly inseparable from the decidedly unheroic pressures of finance and economics. Some Euripidean characters express lucid insights into the economic basis of society: in *Suppliant Women* Theseus' theoretical expositions of the constitution of the Greek city-state relate the conduct of classes of citizen directly to their economic status (238–43, 433–7). The most famous example is Medea's first monologue in *Medea*, which clarifies the socio-economic imperatives underlying her own and other women's predicament:

> Of everything that is alive and has a mind, we women are the most wretched creatures. First of all, we have to buy a husband with a vast outlay of money—we have to take a master for our body . . . divorce brings shame on a woman's reputation and we cannot refuse a husband his rights . . . I would rather stand three times in the battle line than bear one child. (*Medea* 230–51)

She trenchantly exposes the jeopardy in which marriage placed

[21] See Edith Hall, *Inventing the Barbarian* (Oxford, 1989).

[22] This and all subsequent references to the fragments of Euripides are cited from A. Nauck, *Tragicorum Graecorum Fragmenta*, 2nd edn., with supplement by B. Snell (Hildesheim, 1964).

women: besides the insulting dowry system, they were subject to legalized rape in marriage, a hypocritical double standard in divorce, and agonizing mortal danger in childbirth.

This kind of speech outraged the Christian writer Origen, who criticized Euripides for inappropriately making women express argumentative opinions (*Contra Celsum* 7.36.34–6). It is indeed a remarkable feature of Euripidean tragedy that many of his best thinkers and talkers are women: although the finest of Euripides' female orators (Medea and Hecuba, for example) appear in plays not included in this volume, in *Phoenician Women* Jocasta can hold her own during the acrimonious debate between her two sons, and in *Suppliant Women* the persuasively articulated views of Aethra, the Queen Mother of Athens, are listened to attentively.

Women are of course prominent in tragedy generally: patriarchal cultures often use symbolic females to help them imagine abstractions and think about their social order. It is also relevant that women performed the laments at funerals (a reality reflected, for example, in the choral dirges of *Suppliant Women*), that Dionysus' cult in reality (as well as in Euripides' *Bacchae*) involved maenadism and transvestism, and that women were perceived as more emotionally expressive (like Electra in *Orestes*), psychologically erratic (like Evadne in *Suppliant Women*), susceptible to divine interference (like Creusa in *Ion*) or 'in tune' with divinity (like the priestess of Apollo in the same play). They were also regarded as lacking moral autonomy: Athenian men were obsessed with what happened in their households behind their backs, and all the badly behaved women in tragedy—for example Medea and Phaedra, or even Electra in *Orestes*—are permanently or temporarily husbandless. Creusa, for example, only agrees to make an attempt on Ion's life in the physical absence of her husband. The plays are products of an age where huge sexual, financial, and affective tensions surrounded the transfer of women between the households that made up the city-state; the articulate Creusa lucidly expresses the problem women faced in such a society, which fostered distrust of women and misogyny (*Ion* 398–400).

There was, however, a feeling even in antiquity that Euripides' focus on women was sharper than that of either Aeschylus or Sophocles; until recently critics were debating whether Euripides was a misogynist or a feminist. But the only certainties are that he repeatedly chose to create strong and memorable female characters, and that as a dramatist he had a relativist rhetorical capacity for putting both sides of the argument in the sex war.

The position of women in the real world of Athens has itself long been a contentious issue, especially the degree of confinement to which citizen women were subject. But it is clear that most men would have preferred their wives and daughters to stay indoors, to be little discussed in public, to practise thrift, to possess unimpeachable sexual fidelity, and serially to produce healthy sons. Women could not vote or participate in the assembly; nor could they speak for themselves in the courts of law or normally conduct financial transactions except through the agency of their male 'guardian' (*kyrios*)—father, husband, or nearest male relative. A woman known to articulate views in front of men might be regarded as a liability. But women did of course negotiate with the existing power structures (we hear hints in the orators of the need for men to seek their womenfolk's approval), and were prominent in the central arena of public life constituted by religion. This is reflected especially in the figure of the dignified priestess of Apollo in *Ion* and in the chorus of hierodules, likewise bound for the Delphic oracle, in *Phoenician Women*. Other Euripidean tragedies feature important priestesses, such as Iphigenia, a priestess of Artemis in his *Iphigeneia among the Taurians*, and the Egyptian priestess Theonoe in his *Helen*. In a lost play the wise woman Melanippe defended women against practitioners of misogynist rhetoric; one of her strategies was to list the pan-Hellenic cults which women administered (fr. 499):[23]

> Men's criticism of women is worthless twanging of a bowstring and evil talk. Women are better than men, as I will show . . . Consider their role in religion, for that, in my opinion, comes first. We women play the most important part, because women prophesy the will of Zeus in the oracles of Phoebus. And at the holy site of Dodona near the sacred oak, females convey the will of Zeus to inquirers from Greece. As for the sacred rituals for the Fates and the Nameless Ones, all these would not be holy if performed by men, but prosper in women's hands. In this way women have a rightful share in the service of the gods. Why is it, then, that women must have a bad reputation?

EURIPIDES AND RELIGION

Melanippe's words are a fitting introduction to the category of *drama-*

[23] Trans. taken from M. R. Lefkowitz and M. B. Fant, *Women's Life in Greece and Rome: A Source Book in Translation* (London, 1992), 14.

tis personae constituted by the gods. What is to be deduced about Euripides' religious beliefs from his on-stage divinities in these plays (Hermes, Athena, Apollo), and the Aphrodite, Artemis, Death, Iris, Madness, Dioscuri, Poseidon, Thetis, and Dionysus who physically appear in others? One function of Euripides' gods from the machine, such as Apollo in *Orestes*, is certainly to provide a metatheatrical 'alienation' device drawing attention to the author's power over his dramatic narrative. But does that mean that he was an atheist?

Allegations that Euripides was a religious radical began in his lifetime. Aristophanes' caricature includes the charge that Euripides' tragedies had persuaded people 'that the gods do not exist' (*Women at the Thesmphoria* 450–1), and portrays him praying to the Air ('Ether') and 'Intelligence' (*Frogs* 890–2). By later antiquity it was believed that it was at Euripides' house that Protagoras, the great relativist and agnostic thinker, read out his famous treatise on the gods, beginning 'Man is the measure of all things' (fr. 80 B 1 Diels-Kranz; Diogenes Laertius 9.8.5).

Some characters in Euripides undoubtedly articulate views which must have sounded radical, modern, and even 'scientific' to his audience. Ion criticizes the gods for breaking the very laws—for example, their proscription on rape—which they expect humans to obey (437–51). Others depart from traditional theology by attributing the workings of the universe either to physical causes or to the power of the human mind. In *Orestes* Electra refers to the enthroning of 'Nature' (*Physis*) by contemporary natural scientists (126–7), and later hints at ideas associated with the cosmology of the pre-Socratic thinker Anaxagoras (982–5). In *Trojan Women* Hecuba wonders whether Zeus should be addressed as 'the necessity imposed by nature, or human intelligence' (884–6). In one lost play a character asserted that 'the mind that is in each of us is god'; in another the first principle of the cosmos was said to be Air, which 'sends forth the summer's light, and makes the winter marked with cloud, makes life and death'; in a third Air was explicitly equated with Zeus (frr. 1018, 330.3–5, 941).

There has consequently always been a critical tendency to see Euripides as seeking to overturn or challenge traditional religion, especially belief in the arbitrary, partisan, and often malevolent anthropomorphic gods of the Homeric epics. It has been argued that in figures such as the irresponsible rapist Apollo in *Ion*, the vindictive Aphrodite and Artemis in *Hippolytus*, or Dionysus in *Bacchae*,

Euripides portrayed the most 'Homeric' of all Greek tragic gods precisely to undermine them. Thus his tragic divinities, the argument goes, are a literary throwback to the old anthropomorphism, constituting a consciously reductive enactment of the commonly accepted personalities of the Olympians. Alternatively, Euripides is interpreted as a humanist who denies any but human motivation to human action and whose works operate on a similar principle to Thucydides' rationalist and atheological determination that it is human nature, *to anthrōpinon*, which drives and conditions history. Critics have even seen Hecuba in *Trojan Women* as a kind of proselyte advocating a new Euripidean doctrine, emphasizing her assertion that whatever the name 'Zeus' may really mean—necessity or intelligence—it is that principle which disposes 'all human affairs according to justice' (886, see also Theonoe's words in *Helen* 1002–3). This view, allegedly, suggests a belief in a new religion of peace and justice, which Euripides is urging should replace the old Olympian cults.

Yet it is mistaken to confuse Euripidean characters' more innovative theological opinions with his (unknown) personal views. Moreover, many of the expressions of scepticism are more complicated than they seem. One rhetorical function of scepticism is to *affirm* the belief being doubted simply by raising it to consciousness.[24] For the overall impact of Euripidean tragedy does nothing to disrupt the three fundamental tenets of Athenian religion as practised by its citizens: that gods exist, that they pay attention (welcome or unwelcome) to the affairs of mortals, and that some kind of reciprocal allegiance between gods and humans was in operation, most visibly instantiated in sacrifice. The tragic performances were framed by the rituals of the Dionysia, and ritual fundamentally informs tragedy's imagery, plots, and songs: a study of wedding and funeral motifs, for example, has shown how they become conflated into sinister variations of the figure of the 'bride of death', a strikingly important poetic figure, for example in relation to Evadne in *Suppliant Women*.[25] Ritual, moreover, brings group consolidation and profound consolation, as a collective human response in the face of catastrophe.

The plays themselves stage ritual, and frame accounts of it. In *Ion*

[24] See T. C. W. Stinton, '"Si credere dignum est": Some Expressions of Disbelief in Euripides and Others', *PCPS* 22 (1976), 60–89.

[25] Rush Rehm, *Marriage to Death: The Conflation of Wedding and Funeral Rituals in Greek Tragedy* (Princeton, 1994).

the hero instructs the chorus in the correct way to consult the oracle (219–32), and Xuthus stages a sacrificial banquet on the double peak of Parnassus to give thanks for the son he thinks he has rediscovered (1122–7). The *history* of religion certainly seems to have fascinated Euripides, who includes in his tragedies numerous descriptions of specific cults. *Ion* is a goldmine of material on both Athenian cults and the Delphic oracle; in *Suppliant Women* Athena *ex machina* prescribes in detail the sacrificial equipment and victims which are to bind the oath to be made by Adrastus (1196–1207).

Euripidean plots are repeatedly driven by violations of the great taboos and imperatives constituting popular Greek ethics, the boundaries defining unacceptable behaviour which Sophocles' Antigone calls the 'unwritten and unshakeable laws of the gods' (*Antigone* 454–5), and which Euripidean characters are more likely to call 'the laws common to the Greeks' (e.g. *Children of Heracles* 1010). These regulated human relationships at every level. In the family they proscribed incest, kin-killing, and failure to bury the dead. Incest forms the psychological backdrop to *Phoenician Women*, which puts on stage most of the members of Oedipus' family. Kin-killing provides the climax to this play, is only just averted by both the hero and his mother in *Ion*, and is absolutely central to *Orestes*, which comes close to burlesquing the theme. In the aftermath of Orestes' murder of his mother Clytemnestra, Orestes goes on to make additional attempts on the lives of his aunt Helen and cousin Hermione. Failure to bury the dead is the crucial concern of *Suppliant Women*.

At the level of relationships between members of different households and cities the 'common laws' ascribed to Zeus the protection of vulnerable groups such as recipients of oaths, guests and hosts, and suppliants. Supplication at an altar offered protection against physical assault or arrest, and Creusa, condemned to death for the attempted murder of Ion, desperately flees to an altar in the shrine of Apollo (1258). The opening scenes of *Suppliant Women* stage the supplication of Aethra and Theseus by the mothers and sons of the Argive dead, a ritual action whose solemnity is enhanced by the sacred setting. But supplication did not necessarily require an altar: it could also take the form of a formal entreaty, accompanied by ritualized touching of knees, hand, and chin, which is intended to put the recipient under a religious obligation to accede the suppliant's requests. Supplication in Euripides characterizes numerous crucial scenes; the desperate Orestes' first reaction on seeing Menelaus in *Orestes* is to clasp his uncle's knees and beg for help (382–4).

MUSIC, CHORUS, SONG

We have lost the melodies to which the lyrics of tragedy were sung to the accompaniment of a pipes (*auloi*). But it is possible partially to decipher what John Gould has called 'strategies of poetic sensibility'[26] within the formal, conventional media open to the tragedian: besides the choral passages, which were danced and sung, the tragedian had several modes of delivery to choose from for his individual actors. In addition to set-piece speeches and line-by-line spoken dialogue (*stichomythia*), they included solo song, duet, sung interchange with the chorus, and an intermediate mode of delivery, probably chanting to pipe accompaniment, signalled by the anapaestic rhythm (∪ ∪ –). Euripides' songs were extremely popular: the ancients believed that some Athenians in Sicily saved themselves after the disaster at Syracuse in 413 BCE by singing some of his songs to their captors (Plutarch, *Life of Nicias* 29). In a lost comedy named *Euripides-Lover* (Axionicus fr. 3) a character discusses people who hate all but Euripidean lyrics.

In this edition the sung and chanted sections have been labelled and laid out in shorter lines so that the reader can appreciate the shifts between speech and musical passages. In *Ion*, when Creusa recalls the details of her rape and lonely labour, she sings to express her psychological pain (860–922). Evadne's deranged soliloquy, as she prepares to commit suttee on her husband's pyre, is expressed melodically in *Suppliant Women* (990–1008, 1012–30). Awareness of the intermittent use of the singing voice matters because it mattered in antiquity. The musicologist Aristoxenus said that speech begins to sound like song *when we are emotional* (*Elementa Harmonica* 1.9–10). It certainly affects our appreciation of Electra's psychological disturbance, for example, that Euripides chose to make her *sing* about her family's plight in an ode at the heart of *Orestes* (960–1012). It clearly expresses the terror as well as the alien language and ambivalent sexual identity of the Phrygian in *Orestes* that he sings about the assault on *Helen* (1369–1502).

[26] John Gould, 'Dramatic Character and "Human Intelligibility" in Greek Tragedy', *PCPS* 24 (1978) 43–67, especially pp. 54–8.

The chorus, although it can also speak, and even function as an 'umpire' between warring parties in a debate (*Phoenician Women* 497–8), is, however, the primary lyric voice in Euripidean tragedy. Sometimes the chorus' songs 'fill in' time while actors change roles (*Phoenician Women* 202–60) or 'telescope' time while events happen offstage, even a full-scale military encounter such as the battle in *Suppliant Women* (588–633). Often the chorus sings forms of lyric song derived from the world of collective ritual. Passages of choral song may have their roots in hymns of praise to the gods; in *Ion* the Athenian chorus sings an 'anacletic' ('summoning') hymn to Athena, asking her to come from Athens to Delphi to assist their queen (452–509); *Phoenician Women* includes a remarkable hymn which asks the war-god Ares why he does not yield to the joyful, peaceable activities associated with another great Theban divinity, Dionysus (784–833). The opening chorus of *Suppliant Women* is both a formal entreaty to Aethra and a funeral dirge (42–86), and a great antiphonal lament ensues between Adrastus and the chorus when the bodies of the seven war heroes are finally brought into the theatre (778–836).

Some choral odes present a mythical narrative functioning as a form of memory; in *Phoenician Women* the chorus relates the foundation myths of Thebes as a precursor to the destructive violence which is about to afflict the city (638–89). Other choral songs may be more firmly rooted in the time of the action taking place, but likewise offer valuable contextualizing material: a chilling little ode at the heart of *Orestes* records the dress Clytemnestra wore and the words she said to her son at the moment when he killed her (807–43). Yet some choral odes are more philosophical or contemplative in orientation, and meditate in general terms on the issues which have been explored in the concrete situation of the play's previous episode. Thus the chorus of *Ion*, accompanying the apparently childless Creusa on her quest to Delphi, reflect on the blessings which children bestow on their parents, blessings far more important than wealth or palaces (472–87).

SPEECH

In Aristophanes' *Frogs*, a prominent feature of Euripidean tragedy is the 'programmatic' prologue delivered by a leading character, which is characterized in the comedy as predictable in both metrical form and in 'scene-setting' function. But the Aristophanic caricature is unfair: the prologue characteristically establishes expectations, themes, and images which will subsequently become central to the drama. Euripides, moreover, varied the impact by his choice of speaker. The central event of *Phoenician Women*, the deaths of Eteocles and Polynices, is made far more tragic by the choice of their mother, Jocasta, as introductory speaker. Choosing to open *Suppliant Women* with the mature Aethra sets up one of the play's most important concerns—the moral agency of women in time of war.

The Roman rhetorician Quintilian judged Euripides of more use than Sophocles to the trainee orator (10.1.67), and the modern reader will undoubtedly be struck by the series of peculiarly formal debates in these plays: Theseus versus the Theban herald on the political and religious ramifications of the Argives' appeal to Athens in *Suppliant Women* (359–580), and the brothers' debate on statecraft and war in *Phoenician Women*. The debate (*agōn*) is one of the features which Athenian drama assimilated from the oral performances which characterized two other great institutions of the democracy: the lawcourts and the assembly. To meet the increasing need for polished public speaking and its assessment under the widened franchise, the study of the science of persuasion, or the art of rhetoric, developed rapidly around the middle of the fifth century (see also above, 'Euripides the Athenian'); this is reflected in tragedy's increased use of formal rhetorical figures, tropes, 'common topics' such as pragmatism and expediency, and hypothetical arguments from probability. One form of exercise available to the trainee orator was the 'double argument'—the construction or study of twin speeches for and against a particular proposition, or for the defence and prosecution in a hypothetical trial. As a character in Euripides' lost *Antiope* (first staged in the same group as *Phoenician Women*) averred, 'If one were clever at speaking, one could have a competition between two arguments in every single case' (fr. 189). In assessing Euripidean rhetoric it must be remembered that his audience had become accustomed to startling displays by litigants in lawsuits (Aristophanes, *Wasps* 562–86); by the 420s political oratory sometimes descended into competitive exhibitionism in which the medium had superseded the message (Thucydides 3.38).

Euripides' gift for narrative is perhaps clearest in his 'messenger speeches', vivid mini-epics of exciting action, whether it is the exquisite description of Ion's tent in *Ion* (1141–62), the fascinating account of Orestes' trial in the Argive assembly (*Orestes* 866–950), or the messengers' reports of battles in both *Phoenician Women* and *Suppliant Women* (1090–199, 650–730). All Euripides' poetry is marked by exquisite simile and metaphor, often traced thematically through a play: in *Orestes*, for example, there is a complex network of images drawn from the fields of disease, sailing, storm, and fire. Euripides' picturesque style was much admired in antiquity ('Longinus', *On the Sublime* 15.1–4).

Euripides showed infinite versatility of register, and was capable of selecting rare poetic words for special effect (Aristotle, *Poetics* 58^{b}19–24). Yet he still revolutionized the diction of tragedy by making his characters speak in his distinctively 'human way'. This ordinary quality to the language spoken by Euripides' characters attracted emulation by able poets even within his lifetime, yet in Aristophanes' *Frogs* Dionysus dismisses them as insignificant 'chatterers' in comparison (89–95). For Euripides was really doing something extremely difficult in making his unforgettable characters express themselves plausibly and 'like human beings'. Thus the author of an encomium to Euripides in the *Palatine Anthology* justifiably discourages the aspiring imitator (7.50):

> Poet, do not attempt to go down Euripides' road;
> It is hard for men to tread.
> It seems easy, but the man who tries to walk it
> Finds it rougher than if it were set with cruel stakes.
> If you even try to scratch the surface of Medea, daughter of Aeetes,
> You shall die forgotten. Leave Euripides' crowns alone.

NOTE ON THE TRANSLATION

My policy as regards translation has, as usual, been to try to combine, as much as possible, fluency with accuracy. I have not attempted a verse translation: they very rarely work. Of course, the most difficult passages are the choral odes and lyric passages. It is clear that a poetic English version of these passages can be achieved only by taking considerable liberties with the literal meaning of the original Greek; indeed, even apart from such distortion, many translators simply omit whole words or phrases. Therefore, since my policy included the desire to give a faithful translation, I had to ignore most poetic values in favour of accuracy. So other than a tendency to employ more poetic syntax and vocabulary in these passages, the most I have done towards rendering them as verse is to break them up into shorter lines, so that the reader can see at a glance that they are different from—more emotionally charged than—the surrounding material. I have not broken up all the lyric passages into shorter lines like this; occasionally it made better sense not to distinguish them in this way from the surrounding material, for instance where one character is speaking in the usual iambic trimeters, while the other is using lyrics, or the tone is still rather colloquial, or the verses are intrinsically part of the action of the play. Although, then, in most respects I have chosen accuracy of translation over considerations such as the possible modern production of any of the plays, the only major liberty I have taken with the text is to add stage directions, which are lacking in the manuscripts of Greek plays. However, I believe that an intelligent and creative director could still use the following texts as the basis for modern productions, and would thereby come closer to Euripides' original intentions than he might if he used other translations.

Apart from places marked in the translations with an obelus (which refers the interested reader to the Textual Notes, pp. 216–19), I have translated the Oxford Classical Text of J. Diggle (3 vols., 1981, 1984, 1994). Diggle marked quite a few lines, and even some whole passages, as spurious, even though they formed part of the text that has been transmitted to us. His decisions have not always met with approval from other scholars, but after consulting the editions of other modern editors, and my own editorial judgement, I have excluded some, but not all, of the lines which he doubted. I could have translated them within square brackets, but a lot of these lines are bad verse, and/or out of place, and/or corrupt, and so, in order to preserve a smooth translation, I have simply omitted them (this explains the occasional interruptions to the sequence of marginal line numbers). The disadvantage of this policy is that there are lines from the Euripidean manuscript tradition which have simply vanished from this translation; the advantages are that it makes for a more readable text, and one which is closer to what we may suppose Euripides originally wrote. For a volume designed for students and general readers, the advantages seem to me to outweigh the disadvantages. Not many lines are involved—more in *Orestes* and *Phoenician Women* than the other two plays.

I would like to take this opportunity to thank Professor Christopher Collard immensely for his generous notes on an earlier draft of the translations. He saved me from both errors and infelicities. James Morwood and I have found it a pleasure to work with him, Edith Hall, and our editor Judith Luna on this volume.

SELECT BIBLIOGRAPHY

GENERAL BOOKS ON GREEK TRAGEDY

P. E. Easterling (ed.), *The Cambridge Companion to Greek Tragedy* (Cambridge, 1987); Simon Goldhill, *Reading Greek Tragedy* (Cambridge, 1986); Rush Rehm, *Greek Tragic Theatre* (London, 1992); Charles Segal, *Interpreting Greek Tragedy: Myth, Poetry, Text* (Ithaca, NY, 1986); Oliver Taplin, *Greek Tragedy in Action* (London, 1978); J. P. Vernant and P. Vidal-Naquet, *Tragedy and Myth in Ancient Greece* (English trans., Brighton, 1981); John J. Winkler and F. I. Zeitlin (eds.), *Nothing to do with Dionysos? Athenian Drama in its Social Context* (Princeton, 1990).

GENERAL BOOKS ON EURIPIDES

P. Burian (ed.), *New Directions in Euripidean Criticism* (Durham, NC, 1985); Christopher Collard, *Euripides* (Greece & Rome New Surveys in the Classics, 24, Oxford, 1981); D. J. Conacher, *Euripidean Drama* (Toronto, 1967); *Euripide, Entretiens sur l'antiquité classique*, vi, published by the Fondation Hardt (Vandouvres-Geneva 1960); Helene P. Foley, *Ritual Irony: Poetry and Sacrifice in Euripides* (Ithaca, NY, 1985); G. M. Grube, *The Drama of Euripides* (second edn., London, 1962); M. Halleran, *Stagecraft in Euripides* (London, 1985); A. N. Michelini, *Euripides and the Tragic Tradition* (Madison, 1987); Judith Mossman (ed.), *Oxford Readings in Euripides* (Oxford, 2000); E. Segal (ed.), *Euripides: A Collection of Critical Essays* (Englewood Cliffs, NJ, 1968); P. Vellacott, *Ironic Drama: A Study of Euripides' Method and Meaning* (Cambridge, 1976); C. H. Whitman, *Euripides and the Full Circle of Myth* (Cambridge, Mass., 1974).

EURIPIDES' LIFE AND BIOGRAPHIES

Hans-Ulrich Gösswein, *Die Briefe des Euripides* (Meisenheim am Glan 1975); J. Gregory, *Euripides and the Instruction of the Athenians* (Ann Arbor, 1991); M. R. Lefkowitz, *The Lives of the Greek Poets* (London, 1981) 88–104, 163–9; P. T. Stevens, 'Euripides and the Athenians', *JHS* 76 (1956), 87–94; R. E. Wycherley, 'Aristophanes and Euripides', *G&R* 15 (1946), 98–107.

OPINIONS AND INTERPRETATIONS

R. Aélion, 'La Technique dramatique d'Euripide et sa conception de la destinée humaine', in J. Duchemin and F. Jouan (eds.), *Visages du destin dans les mythologies* (Paris, 1983), 69–85; R. B. Appleton, *Euripides the Idealist* (London, 1927); Robert Eisner, 'Euripides' Use of Myth', *Arethusa*, 12 (1979), 153–74; for 'historicist' approaches see E. Delebecque, *Euripide et la guerre du Péloponnèse* (Paris, 1951), and V. Di Benedetto, *Euripide: teatro e società* (Turin, 1971); E. R. Dodds, 'Euripides the Irrationalist', *CR* 43 (1929), 97–104; H. Reich, 'Euripides, der Mystiker', in *Festschrift zu C. F. Lehmann-Haupts sechzigsten Geburtstage* (Vienna, 1921), 89–93; K. Reinhardt, 'Die Sinneskrise bei Euripides', *Eranos*, 26 (1957), 279–317—Euripides as a Nihilist; in his *Existentialism and Euripides* (Victoria, BC, 1977) William Sale draws on both Heidegger and Freud; A. W. Verrall, *Euripides the Rationalist* (Cambridge, 1895).

RECEPTION OF EURIPIDEAN TRAGEDY

Peter Burian, 'Tragedy Adapted for Stages and Screens: The Renaissance to the Present', in Easterling, *Cambridge Companion to Greek Tragedy* (see above), 228–83; Pat Easterling, 'Gilbert Murray's Readings of Euripides', *Colby Quarterly*, 33 (1997), 113–27; Stuart Gillespie, *The Poets on the Classics* (London, 1988) 90–4; Edith Hall, 'Talfourd's Ancient Greeks in the Theatre of Reform', *International Journal of the Classical Tradition*, 3 (1997), 283–407 (on *Ion*); Edith Hall, 'Medea and British Legislation before the First World War', *G&R* 46 (1999), 42–77; Edith Hall, 'Greek Tragedy and the British Stage', *Cahiers du GITA*, 12 (1999), 113–34; Edith Hall, Fiona Macintosh, and Oliver Taplin (eds.), *Medea in Performance 1500–2000* (Oxford, 2001); F. L. Lucas, *Euripides and his Influence* (New York 1928); K. Mackinnon, *Greek Tragedy into Film* (London, 1986); Fiona Macintosh, 'Tragedy in Performance: Nineteenth and Twentieth-Century Productions', in Easterling, *Cambridge Companion to Greek Tragedy* (see above), 284–323; Fiona Macintosh, 'Alcestis on the British Stage', *Cahiers du GITA*, 14 (2001); Martin Mueller, *Children of Oedipus and Other Essays on the Imitation of Greek Tragedy 1550–1800* (Toronto, 1980), 46–63; Ruth Padel, '*Ion*: Lost and Found', *Arion*, 4 (1996), 216–24.

VISUAL ARTS

Vase-paintings illustrating scenes from Euripides are collected in A. D. Trendall and T. B. L. Webster, *Illustrations of Greek Drama* (London, 1971), 72–105, and supplemented in the articles under the names of each important mythical character (e.g. 'Theseus') in the multi-volume ongoing *Lexicon Iconographicum Mythologiae Classicae* (Zurich, 1984–). See also Richard Green, *Theater in Ancient Greek Society* (London, 1994); Richard Green and Eric Handley, *Images of the Greek Theatre* (Austin, Tex., 1995); Oliver Taplin, 'The Pictorial Record', in Easterling, *Cambridge Companion to Greek Tragedy* (see above), 69–90; Kurt Weitzmann, 'Euripides Scenes in Byzantine Art', *Hesperia*, 18 (1949), 159–210.

PRODUCTION AND PERFORMANCE CONTEXT

Giovanni Comotti, *Music in Greek and Roman Culture* (English trans., Baltimore, 1989), 32–41; E. Csapo and W. J. Slater, *The Context of Ancient Drama* (Ann Arbor, 1995), 79–101; P. Easterling and Edith Hall (eds.), *Greek and Roman Actors* (forthcoming, Cambridge, 2002); S. Goldhill, 'The Great Dionysia and Civic Ideology', in Winkler and Zeitlin, *Nothing to Do with Dionysos?* (see above), 97–129; John Gould, 'Tragedy in Performance', in B. Knox and P. E. Easterling (eds.), *The Cambridge History of Classical Literature*, i (Cambridge, 1985) 258–81; John Gould, 'Dramatic Character and "Human Intelligibility" in Greek Tragedy', *PCPS* 24 (1978), 43–67; Edith Hall, 'Actor's Song in Tragedy', in Simon Goldhill and Robin Osborne (eds.), *Performance Culture and Athenian Democracy* (Cambridge, 1999), 96–122; Nicolaos C. Hourmouziades, *Production and Imagination in Euripides: Form and Function of the Scenic Space* (Athens, 1965); Maarit Kaimio, *Physical Contact in Greek Tragedy* (Helsinki, 1988); Solon Michaelides, *The Music of Ancient Greece: An Encyclopaedia* (London, 1978), 117–19; A. Pickard-Cambridge, *The Dramatic Festivals of Athens*[3], revised by J. Gould and D. M. Lewis (Oxford, 1988); Erika Simon, *The Ancient Theater* (London, 1982); Oliver Taplin, *The Stagecraft of Aeschylus* (Oxford, 1977), and 'Did Greek Dramatists write Stage Instructions?', *PCPS* 23 (1977), 121–32.

On satyr drama see P. E. Easterling, 'A Show for Dionysos', in Easterling, *Cambridge Companion to Greek Tragedy* (see above), 36–53; Richard Seaford (ed.), *Euripides' Cyclops* (Oxford, 1984), 1–45; E. Hall

'Ithyphallic Males Behaving Badly: Satyr Drama as Gendered Tragic Ending', in M. Wyke (ed.), *Parchments of Gender: Deciphering the Bodies of Antiquity* (Oxford, 1998), 13–37.

SOCIAL AND HISTORICAL CONTEXT

See J. K. Davies, *Democracy and Classical Greece* (Glasgow, 1978), 63–128, and 'Athenian Citizenship: The Descent Group and the Alternatives', *CJ* 73 (1977–8), 105–21; Paul Cartledge, *The Greeks* (Oxford, 1996), and (ed.), *The Cambridge Illustrated History of Ancient Greece* (Cambridge, 1997); Colin McLeod, 'Thucydides and Tragedy', *Collected Essays* (Oxford 1983) 140–58; Christopher Pelling (ed.), *Greek Tragedy and the Historian* (Oxford, 1997); Anton Powell, *Athens and Sparta: Constructing Greek Political and Social History from 478 BC* (London, 1988).

For an overview of the problems in reconstructing Athenian women's lives, see Josine Blok's review in J. Blok and H. Mason (eds.), *Sexual Asymmetry: Studies in Ancient Society* (Amsterdam, 1987), 1–57. For a recent range of views on gender issues see D. Cohen, *Law, Sexuality, and Society: The Enforcement of Morals in Classical Athens* (Cambridge, 1991); Elaine Fantham *et al.* (eds.), *Women in the Classical World* (New York, 1994); John Gould, 'Law, Custom, and Myth: Aspects of the Social Position of Women in Classical Athens', *JHS* 100 (1980) 38–59; Virginia Hunter, *Policing Athens* (Princeton, 1994), 9–42; R. Just, *Women in Athenian Law and Life* (London, 1989).

SPECIFIC ASPECTS OF EURIPIDEAN DRAMA

Rachel Aélion, *Euripide. Héritier d'Eschyle* (Paris, 1983, two vols.); Luigi Battezzatto, *Il monologo nel teatro di Euripide* (Pisa, 1995); Francis M. Dunn, *Tragedy's End: Closure and Innovation in Euripidean Drama* (New York, 1996); H. Erbse, *Studien zum Prolog der euripideischen Tragödie* (Berlin, 1984); M. Fusillo, 'Was ist eine romanhafte Tragödie? Überlegungen zu Euripides' Experimentalismus', *Poetica*, 24 (1992), 270–99; Richard Hamilton, 'Prologue, Prophecy and Plot in Four Plays of Euripides', *AJP* 99 (1978), 277–302, and 'Euripidean Priests', *HSCP* 89 (1985), 53–73; Rosemary Harriott, 'Aristophanes' Audience and the Plays of Euripides', *BICS* 9 (1962), 1–9; Martin Hose, *Studien zum Chor bei Euripides* (Berlin, 1990–1);

E. O'Connor-Visser, *Aspects of Human Sacrifice in the Tragedies of Euripides* (Amsterdam, 1987); Bernd Seidensticker, 'Tragic Dialectic in Euripidean Tragedy', in M. S. Silk (ed.), *Tragedy and the Tragic: Greek Theatre and Beyond* (Oxford, 1996), 377–96; H. P. Stahl, 'On Extra-dramatic Communication of Characters in Euripides', *YCS* 25 (1977), 159–76; Sophie Trenkner, *The Greek Novella in the Classical Period* (Cambridge, 1958), 31–78; R. P. Winnington-Ingram, 'Euripides: *poiētēs sophos*', *Arethusa*, 2 (1969), 127–42; Froma Zeitlin, 'The Artful Eye: Vision, Ecphrasis and Spectacle in Euripidean Theatre', in S. Goldhill and R. Osborne (eds.), *Art and Text in Ancient Greek Culture* (Cambridge, 1994), 138–305.

For the lost plays of Euripides see C. Collard, M. J. Cropp, and K. H. Lee (eds.), *Euripides: Selected Fragmentary Plays*, i–ii (Warminster, 1995, 1999); T. B. L. Webster, *The Tragedies of Euripides* (London, 1967).

On slaves in Euripides see H. Kuch, *Kriegsgefangenschaft und Sklaverei bei Euripides* (Berlin, 1974); K. Synodinou, *On the Concept of Slavery in Euripides* (English trans., Ioannina, 1977); Edith Hall, *Inventing the Barbarian* (Oxford, 1989); Edith Hall, 'The Sociology of Athenian Tragedy', in Easterling, *Cambridge Companion to Greek Tragedy* (see above) 93–126; D. P. Stanley-Porter, 'Mute Actors in the Tragedies of Euripides', *BICS* 20 (1973), 68–93. On children see G. Sifakis, 'Children in Greek Tragedy', *BICS* 26 (1979), 67–80. On women see H. Foley, 'The Conception of Women in Athenian Drama', in H. P. Foley (ed.), *Reflections of Women in Antiquity* (London, 1981), 127–67; Ruth Herder, *Die Frauenrolle bei Euripides* (Stuttgart 1993); Nicole Loraux, *Tragic Ways of Killing a Woman* (English trans., Cambridge, Mass., 1987); Rush Rehm, *Marriage to Death: The Conflation of Wedding and Funeral Rituals in Greek Tragedy* (Princeton, 1994); Richard Seaford, 'The Structural Problems of Marriage in Euripides', in A. Powell (ed.), *Euripides, Women and Sexuality* (London, 1990), 151–76; Nancy Sorkin Rabinowitz, *Anxiety Veiled: Euripides and the Traffic in Women* (Ithaca, NY, 1993); Froma Zeitlin, *Playing the Other: Gender and Society in Classical Greek Literature* (Chicago, 1996).

For religion in Euripides see C. Sourvinou-Inwood, 'Tragedy and Religion: Constructs and Meanings', in Christopher Pelling (ed.), *Greek Tragedy and the Historian* (Oxford, 1997), 161–86. For sceptical discussions see M. R. Lefkowitz, 'Was Euripides an Atheist?', *Studi Italiani*, 5 (1987), 149–65, and '"Atheism" and "Impiety" in Euripides' Dramas', *CQ* 39 (1989), 70–82; G. E. Dimock, *'God or Not God, or between the Two': Euripides' Helen* (Northampton, Mass., 1977)—Euripides' evangelism; T. C. W. Stinton, '"Si credere dignum est": Some Expressions of Disbelief in Euripides and Others', *PCPS* 22 (1976), 60–89; Harvey Yunis, *A New Creed: Fundamental Religious Beliefs in the Athenian Polis and Euripidean Drama* (= *Hypomnemata*, 91, Göttingen, 1988). On supplication scenes, see J. Gould, 'Hiketeia', *JHS* 93 (1973), 74–103.

On the sophists, philosophy, and the intellectual background see D. J. Conacher, *Euripides and the Sophists: Some Dramatic Treatments of Philosophical Ideas* (London, 1998); J. H. Finley, 'Euripides and Thucydides', in *Three Essays on Thucydides* (Cambridge, Mass., 1967), 1–24; S. Goldhill, *Reading Greek Tragedy* (Cambridge, 1986) 222–43; G. B. Kerferd, *The Sophistic Movement* (Cambridge, 1981); W. Nestle, *Untersuchungen über die philosophischen Quellen des Euripides, Philologus* suppl. 8.4 (1901), 557–655, and *Euripides: der Dichter der griechischen Aufklärung* (Stuttgart, 1901); F. Solmsen, *Intellectual Experiments of the Greek Enlightenment* (Princeton, 1975), 24–31, 132–41.

On rhetoric see V. Bers, 'Tragedy and Rhetoric', in I. Worthington (ed.), *Greek Rhetoric in Action* (London, 1994), 176–95; Richard Buxton, *Persuasion in Greek Tragedy* (Cambridge, 1982); C. Collard, 'Formal Debates in Euripidean Drama', in I. McAuslan and P. Walcot, *Greek Tragedy* (Oxford, 1993), 153–66; D. J. Conacher, 'Rhetoric and Relevance in Euripidean Drama', *AJP* 102 (1981), 3–25; E. Hall, 'Law-court Dramas: The Power of Performance in Greek Forensic Oratory', *BICS* 40 (1995), 39–58; M. Lloyd, *The Agon in Euripides* (Oxford, 1992).

On characterization, see H. P. Stahl, 'On "Extra-dramatic" Communication in Euripides', *YCS* 25 (1977), 159–76; J. Griffin, 'Characterization in Euripides', in C. Pelling (ed.), *Characterization and Individuality in Greek Literature* (Oxford, 1990) 128–49.

On speech, language, style, and imagery, see Shirley Barlow, *The Imagery of Euripides* (London, 1971); I. J. F. de Jong, *Narrative in Drama: The Art of the Euripidean Messenger-Speech* (Leiden, 1991); Ewald Kurtz, *Die bildliche Ausdrucksweise in den Tragödien des Euripides* (Amsterdam, 1985); P. T. Stevens, *Colloquial Expressions in Euripides* (Wiesbaden, 1976); Ernst Schwinge, *Die Verwendung der Stichomythie in den Dramen des Euripides* (Heidelberg, 1968).

ION

Editions

A. S. Owen (ed.), *Euripides' Ion* (Oxford, 1939); K. H. Lee (ed.), *Euripides, Ion* (Warminster, 1997).

Studies

A. P. Burnett, 'Human Resistance and Divine Persuasion in Euripides' *Ion*', *CP* 57 (1962), 89–103; H. Erbse, 'Der Gott von Delphi in *Ion* des Euripides', in B. Allemann and E. Koppen (eds.), *Festschrift für H. Rüdiger* (Berlin, 1975), 40–54; B. Gauger, *Gott und Mensch im Ion des Euripides* (Bonn, 1977); G. Gellie, 'Apollo in the *Ion*', *Ramus*, 13 (1985), 93–101; V. Giannopoulou, 'Divine Agency and *tyche* in Euripides' *Ion*: Ambiguity and Shifting Perspectives', in M. Cropp *et al.* (eds.), *Studies in Euripides* (forthcoming, 2001); Barbara Goff, 'Euripides' *Ion* 1132–1165: The Tent', *PCPS* 34 (1988), 42–54; K. Hartigan, *Ambiguity and Self-Deception: The Apollo and Artemis Plays of Euripides* (Frankfurt 1991); M. Huys, *The Tale of the Hero who was Exposed at Birth in Euripidean Tragedy: A Study of Motifs* (Leuven, 1995); M. Imhof, *Euripides' "Ion": Ein literarische Studie* (Berne, 1966); H. I. Immerwahr, 'Athenian Images in Euripides' *Ion*', *Hellenica*, 25 (1972) 277–97; K. Lee, 'Shifts of Mood and Concepts of Time in Euripides' *Ion*', in Michael Silk (ed.), *Greek Tragedy and the Tragic* (Oxford, 1996), 85–109; Michael Lloyd, 'Divine and Human Action in Euripides' *Ion*', *A&A* 32 (1986), 33–45; Nicole Loraux, 'Autochthonous Kreousa: Euripides, *Ion*', in *The Children of Athena* (English trans. by C. Levine, Princeton, 1993), 184–236; D. J. Mastronarde, 'Iconography and Imagery in Euripides' *Ion*', *CSCA* 8 (1975), 163–76; K. Matthiessen, 'Der *Ion*—eine Komödie des Euripides?', in M. Geerard (ed.), *Opes Atticae: Miscellanea Philologica et Historica R. Bogaert et H. Van Looy Oblata* (The Hague, 1990), 271–91; Gerhard Mueller, 'Beschreibung von Kunstwerken im *Ion* des Euripides', *Hermes*, 103 (1975), 25–44; V. J. Rosivach, 'Earthborns and Olympians: The Parodos of the *Ion*', *CQ* 27 (1977), 284–94; A. Saxonhouse, 'Myths and the Origins of Cities: Reflections on the Autochthony Theme in Euripides' *Ion*', in J. P. Euben (ed.), *Greek Tragedy and Political Theory* (Berkeley, 1986), 252–73; G. B. Walsh, 'Rhetoric of Birthright and Race in Euripides' *Ion*', *Hermes*, 106 (1978), 301–15; F. Wassermann, 'Divine Violence and Providence in Euripides' *Ion*', *TAPA* 71 (1940), 587–604; C. Wolff, 'The Design and Myth in Euripides' *Ion*', *HSCP* 69 (1965), 169–94;

K. Zacharia, 'The Marriage of Tragedy and Comedy in Euripides' *Ion*', in S. Jäkel and A. Timonen (eds.), *Laughter down the Centuries* (Turku, 1995), 45–62; Froma Zeitlin, 'Mysteries of Identity and Designs of the Self in Euripides' *Ion*', *PCPS* 35 (1989), 144–97.

ORESTES

Editions

C. W. Willink (ed.), *Euripides' Orestes* (Oxford, 1986); Martin West (ed.), *Euripides' Orestes* (Warminster, 1987).

Studies

W. G. Arnott, 'Euripides and the Unexpected', *G&R* 20 (1973), 49–64; P. N. B. Boulter, 'The Theme of *agria* in Euripides' *Orestes*', *Phoenix*, 16 (1962), 102–6; W. Burkert, 'Die Absurdität der Gewalt und das Ende der Tragödie: Euripides' *Orestes*', *A&A* 20 (1974), 97–109; J. de Romilly, 'L'Assemblée du peuple dans l'Oreste d'Euripide', *Studi Classici in onore di Quintino Cataudella* (Catania, 1972), 237–51; H. Erbse, 'Zum *Orestes* des Euripides', *Hermes*, 103 (1975), 434–59; T. M. Falkner, 'Coming of Age in Argos: *physis* and *paideia* in Euripides' *Orestes*', *CJ* 78 (1983), 289–300; C. Fuqua, 'Studies in the Use of Myth in Sophocles' *Philoctetes* and Euripides' *Orestes*', *Traditio*, 32 (1976), 29–95; C. Fuqua, 'The World of Myth in Euripides' *Orestes*', *Traditio*, 34 (1978), 1–28; N. Greenberg, 'Euripides' *Orestes*: An Interpretation', *HSCP* 66 (1962), 157–92; Edith Hall, 'Political and Cosmic Turbulence in Euripides' *Orestes*', in Alan Sommerstein *et al.* (eds.), *Tragedy, Comedy and the Polis* (Bari, 1993), 263–85; H. G. Mullens, 'The Meaning of Euripides' *Orestes*', *CQ* 34 (1940), 153–8; H. Parry, 'Euripides' *Orestes*: The Quest for Salvation', *TAPA* 100 (1969) 337–53; Elizabeth Rawson, 'Aspects of Euripides' *Orestes*', *Arethusa*, 5 (1972), 155–67; A. M. S. Scarcella, 'L'Oreste e il problema dell'unità', *Dioniso*, 19 (1956), 266–76; Seth Schein, 'Mythical Allusion and Historical Reality in Euripides' *Orestes*', *WS* 88 (1975), 49–66; W. D. Smith, 'Disease in Euripides' *Orestes*', *Hermes*, 95 (1967), 291–307; F. Will, 'Tyndareus in the *Orestes*', *SO* 37 (1961), 96–9; C. Wolff, '*Orestes*', in E. Segal (ed.), *Oxford Readings in Greek Tragedy* (Oxford, 1983), 340–56; Froma Zeitlin, 'The Closet of Masks: Role-playing and Myth-making in the *Orestes* of Euripides', *Ramus*, 9 (1980), 51–77.

PHOENICIAN WOMEN

Editions

D. J. Mastronarde (ed.), *Euripides' Phoenissae* (Cambridge, 1994); E. Craik (ed.), *Euripides' Phoenician Women* (Warminster, 1988).

Studies

M. B. Arthur, 'The Curse of Civilization: The Choral Odes of the *Phoenissae*', *HSCP* 81 (1977), 163–85; J. M. Bremer, 'The Popularity of Euripides' *Phoenissae* in Late Antiquity', *Actes du VIIe Congrès de la FIEC*, i (Budapest, 1985), 281–8; P. Burian, 'Introduction', in P. Burian and B. Swann (trans.), *Euripides, The Phoenician Women* (New York, 1971) 3–17; D. J. Conacher, 'Themes in the Exodos of Euripides' *Phoenissae*', *Phoenix*, 21 (1967) 92–101; J. de Romilly, '*Phoenician Women* of Euripides: Topicality in Greek Tragedy', *Bucknell Review*, 15 (1967), 108–32; H. Erbse, 'Beiträge zum Verstandnis der euripideischen Phönissen', *Philologus*, 110 (1970), 1–34; Y. Garlan, 'De la poliorcétique dans les Phéniciennes d'Euripide', *REA* 68 (1966), 264–77; Barbara Goff, 'The Shields of the *Phoenissae*', *GRBS* 29 (1988), 135–52; J. Jouanna, 'Texte et espace théâtral dans les Phéniciennes d'Euripide', *Ktema*, 1 (1976), 81–97; J. Jouanna, 'Remarques sur le texte et la mise en scène de deux passages des Phéniciennes d'Euripides', *REG* 89 (1976), 40–56; A. Masaracchia, 'Ares nelle *Fenicie* di Euripide', in *Filologia e forme letterarie* (Studi F. della Corte) (Urbino, 1987), 169–81; D. Mastronarde, 'The Optimistic Rationalist in Euripides: Theseus, Jocasta, Teiresias', in M. Cropp, E. Fantham, and S. Scully (eds.), *Greek Tragedy and its Legacy: Essays Presented to D. J. Conacher* (Calgary, 1987), 201–11; C. Mueller-Goldingen, *Untersuchungen zu den Phönissen des Euripides* (Stuttgart, 1985); A. J. Podlecki, 'Some Themes in Euripides' *Phoenissae*', *TAPA* 93 (1962) 355–73; E. Rawson, 'Family and Fatherland in Euripides' *Phoenissae*', *GRBS* 11 (1970), 109–27; S. Saïd, 'Euripide ou l'attente déçue: l'example des Phéniciennes', *ASNP* 15 (1985), 501–27; A. Tirelli, 'La crisi dei modeli ideologici nelle Fenicie di Euripide', in I. Gallo (ed.), *Miscellanea Filologica* (Salerno, 1986), 7–55; Froma Zeitlin, 'Thebes: Theater of Self and Society in Athenian Drama', in Winkler and Zeitlin, *Nothing to do with Dionysos?* (see above), 130–67.

SUPPLIANT WOMEN

Edition

C. Collard (ed.), *Euripides' Supplices* (Groningen, 1975).

Studies

A. M. Bowie, 'Tragic Filters for History: Euripides' *Supplices* and Sophocles' *Philoctetes*', in Christopher Pelling (ed.), *Greek Tragedy and the Historian* (Oxford, 1997), 39–62; P. Burian, '*Logos* and *pathos*: The Politics of the *Suppliant Women*', in P. Burian (ed.), *Directions in Euripidean Criticism* (Durham, NC, 1985), 239–55; C. Collard, 'The Funeral Oration in Euripides' *Supplices*', *BICS* 19 (1972), 39–53; D. J. Conacher, 'Religious and Ethical Attitudes in Euripides' *Suppliants*', *TAPA* 87 (1956), 8–26; W. R. Connor, 'Theseus in Classical Athens', in A. G. Ward (ed.), *The Quest for Theseus* (London, 1970), 143–74; J. Davie, 'Theseus the King in Fifth-century Athens', *G&R* 29 (1982), 25–34; J. W. Fitton, 'The *Suppliant Women* and the *Herakleidai* of Euripides', *Hermes*, 89 (1961) 430–61; R. B. Gamble, 'Euripides' *Suppliant Women*: Decision and Ambivalence', *Hermes*, 98 (1970), 385–405; A. Michelini, 'The Maze of the *logos*: Euripides, *Suppliants* 163–249', *Ramus*, 20 (1991), 16–36; A. Michelini, 'Political Themes in Euripides' *Suppliants*', *AJP* 115 (1994), 219–52; A. Michelini, 'Alcibiades and Theseus in Euripides' *Suppliants*', *Colby Quarterly*, 33 (1997), 177–84; Sophie Mills, *Theseus, Tragedy and the Athenian Empire* (Oxford, 1997) 87–128; G. Paduano, 'Interpretazione delle *Supplici* di Euripide', *ASNP* 35 (1966) 193–249; M. H. Shaw, 'The *ethos* of Theseus in the "Suppliant Women"', *Hermes*, 109 (1982), 3–19; W. D. Smith, 'Expressive Form in Euripides' "Suppliants"', *HSCP* 71 (1966), 151–70; Henry J. Walker, *Theseus and Athens* (New York, 1995), 143–69; John E. G. Whitehouse, 'The Dead as Spectacle in Euripides' "Bacchae" and "Suppliant Women"', *Hermes*, 114 (1986), 59–72.

A CHRONOLOGY OF EURIPIDES' WORK AND TIMES

Dates of productions of extant plays (adapted from C. Collard, *Euripides* (Oxford, 1981), 2)		Dates in the history of Athens	
		462	Radical democracy established in Athens
455	first production		
		448	Building of Parthenon begun
441	first prize (play unknown)		
438	*Alcestis*—second prize		
431	*Medea*—third prize	431	Outbreak of Peloponnesian war between Athens and Sparta
430–428	*Heraclidae*	430	Outbreak of plague in Athens
428	*Hippolytus* (revised from earlier production)—first prize		
?425	*Andromache*		
before 423	*Hecuba*		
?423	*Supplices*		
?before 415	*Hercules Furens*	416	Slaughter by the Athenians of the men of the island of Melos and the enslavement of its women and children
before 415	*Electra*		
415	*Troades*—second prize	415–413	Disastrous Athenian expedition to Sicily
before 412	*Iphigenia at Tauris*		
?before 412	*Ion*		
412	*Helen*		
?412	*Cyclops* (satyr play)		
411–408, ?409	*Phoenissae*—second prize	411	Oligarchic revolution in Athens
408	*Orestes*		
after 406	*Iphigenia at Aulis* and *Bacchae*—first prize	404	Defeat of Athens by Sparta in the Peloponnesian war

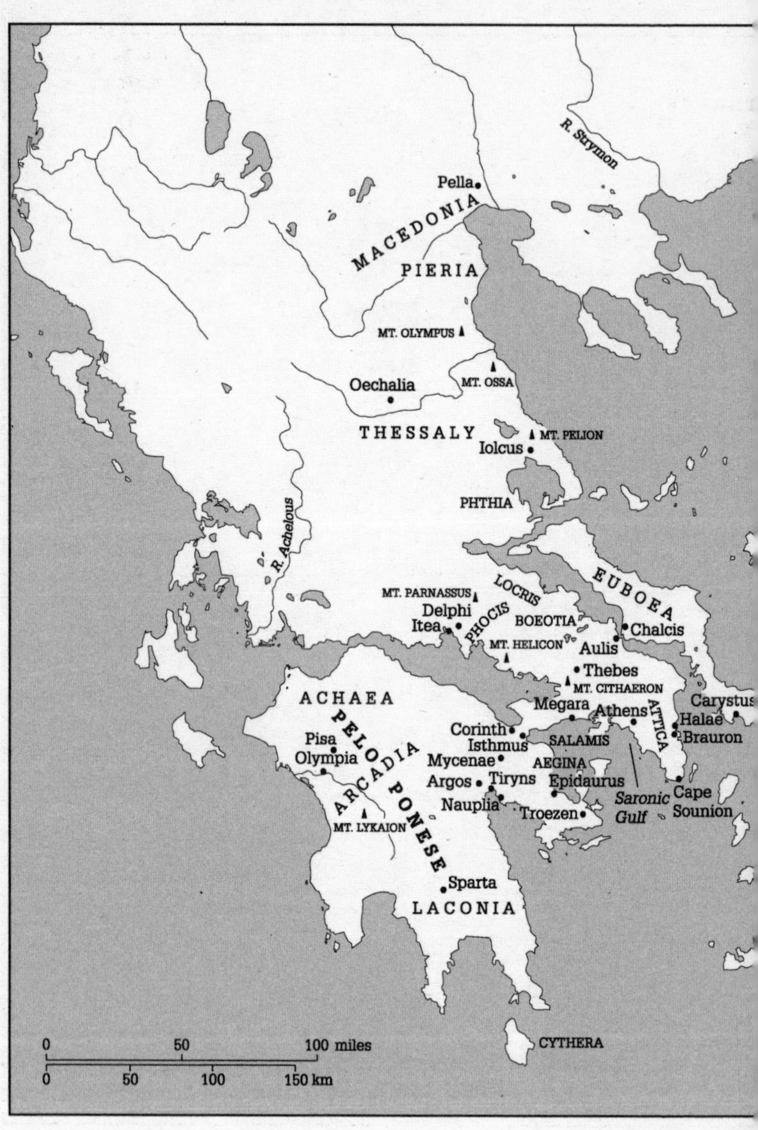
R. Strymon
Pella
MACEDONIA
PIERIA
MT. OLYMPUS
MT. OSSA
Oechalia
THESSALY
MT. PELION
Iolcus
PHTHIA
R. Achelous
EUBOEA
LOCRIS
MT. PARNASSUS
Delphi
Itea
PHOCIS
BOEOTIA
Chalcis
MT. HELICON
Aulis
Thebes
MT. CITHAERON
ACHAEA
Megara
Athens
ATTICA
Carystus
Halae
Brauron
PELOPONNESE
Corinth
Isthmus
SALAMIS
Pisa
Olympia
ARCADIA
Mycenae
AEGINA
Argos
Tiryns
Epidaurus
Saronic Gulf
Cape Sounion
Nauplia
Troezen
MT. LYKAION
Sparta
LACONIA
CYTHERA
0 50 100 miles
0 50 100 150 km

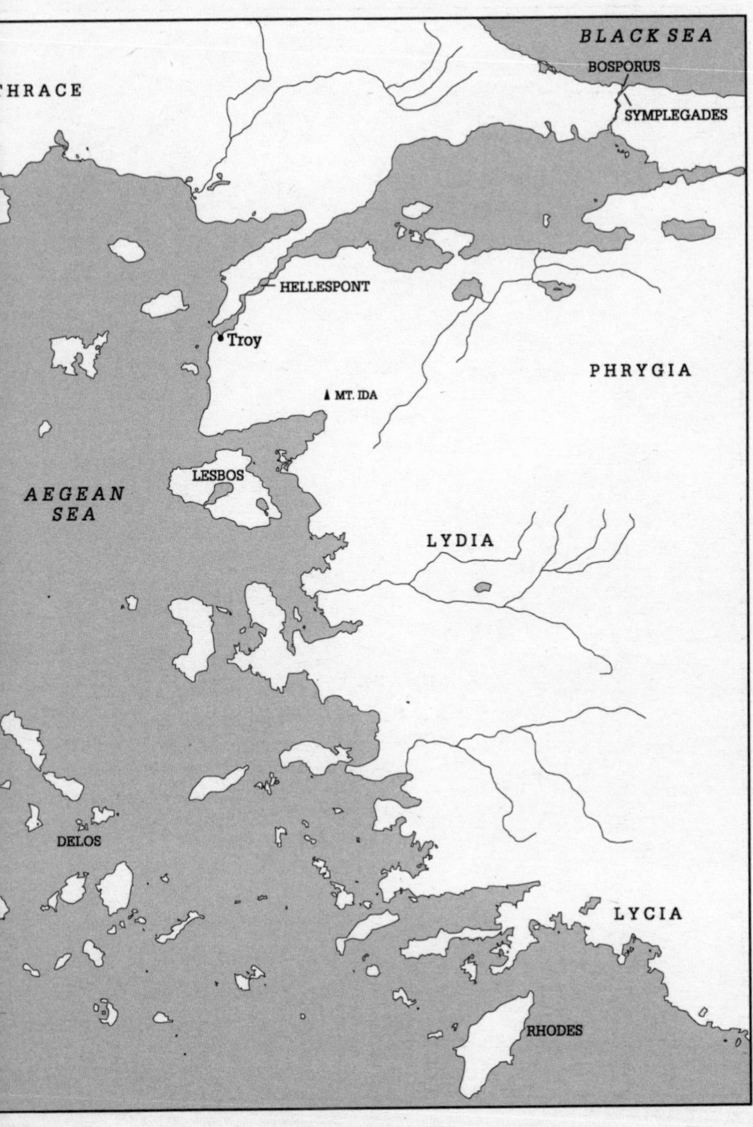
THRACE
BLACK SEA
BOSPORUS
SYMPLEGADES
HELLESPONT
Troy
PHRYGIA
MT. IDA
LESBOS
AEGEAN
SEA
LYDIA
DELOS
LYCIA
RHODES

ION

Characters

HERMES
ION, *lost son of Creusa and Apollo*
CREUSA, *daughter of Erechtheus, king of Athens*
XUTHUS, *Creusa's husband, king of Athens*
OLD MAN, *a slave of Creusa*
SLAVE *of Creusa*
PRIESTESS *of Apollo*
ATHENA

CHORUS of Creusa's female slaves

Scene: In front of the temple of Apollo at Delphi. There is an altar on the stage. When the play starts, it is just before sunrise. Enter HERMES.*

HERMES. Atlas, whose adamantine back wears out the sky,* the ancient home of the gods, fathered Maia by one of the goddesses,* and Maia bore me to almighty Zeus. For I am Hermes, the servant of the gods. And this spot is Delphi,* where Phoebus sits at the central navel-stone, chanting his oracles, regularly revealing for mortal men what is and what shall be. Why have I come here? There is a rather famous city in Greece,* named after Pallas of the golden spear. Once, under Pallas' hill in the land of the Athenians, by the north-facing cliffs—the Long Rocks, as they are called by the lords of Attica—Phoebus took Creusa, the child of Erechtheus,* against her will to be his lover. Through long months she bore the burden of her womb without her father's knowledge, as Phoebus wanted. When her time came, she gave birth at home to a child. Afterwards she took the baby out of the house and brought it to the same cave in which she and the god had lain together,* and left it there to die untended within the rounded hollow of a crib.* She observed the custom of her ancestors and of earth-born Erichthonius. For when Zeus' daughter gave Erichthonius to Aglaurus' daughters* for safe keeping, she set two snakes to guard and protect him, and ever since it has been the custom in Athens for the descendants of Erechtheus to have their children wear golden snake-ornaments* while they are growing up. However, when the young woman had put on her child the finery that she owned, she left him to die.

'Brother,' Phoebus asked me (for he is my brother), 'you are familiar with Pallas' city, so go to the people of illustrious Athens, whose roots lie in the land where they live,* and fetch the new-born baby out of the cavern along with his cradle and the baby clothes he's wearing. Bring him to my oracle at Delphi and put him right by the entrance to my temple. I'll take care of him after that*—I should explain that the child is mine.' So I did my brother Loxias* this favour. I fetched the wicker cradle and brought it here. I put the child on the steps of this temple, once I had folded back the crib's rounded cover, so that the child would be visible. It so happened that just then, as the sun's orb was embarking on its chariot journey, the prophetess entered the god's oracular shrine. She noticed the infant child and wondered at the effrontery of the local girl, whoever it was, who had abandoned her secret offspring at the god's temple. She felt she ought to remove him from the bounds of the precinct, but pity melted her harshness; and the god was on the child's side too, working to prevent his removal from the temple, so she took him in and brought him up. She has no idea that the father is Phoebus, and doesn't know who the mother is either; nor does the boy know who his parents are.

As a child he used to roam and play around the altars that fed him, and when he reached manhood* the people of Delphi made him the keeper of the god's treasures and the trusted caretaker of the whole sanctuary. So up till now he has lived a life of devotion in the god's temple. Meanwhile, the young man's mother, Creusa, became the wife of Xuthus.* This came about as follows. Hostilities surged up between Athens and the descendants of Chalcodon, who live in Euboea.* During the war, Xuthus supported the Athenian effort and helped them to victory; his reward was marriage with Creusa,* though he was no Athenian, but Achaean by birth, descended from Zeus through Aeolus. Although they've been married for a long time, he and Creusa have no children—and that is why they have come here to Apollo's oracle, because they long for children. Loxias is behind this turn of events; despite appearances, he has not been remiss. When Xuthus enters the shrine, Apollo is going to give him his own son, telling him that he is the father. And so, once inside his mother's house and recognized by Creusa,* the boy will come into his proper station in life, while Loxias' ravishing of her will remain a secret. And Apollo will make him known throughout Greece as Ion, the founding father of Asia.*

Well, I had better hide among the laurels of this dell here, from where I can learn everything that happens to the boy.* For over there I can see Loxias' son coming out to brighten up the entrance of the temple with his laurel branches.* Here Ion comes, then; no other god before me has called him by this name—the name that awaits him.*

Exit HERMES.

Enter ION *from the temple with bow and arrows, a broom, and golden jugs of water. Some temple attendants also enter.*

ION (*sings*). Here is the gleaming four-horse chariot!*
Now the Sun-god is shedding his light over the earth!
See how his celestial fire chases the stars into the holy night,
and how the untrodden peaks of Parnassus light up
as they catch the day-long wheel of his chariot!
What a boon for mortal men! The smoke of desert incense*
wafts into Phoebus' roofs; the Delphic priestess is seated
on her sacred three-footed stool, chanting loud and clear for Greece
the utterances declared by Apollo.
Go, you men of Delphi who minister to Phoebus,
go to the silvery eddies of the Castalian spring;*
sprinkle yourselves with its pure, cool waters, and then enter the temple.
Guard your tongues, keep your mouths pure, uttering as you speak
only words of good omen to those who desire to consult the oracle.
As for me, I shall occupy myself with the jobs I have carried out

since childhood. I shall clean Phoebus' entrance with boughs of laurel
bound with holy ribbons and dampen the ground with sprinkled water;*
and with my arrows I shall scare away the flocks of birds
which spoil the holy treasures. For I tend the shrine of Phoebus
which brought me up when I had no mother or father to look after me.*

Exeunt temple attendants.

Onward, implement of lovely, fresh laurel!
Sweep the steps leading up to Phoebus' temple—
this broom plucked from undying gardens
where sacred waters send forth their never-failing spring,
and moisten the sacred bush of myrtle.
With this laurel each day I sweep the god's floor,
as soon as the sun's swift wing* appears,
as part of my daily round of work.

Paean,* blessings on you; blessings, Paean, son of Leto.*

Phoebus, out of reverence for your oracular shrine
I work for you here in front of your temple and count the toil fair.*
Since my master is not human but an immortal god,
my work, however menial, is a source of glory.
I never get tired of labouring at my sacred tasks.
Phoebus is my father, for I honour the one who feeds me
and call by the name of father Phoebus,
whose temple this is and from whose bounty I benefit.

Paean, blessings on you; blessings, Paean, son of Leto.

But now I shall stop working with the laurel broom.
Instead, as one celibate and undefiled,
I shall dampen the ground with water,
sprinkling from golden vessels Earth's stream,
collected from the eddying Castalian spring.
I pray that this service of mine to Phoebus may never end—
or that if it does, I meet with good fortune.

Aha! Here they come now!* The birds are leaving their nests on Parnassus.
I forbid you to approach the caves or the gold-decked halls!
Herald of Zeus,* I've shot you before with my arrows, and shall do so again,
for all that the strength of your beak is unrivalled among birds.
But here is another bird sailing in towards the temple—a swan!
Why don't you take your red feet off elsewhere? So Phoebus' lyre
harmonizes with your song—but that will not protect you from my shafts.
Fly on past here! Settle on the lake of Delos!* Your beautiful song
will turn to lamentation if you fail to heed my command!
Aha! What's this? Another bird of some kind.* I suppose it plans
to build a nest of straw for its young under the eaves.
The twanging of my bow will stop you. Won't you do as you're told?
Go and rear your fledglings by the swirling Alpheus
or in the sacred grove on the Isthmus*—anywhere,
so long as the treasures and Phoebus' temple remain unspoiled.
And yet I shrink from killing you birds, who bring the gods' messages to men. Still, I shall perform in Phoebus' service the work I have been given.
I shall never stop serving those who feed me and look after me.

Enter CHORUS.* *They divide into two Semichoruses.*

SEMICHORUS A. So sacred Athens is not the only place with porticoed courtyards for the gods and worship of the divine protector of highways. Here too, in the temple of Leto's son Loxias, twin faces gleam with fair-eyed light.*

SEMICHORUS B. See here! Look! The son of Zeus is slaying the Lernaean Hydra* with a golden sword! Do come and look, my dear!

SEMICHORUS A. I can see him. And next to him there's

someone else, raising on high a blazing brand. I wonder if it's the warrior Iolaus, whose story I hear while at work on my loom,* and who shared with the son of Zeus the burden and suffering of his labours.

SEMICHORUS B. And look at this man riding a winged horse! He's slaying a three-bodied, fire-breathing monster!*

SEMICHORUS A. Yes, my eyes dart in all directions. Look at the rout of the giants depicted on the marble walls!

SEMICHORUS B. We can see it from here, dears.

SEMICHORUS A. Well, can you see the goddess wielding against Enceladus her shield with its Gorgon heads?*

SEMICHORUS B. Yes, it's Pallas, my native city's goddess!

SEMICHORUS A. Of course. And what about the mighty thunderbolt, flaming at both ends,* Zeus holds in his far-striking hands?

SEMICHORUS B. I can see it: he's incinerating dread Minas.*

SEMICHORUS A. And Bromius, the Bacchants' god, is slaying another of Earth's children with his ivy-entwined wand, unwarlike though it is.*

They catch sight of ION.

CHORUS. You there, near the temple! Are we allowed to enter the sanctuary and walk there, provided our feet are unshod?

ION. No, strangers, it's not allowed.

CHORUS. But may I ask you a question?

ION. Yes, go on: what do you want?

CHORUS. Is it true that Phoebus' temple occupies the exact centre of the world?

ION. Yes, the navel-stone is here, adorned with wreaths and surrounded by Gorgons.

CHORUS. That's what we had heard.

ION. To enter the sanctuary, you need to have a question for Phoebus and to have offered up a honey-cake* in front of the temple; and to enter the inner chambers of the temple, you need to have sacrificed a sheep.

CHORUS. I see. We won't break the temple rules. We'll just enjoy the sight of what's outside the sanctuary.

ION. Yes, there's nothing to stop you doing that. Look around everywhere.

CHORUS. It was my mistress who gave me permission to come and see this sanctuary of Apollo.

ION. Tell me, whose slaves are you? To what household do you belong?

CHORUS. The royal palace where my mistress grew up is next to Pallas' temple. But here she is—here's the person you're asking about.

Enter CREUSA.

ION. I don't know who you are, my lady, but I can see the stamp of nobility in the way you bear yourself. Usually, where a person is concerned, his bearing tells you whether he is nobly born. (*CREUSA begins to weep*) Oh, how disturbing! The sight of Loxias' holy oracle has made you close your eyes and wet your noble cheeks with tears. What's the matter, my lady? Why are you crying, when everyone else enjoys the sight of the god's sanctuary?

CREUSA. Your surprise at my tears, sir, shows sensitivity on your part. When I saw this temple of Apollo, I went back over some old memories. I was here, but I had turned my mind elsewhere. Oh, how wretched we women are! And how shamefully the gods behave! So where shall we go for justice when our masters do us wrong and ruin us?*

ION. You're being rather mysterious, my lady. Why are you so miserable?

CREUSA. It's nothing. I've shot my bolt. I won't mention it again and you needn't concern yourself about it.

ION. All right, but who are you? Where have you come from, and what is the country of your birth? What should I call you?

CREUSA. My name is Creusa. I am the daughter of Erechtheus, and my homeland is the city of Athens.

ION. An illustrious city, madam, and a noble lineage. Very impressive.

CREUSA. In fact, that is as far as my good fortune goes, sir.*

ION. Do tell me, please, is the story people tell true?

CREUSA. What are you getting at, sir? What do you want to know?

ION. Was your father's father really born from the earth?

CREUSA. Erichthonius, yes—not that having him as an ancestor has done me any good.

ION. And was it Athena who raised him up out of the ground?*

CREUSA. Yes, and entrusted him to the care of some maidens, since she wasn't his mother.

ION. Are the traditional paintings correct?* Did she hand him over . . .?

CREUSA. To Cecrops' daughters, yes. They were supposed to keep him safe without looking at him.

ION. I've heard that the young women did undo Athena's casket, though.

CREUSA. That's right, and they paid for it with their deaths. Their blood stained the rocks at the foot of the cliff.

ION. Well now, here's another question for you. Is it true or false . . .?

CREUSA. What's your question? I don't mind—I'm in no hurry.

ION. Did your father Erechtheus offer up your sisters in sacrifice?

CREUSA. Yes, he hardened his heart and used young girls as his victims. It was done to defend his country.*

ION. Why were you the only one of the sisters to survive?

CREUSA. I was just a new-born baby at the time, in my mother's arms.

ION. And is it true that the earth opened up and swallowed your father?*

CREUSA. It was the sea-god's doing: he struck the ground with his trident and killed him.

ION. Is there a place in your country called the Long Rocks?

CREUSA. Why do you ask? You've brought back memories . . .

ION. It's just that the place is famous for its association with Phoebus† and the Pythian lightning.*

CREUSA. ⟨. . .⟩† I wish I'd never seen it.

ION. What's this? Do you hate something the god likes so much?

CREUSA. It's nothing—only that I know well something that brings the caves there into disrepute.

ION. And which Athenian married you and made you his wife?

CREUSA. My husband is no Athenian, but a foreigner from abroad.

ION. Who is he? He must be a man of noble birth.

CREUSA. His name is Xuthus, and he is descended from Aeolus and Zeus.

ION. And how did he, a foreigner, come to marry you, an Athenian?

CREUSA. Next to Athens lies the land of Euboea . . .

ION. Which is surrounded with water on all sides, I hear.

CREUSA. Xuthus joined forces with us Athenians and sacked the island.

ION. As your ally? And then he took you in marriage?

CREUSA. Yes, gaining my dowry as a reward for his help in the war.*

ION. Has he come here to the oracle with you or are you alone?

CREUSA. He's here too, but he's been delayed at the precinct of Trophonius.*

ION. Has he come to see the sights or to consult the oracles?

CREUSA. There's just one response he wants to hear from both Trophonius and Phoebus.

ION. What has brought you both here? To ask about crops or what?†

CREUSA. We're childless, even after all these years of marriage.

ION. You've never had any children? None at all?

CREUSA (*ironically*). Phoebus knows the truth of my childlessness.

ION. You poor thing—so lucky otherwise, but still unlucky.

CREUSA. And what about you? Who are you? How fortunate your mother is!

ION. My lady, I am known as a slave of the god, and that is what I am.

CREUSA. Were you sold by some individual, or were you an offering made by a city?

ION. All I know is that I am said to belong to Loxias.

CREUSA. Now it's my turn to feel sorry for you, sir.

ION. Because I don't know who my mother and father were.

CREUSA. And do you live in this temple or in a house?

ION. The whole of the god's dwelling is mine. I sleep wherever sleep overtakes me.

CREUSA. Were you a boy when you arrived at the temple, or a young man?

ION. People who seem to know what they're talking about say I was a baby.

CREUSA. And which woman of Delphi nursed you and gave you milk?

ION. I never knew the breast. The woman who brought me up . . .*

CREUSA. Who was she? You poor boy. Here I find suffering to match my own.

ION. I look on Phoebus' priestess as my mother.

CREUSA. But you're a man now. From where did you get food?

ION. The altars and the constant stream of visitors fed me.

CREUSA. You do all right, to judge by the clothes you're wearing.

ION. This finery belongs to the god whose slave I am.

CREUSA. Didn't you rush to try to find out who your parents were?

ION. No, because I had no clues, my lady.

CREUSA. Then your mother deserves pity, whoever she may be.

ION. Perhaps I was born as a result of some woman's sin.

CREUSA. Ah! Then there's another woman who shares your mother's experience.

ION. Who's that? I'd welcome any support in my efforts.

CREUSA. She's the reason I've come here ahead of my husband.

ION. What is it you want? If I can be of any help, my lady . . .

CREUSA. I want Phoebus to give me an oracle in secret.

ION. Please explain. I'll take care of everything else.

CREUSA. All right, here's the story I have to tell. But I feel ashamed.

ION. That will get you nowhere. Shame is a sluggish deity.

CREUSA. One of my friends* claims she lay with Phoebus.

ION. A mortal woman with Phoebus? How can you say such a thing, stranger?

CREUSA. And what's more she bore the god a child without her father's knowledge.

ION. Impossible! She's just ashamed at the wrong done her by a man.

CREUSA. That's not what she says. And she has suffered dreadfully.

ION. Why would she have suffered, with a god as her lover?

CREUSA. She abandoned the child she bore, her son.

ION. Where is the boy who was exposed? Is he alive?

CREUSA. No one knows. That's exactly what I want to ask the oracle.

ION. If he's dead, how did he die?

CREUSA. She assumes that wild animals killed the poor child.

ION. What evidence does she have for this idea?

CREUSA. She went back to where she'd left him and found him gone.

ION. Were there spots of blood on the trail?

CREUSA. She says not. And yet she went back and forth over the ground time and time again.

ION. How long is it since the boy was disposed of?

CREUSA. If he was alive, he'd be the same age as you.

ION. I wonder if Phoebus took him and brought him up in secret.

CREUSA. If so, he's wrong to enjoy alone pleasures meant to be shared.

ION. The god does wrong, and the mother suffers.

CREUSA. Yes, and she hasn't subsequently had another child.

ION. Alas! Her misfortune and my pain are so similar!*

CREUSA. I imagine your poor mother longs for you too, sir.

ION. Ah! Don't make me upset! I don't dwell on that.

CREUSA. I'll say no more. Go on with what I was asking you about.

ION. All right. Do you know the main problem your cause faces?

CREUSA. Everything is a painful struggle for that poor woman.

ION. Why would the god reveal in an oracle something he wants to keep hidden?

CREUSA. Because the tripod on which he sits is open to all Greeks.*

ION. He feels shame for what he did. Don't put him to the test.

CREUSA. But she feels pain—she suffers in her misfortune.

ION. No one will act as the god's spokesman for you on this matter.* Were it to be revealed, within his own house, that Phoebus had done wrong, he would be justified in injuring the person who announced the oracle to you. Forget it, my lady. Questions inimical to the god should not be put to the oracle. Advantages we gain after striving for them with all our might against the will of the gods do us no good, my lady. It is the things they give us of their own accord that benefit us.

CHORUS. There are many mortal men, and many indeed and varied are the calamities to which they are subject. It would be hard to find a single man whose life is filled with good fortune.

CREUSA. Phoebus, you wrong her—both here and in Athens you wrong the woman who is not here in person but is represented by her story. Not only did you fail in your duty to save your child, but now you betray your gift of prophecy by refusing to respond to the mother's question, when an answer would allow him either to have a tomb heaped up over him, if he's dead, or, if alive, to meet his mother one day. Still, I had better leave off such complaints,† since it is the god who prevents me from learning what I want to know. But here comes my noble husband Xuthus, sir: I can see him drawing near, now that he has left the chambers of Trophonius. Please don't mention to my husband what we've been talking about: I'd rather avoid any embarrassment that might be caused me by my performance of this secret favour, and your conversation with him might not proceed along the same course as ours. Women's business is distasteful to men, and, good or bad, we all meet indiscriminately with loathing. This is the measure of our misfortune.

Enter XUTHUS.

XUTHUS. The first-fruits of my salutation belong to the god, and so I greet him first. As for you, wife, I hope my delay in coming did not fill you with dread.

CREUSA. No, but I had just begun to get worried. But tell me, what response do you bring from Trophonius? How may the child-seed from the two of us be blended together?*

XUTHUS. He chose not to anticipate the god's oracle. Still, he did say one thing—that neither you nor I would return home childless from the oracular shrine.*

CREUSA. I pray to you, divine lady, mother of Phoebus,* for fair prospects for our visit here, and for a favourable outcome, in so far as it is up to your son, to the earlier business between the two of us.

XUTHUS. It shall be so. But who will act as spokesman for the god?

ION. I shall take care of procedure outside the shrine, but what happens inside, sir, is the responsibility of others, who sit near the tripod. They have been chosen by lot from among the élite of Delphi.

XUTHUS. Excellent. I have everything I wanted. I shall go inside now. I've been informed that the victim offered in front of the temple for all visitors* has already fallen. The day is favourable, and I'd like to receive the god's oracle today. As for you, wife, take branches around the laurel-laden altars* and pray to the gods that I return from Apollo's house with oracles that augur well for children.

Exit XUTHUS into the temple.

CREUSA. It shall be so, it shall be so. And if Loxias is now finally prepared to make amends for his earlier wrongdoing, although I won't be completely reconciled to him, I shall at least bow to his will. He is a god, after all.

Exit CREUSA.

ION. Why is the visitor constantly railing against the god in dark and riddling speech? I suspect it's because she's close to the woman on whose behalf she's consulting the oracle, but it may be that she's not mentioning something she has to keep to herself. But what business of mine is the daughter of Erechtheus? She's nothing to me.

Anyway, now I'll go to fill the lustral bowls with water poured from golden jugs. (*He pauses on his way*) But I must take Phoebus to task. What's got into him? Raping and then abandoning virgins? Secretly fathering children and then nonchalantly letting them die? You should be the last to do this, Phoebus: you have the power, so you should make virtue your goal. Human wickedness is punished by the gods, so how can it be right for you gods to make laws for us and then to be guilty of breaking those same laws yourselves? If—not that it will happen, but just for the sake of argument—if you and Poseidon and Zeus, the lord of the heavens, are going to be brought to book by humans for all the rapes you've committed,* the penalties will empty your temples. Where you go wrong is in indulging your whims beyond the limits of prudence. It stops being fair to call men 'bad' if all we're doing is imitating what is acceptable behaviour among the gods. No, it should be those who educate us in these ways who are called 'bad'.

Exit ION.

CHORUS (*sings*). Athena, goddess of my native city, you in whose birth
Eleithuia with her labour-pains played no part,
you who were born thanks to the Titan Prometheus
from the very crown of Zeus' head, come, blessed Victory,*
I implore you, come to the dwelling of the Pythian god,*
fly from your golden chambers on Olympus* to the streets of Delphi,
where by the tripod celebrated in song and dance
Phoebus' altar, at the navel-centre of the earth,
reveals true oracles. I call on you and Leto's daughter—
both goddesses, both virgins,* revered sisters of Phoebus.
Young maidens, pray with me that the ancient line of Erechtheus
may meet at last with fertility thanks to oracles that are clear.

Men with ancestral chambers illuminated by the fruitful young vigour
of children possess a sure fund of overwhelming happiness,
for then the children themselves will keep the wealth
inherited from their fathers for further children.
Children offer protection in times of trouble and affection
in times of good fortune, and in war they wield
protective might for the land of their fathers.
I, at any rate, would rather have trusty children to nurture
and care for than wealth and a royal palace.
Abominable to me is a life without children,
and I deplore those who find it to their liking.
I pray that I may embrace a life of moderate means and many children.

O abode of Pan, rocky neighbour to the Long Rocks with their caverns,
where the three maiden daughters of Aglaurus dance*
and tread with their feet the grassy swards before Pallas' temple,
to the quavering sound of the songs of the pipes when you play them,
Pan, in your sunless caves. There once a wretched young woman,

unmarried, the mother of Phoebus' child, exposed the baby to be a feast for birds and bloody meal for beasts, the terrible outcome of a bitter union. Neither when working at my loom nor in the telling of stories have I heard that children born to the gods by mortals meet with happiness.

Enter ION, carrying bowls of water, which he puts down.

ION. Since you serving-women are waiting here by the steps of the sacrificial temple and watching out for your mistress, could you tell me whether Xuthus has already left the sacred tripod and the oracle, or whether he's still inside enquiring about his childless state?

CHORUS. He's inside, sir. He hasn't yet emerged from the temple. But I can hear the sound of the doors, suggesting that he's on his way out—and now I can see him stepping outside.

Enter XUTHUS from the temple.

XUTHUS. My son—an opening I may appropriately use—I wish you well!*

ION. Thank you, I am well. And if you are in your right mind, both of us will be fine.

XUTHUS. Give me your hand as a token of affection, and let me take you in my arms!

ION. Are you sure you're in your right mind? Perhaps some god has driven you out of your wits.

XUTHUS. Isn't it a sign of sanity for me to want to embrace my nearest and dearest now that I've found him?

XUTHUS tries to embrace ION.

ION. Stop! If you touch the sacred garlands you might break them!

XUTHUS. I will clasp you in my arms! I'm not stealing what doesn't belong to me, but discovering what is my own, and dear to me!

ION makes a move to take the bow off his shoulders.

ION. Back off, before you get an arrow in your guts!

XUTHUS. Why are you frightened of recognizing me as your nearest and dearest?

ION. I don't usually explain myself to rude, crazy strangers.

XUTHUS. Do your worst—kill me, burn my corpse. But if you do, you'll be murdering your father.

ION. What do you mean, you're my father? Is this some kind of joke?

XUTHUS. No. You'd see what I'm getting at if you'd let me carry on with my tale.

ION. What do you have to tell me?

XUTHUS. I am your father and you are my son.

ION. Says who?

XUTHUS. Loxias, who brought you up even though you were mine.

ION. I have only your word for it.

XUTHUS. Yes, but this is what I was given to understand by the god's oracle.

ION. You must have misinterpreted a riddling response.

XUTHUS. Not if I heard correctly.

ION. What did Phoebus say?

XUTHUS. That whoever I met . . .

ION. Where? When?

XUTHUS. . . . as I came out of the god's temple here . . .

ION. What would happen to him?

XUTHUS. . . . was my son.

ION. Your natural son, or given you by others?

XUTHUS. Given to me, despite being my natural son.

ION. And I was the first person you came across?

XUTHUS. Exactly, my son.

ION. How on earth did this happen?

XUTHUS. That's just what I'm wondering too.

ION. Which woman bore me for you? Who is my mother?

XUTHUS. I couldn't tell you.

ION. And Phoebus didn't tell you either?

XUTHUS. I was happy enough with what he'd already said, and didn't ask him that question.

ION. So was the earth my mother?

XUTHUS. Children aren't born from the ground.*

ION. Then how can I be your son?

XUTHUS. I don't know, but I refer you to the god.

ION. Let's come at this from another angle.

XUTHUS. That would be better, my son.

ION. Did you ever have an illicit liaison?

XUTHUS. Yes, when I was young and foolish.

ION. Before marrying Erechtheus' daughter?

XUTHUS. Of course—certainly not afterwards.

ION. So that must have been where you fathered me.

XUTHUS. The time is right.

ION. But how did I subsequently get to Delphi . . .

XUTHUS. I've no idea.

ION. . . . from so far away?

XUTHUS. That puzzles me too.

ION. Have you visited rocky Delphi before?

XUTHUS. Yes, for the torchlit ceremony in honour of Bacchus.*

ION. Did you stay in one of the official guest-houses?

XUTHUS. Yes, and my host took me and some young local women . . .

ION. . . . and formed you into a Bacchic coven? What else might you mean?

XUTHUS. Yes, and they were under the influence of Bacchus.

ION. And were you sober or drunk?

XUTHUS. I had succumbed to the delights of Bacchus.

ION. That's it! The place were I was conceived . . .

XUTHUS. . . . has been revealed by destiny, my son.

ION. I wonder how I got to the temple.

XUTHUS. Perhaps the young woman abandoned you there.

ION. At least there's no chance of my being a slave.

XUTHUS. Accept me as your father, my son.

ION. Well, I suppose it would be wrong to disbelieve the god.

XUTHUS. This shows that you're in your right mind.

ION. And what could be preferable . . .

XUTHUS. Now you're seeing things clearly.

ION. . . . to being the son of offspring of Zeus?

XUTHUS. And that's just what you are.

ION. Shall I then embrace my father?

XUTHUS. Yes, with confidence in the god.

They embrace, somewhat stiffly.

ION. I wish you well, father . . .

XUTHUS. That's a lovely thing for me to hear.

ION. . . . and I salute today as well.

XUTHUS. It has certainly made me happy.

ION. Dear mother, when, I wonder, shall I see your face too?

Now even more than before I long to look on you, whoever you are. But perhaps you're dead, and I won't be able to see you even in a dream.

CHORUS. When the royal house prospers, we share in that prosperity. But I would like our mistress and Erechtheus' line to be blessed with children too.

XUTHUS. My son, the god's oracle about your discovery came true and joined you to me. And for your part you have discovered your nearest and dearest, previously unknown to you. But you're right to jump on to the next step, and I share your longing: I would love you to find your mother, my son, and, for myself, I would love to see what kind of woman gave you life. If we trust to time we may perhaps realize these goals. But now it's time to leave the god's domain and your rootless life and go to Athens in unanimity with your father. (*ION is silent and glum*) Do you have nothing to say? Why do you hang your head and give yourself over to worries? Why has your mood changed again from happiness? It makes your father anxious.

ION. Things look different close to and from far away. I'm delighted with what's happened—with finding out that you're my father—but here's what's on my mind, father. It's said that the people of glorious Athens, whose roots lie in the land where they live, are not incomers from abroad. I shall arrive there, then, with two defects—being the son of a foreigner, and being illegitimate. With this stigma, if I remain a political lightweight I'll be said to be a nothing born of nobodies,† and if I set my sights on the first ranks of the city and endeavour to make something of myself, I shall incur the hatred of the lower classes, since greater power always provokes rancour. At the same time, any decent man from the upper class, who has the sense to keep his views to himself and to remain aloof from politics, will laugh at me and count me foolish for taking an active part in a city which is riddled with fault-finders. On the other hand, if I acquire a more prestigious position in society than the orators† and statesmen, they will use their votes to keep me down. For what usually happens, father, is that the powers that be in a city, the men with prestige, are deadly enemies of their rivals.

Then there's the fact that I shall be coming as an outsider

into someone else's home and living with a childless woman, who may have been your partner in your earlier situation, but has now been deprived of that position: in her isolation, she will bitterly resent her misfortune. I am bound to be hated by her—and who could blame her?—when I stand close by your side. In her childless condition she will look on any children of yours with resentment. You will have a choice, then: either to let me down and side with your wife, or to respect my rights and have a house torn with constant disruption. Look at all the wives who have stabbed or poisoned their husbands! In any case, I feel sorry for your wife, father, growing old without children. With her noble ancestry she doesn't deserve to be afflicted with childlessness.

Kingship does not deserve the praise that is lavished upon it: all smiles on the surface, it is racked with pain inside. For no one can be content or happy if they spend their lives in fear and expectation of violence. I'd rather limit my fortune to the lot of a commoner than live as a king, who can find pleasure only in the friendship of bad men, and who is so afraid of being killed that he loathes the company of good men. You might argue that riches more than compensate for this, and that wealth is pleasant, but I find no satisfaction in hoarding wealth with condemnation ringing in my ears and with troubles plaguing me. No, I pray for moderate wealth and a carefree life!

Let me tell you, father, all the advantages I enjoyed here. First, I had spare time, which everyone prizes above all else, and few problems. No lout ever elbowed me out of his way—it is intolerable to yield and give way to such people. In my prayers to the gods and my conversations with others, I was serving those who were happy, not miserable. New visitors would arrive to replace those I had sped on their way, and so I was always welcome, and no one grew tired of my company, nor I of theirs. Finally, both convention and my natural inclination made me behave with integrity towards the god, and that is what all men pray for, albeit reluctantly at times. In view of all this, father, I think my circumstances here are preferable to what I would find in Athens. So please let me live here. After all, there's no difference in feeling between the pleasures of simplicity and enjoyment of the high life.

CHORUS. Your sentiments are sound, but I only hope that those who are dear to me will find happiness if you get your way.

XUTHUS. I'll hear no more of this talk! Learn to be happy! I'd like to make a start at the place where I found you, my son, with a communal table, since I am moved to set up a feast in which all can share, and I want to perform the birthday sacrifices* for you that I never performed before. What I'll do now is take you to the feast (making out that you are a guest-friend, of course), which I'm sure you'll enjoy, and then I'll take you to Athens, as if you had come to see the sights, not as a member of my family. I too don't want my good fortune to upset my wife in her childless state. But in due course I'll seize the opportunity to prevail upon my wife to let you take over my kingdom. And I name you 'Ion', in keeping with what has happened, because you were the first to cross my path as I came out of the god's shrine.* Anyway, round up the full complement of your friends and find time during the celebrations accompanying the sacrifice of the ox to make your farewells, since you're about to leave Delphi. As for you, serving-women, I command you not to breathe a word of this to my wife, on pain of death if you do.

ION. Off I go, then. But there's one thing that spoils my happiness, father: if I fail to find my mother, my life won't be worth living. If this is something I should pray for, then I pray that my mother is of Athenian descent, so that from her side I may possess freedom of speech.* For if a stranger arrives in a city which is untainted by foreign blood, he may nominally be a citizen, but in fact he has the tongue of a slave, with no freedom of speech.

Exeunt ION *and* XUTHUS.

CHORUS (*sings*). I see tears, cries of grief, and the onset of woe when my lady,
the queen, learns that her husband has been blessed with children
while she remains childless, bereft of offspring.
Son of Leto, chanter of prophecies, what kind of response did you give?
What are the origins of this boy, the nursling of your temple?
What woman bore him? I have misgivings; within the oracle

I suspect treachery. I fear what may happen and feel anxious
for the future. Weird are the words of the god, and weird are the feelings
they provoke in me. The boy weaves cunning lies; he was born
and bred a foreigner. Surely all of you agree with me in this?

Friends, shall I speak plainly in my mistress's ear of her husband, on whom
the poor woman depends utterly, in whom she found a partner for her hopes?
As things are, in her declining years—what a contrast with his happiness!—
she is overwhelmed, devastated, while her husband dishonours
those who should be dear to him. How despicable to have come as an outsider
to a house, to have enjoyed its great wealth, without sharing equally in its fortunes!
Damn him! Damn him for deceiving my royal mistress! May he meet with no success
when on the fire he sacrifices to the gods the brightly burning cake.*
He will soon discover my feelings ⟨if he abuses⟩† things dear to the royal family.
Right now father and son, each new to the other, are prey to catastrophe!

O Parnassian ridge with sheer cliff and terrace as high as heaven,
where Bacchus, pine torches in either hand, prances light of foot
with his night-roaming Bacchants! I pray that the boy
may never reach my city! I pray that his young life
may come to an abrupt end! For in defending itself
against foreign invasion the city might have a pretext ⟨. . .⟩†
when our former leader, King Erechtheus, mustered his troops.

Enter CREUSA *and* OLD MAN, *who has a staff. She is helping him along.*

CREUSA. Up you come, old friend—up to the god's oracular

shrine. You once were tutor to my father Erechtheus,* when he was alive, and I'd like you to share my happiness, if the lord Loxias spoke an oracle of some kind about my giving birth to children. The company of friends at times of good fortune is a joy, and it's also pleasant to have a sympathetic face to look on if something bad happens—not that it will, I hope! In times past you took care of my father, and now, although I am your mistress, it's my turn to take care of you, as if you were my father.

OLD MAN. Daughter, the noble ways of your forebears are kept nobly alive by you. You are a credit to your family, the descendants of the men of old whose roots lie in the land where they live. Give me your hand and pull me up towards the shrine—I find the way steep. But if you help me out, you'll bring relief to my aged body.

CREUSA. Stay close to me, then, and tread carefully.

OLD MAN. There. Slow of foot, quick of mind—that's me.

CREUSA. Lean on your stick. The path is uneven.

OLD MAN. My poor sight makes my stick blind too.

CREUSA. True, but you mustn't give up, however hard you find it.

OLD MAN. It's not that I want to, but I'm not as strong as I used to be.

CREUSA. Hello there, women, trusty workers with the shuttle at my looms! Before he left the shrine, what was my husband told? We came here to learn about children, so what does the future hold for us in that regard? Tell me. If you give me good news, you can trust me to be less ungrateful than some masters are. You won't be doing me a wasted favour.

CHORUS. Such wretched luck!

CREUSA. This is hardly an auspicious beginning.

CHORUS. Poor you!

CREUSA. Has the oracle brought pain to your mistress, then?

CHORUS. Oh, what am I to do? The outcome could be fatal!

CREUSA. Why such a mournful strain? What has made you afraid?

CHORUS. Shall I speak or be silent? What shall I do?

CREUSA. Speak—though it looks as if your words will spell doom for me.

CHORUS. I shall speak, then, even at the risk of doubling the threat of death.* Mistress, you will never have children to hold in your arms or clasp to your breast.

CREUSA. Alas! Then I pray for death!

OLD MAN. Daughter . . .

CREUSA. What a cruel blow! I am wounded! The pain I suffer is more than life can bear, my friends. This is the end of me!

OLD MAN. My child . . .

CREUSA. Ah, woe, woe! The pain! It pierces me to the heart!

OLD MAN. Don't cry yet . . .

CREUSA. But I already have reason for tears!

OLD MAN. . . . not until we find out . . .

CREUSA. What? What might I hear?

OLD MAN. . . . whether my master is in the same situation. Has the catastrophe overwhelmed him too, or are you alone in your misfortune?

CHORUS. In fact, old man, Loxias has given *him* a child. He's happy, but it's his own personal happiness, and she has no part in it.

CREUSA (*sobbing*). This too, on top of the troubles I already have? You could not have said . . . said anything more painful, more certain to cause me grief.

OLD MAN. This child you mentioned—is he to be born from some woman, or is he already alive? What did the god say?

CHORUS. Loxias gave him a son born long ago, now a full-grown young man. I was there.

CREUSA. What do you mean? I can't . . . no, I can't bear to hear what you're saying!

OLD MAN. Nor can I. But please explain how the oracle came to be fulfilled, and who the boy is.

CHORUS. The god gave your husband as his son the first person he would meet as he hastened out of the temple.

CREUSA. Aaaaaah! Then he has condemned my life to be childless, childless! I shall live in isolation in a house deprived of children!

OLD MAN. So who did the oracle mean? Who did this poor woman's husband meet? How did he see him? Where?

CHORUS. Mistress, you know the young man who was sweeping this temple? He's his son.

CREUSA. May I fly on the supple air far from the land of Greece to the western stars! That is my wish, friends, to escape from this pain, this terrible pain I suffer!*

OLD MAN. What does his father call him? Do you know, or does it remain uncertain, cloaked in silence?

CHORUS. He calls him 'Ion', since he was the first his father met. But I cannot say who the mother was. And now he's gone off—just so that you know all the news I have, old man—secretly, without his wife's knowledge, to a consecrated tent to perform birthday and guest-friend sacrifices, and to inaugurate with his new-found son a communal feast.

OLD MAN. Mistress, I share your pain. We have been betrayed by your husband, and we are being deliberately abused and expelled from Erechtheus' house. I say this not out of hatred for your husband, but because you are more dear to me than he is. For he came to Athens a foreigner,* took you as his wife, was given your house and all your property—and now it turns out that he was secretly spawning children by another woman! I'll tell you how it all remained secret. When he realized you were childless, he had no mind to be the same and to share the burden of this misfortune. No, he secretly took a slave into his bed, had sex with her, and fathered the child, who was then sent away and given to an inhabitant of Delphi to bring up. The boy's childhood was spent loose in the god's temple, because that was a good way to hide him. When he realized that the boy had grown to be a young man, he used your childlessness as a means of persuading you to come here. And so it was not the god who lied, but he who lied, since he had long been bringing the child up, and was weaving this web of treachery. If he had ever been found out, he would have blamed the god; but, having got away with it,† and wanting to ward off the effects of time, he was intending to invest his son with the rulership of our country.

CHORUS. Oh, how I hate, and always will, evil men who disguise their wicked schemes with fair contrivances! Give me as a friend a plain but honest man, rather than someone with more intelligence who is bad!

OLD MAN. But the worst of all your troubles is this: into your house as its master he brings a motherless good-for-nothing, the child of some slave or other. It would have been less devious had he prevailed upon you, citing your childlessness, and then introduced into the house the child of a well-born mother. And if that was distasteful to you, he should have sought marriage with the house of Aeolus.* And so you must act as women do. You must take up a sword, or resort to trickery or poison, and kill your husband and his son before death comes your way from them. For be assured that if you shrink from this, you will lose your life. After all, when two hostile forces meet under one roof things are bound to go badly for one or the other of them. Now, I am willing to help you out by murdering the boy: I'll sneak into the place where he's preparing the feast and repay the debt I owe my masters for keeping me, whether in the attempt I die or live to see the light of day. For the only source of shame for slaves is their name: in all other respects a slave is no worse than a free man, as long as he is good.

CHORUS. The same goes for me, mistress: whether it brings death or life with honour I shall make this catastrophe mine as well as yours.†

CREUSA (*sings*). O my heart, how shall I keep silent?
But how shall I disclose my secret union
and yet be free of shame?
But what is there now to stop me?
The contest now is not one of virtue.*
Has my husband not become my betrayer?
I am robbed of my home, robbed of children.
Gone are my hopes. I failed in my desire
to set them right, though silent I remained
about the union and the birth, the source of all my tears.
No, by the star-studded seat of Zeus,
by the goddess who dwells on the cliffs of my city,
and by the august shore of Triton's deep-watered lake,*
I shall no longer conceal the liaison,
and with this burden removed from my heart
I shall be more easy. My eyes shed tears,
and my heart is hurt by the evil schemes
it suffers at the hands of both men and gods,
ungrateful traitors to their lovers, as I shall show.
You whose song accompanies the music
of the seven-stringed lyre, which on the lifeless horns

of field-dwelling beasts resounds the melodious songs
of the Muses,* son of Leto, your blame
I shall proclaim to the clear light of day.
You came to me, your hair gleaming like gold,
while I was gathering yellow petals in my lap,
their golden light reflected on my robe,
for a flower festival.* Clasping the white
of my wrists you took me, a god, my lover.
You laid me down in a cavern while I cried out 'O mother',
and you gratified Cypris* in a shameless manner.
And then—poor me!—I bore you a son,
and filled with maternal terror I cast him into that love-bed of yours,
the very place where you had coupled with me—poor me!—
in the wretched union that brought about my misery.
Oh, woe is me! And now he is gone, my son and yours,
seized by birds for them to feast upon. And you, callous one,
you just sing paeans* while strumming on your lyre.
Oh, yes! I accuse you, son of Leto, whose voice is heard
by the queueing visitors† to the golden seat*
and the shrine at the centre of the earth.
I shall proclaim my accusation in the open!
Ah! Ah, you vile lover! Into my house you bring a son
for my husband, though no favour did he do you first.
But my child—mine and yours—vanished, while still an infant,
a prey to birds, shedding his mother's baby clothes.
You are abhorrent to Delos* and to the shoots of laurel
growing alongside the delicate palm fronds
in the gardens of Zeus where Leto bore you in august birth.

CHORUS. Ah, how vast is the vault of misery here opened up!
No eye could remain dry at this.

OLD MAN. Daughter, the sight of your face fills me with sadness and scatters my wits. Scarcely have I finished bailing out my mind from one wave of grief, when another comes from behind and upends me. This second wave was driven by words of yours which, once uttered, take you down paths of evil formed by different woes, not the troubles confronting you now. What are you saying? What charge are you bringing against Loxias? Who is this child you say you bore? Whereabouts in the city did you abandon him? Where was this grave which wild animals relished? Please resume your tale.

CREUSA. It shames me to speak of it to you, old friend, but I shall.

OLD MAN. Don't worry. I know how to sympathize in full with the grief of those I love.

CREUSA. Listen, then. You know the north-facing cave in Cecrops' crags—the Long Rocks, as we call them?

OLD MAN. Yes, close to where Pan has his shrine and altar.*

CREUSA. That's where I was involved in a terrible struggle.

OLD MAN. What struggle? See how my tears meet your words.

CREUSA. I lay with Phoebus against my will—a union that has brought me misery.

OLD MAN. Could this have been what I noticed, daughter?

CREUSA. I've no idea, but I'll tell you if you're on the right track.

OLD MAN. It was when some hidden ailment used to make you grieve in secret.

CREUSA. That was the time of the troubles I'm now telling you about openly.

OLD MAN. So how did you conceal the fact that you lay with Phoebus?

CREUSA. I gave birth—be strong, old man, as you listen to what I have to say.

OLD MAN. Where? Did you have any help at the birth, or did you endure this pain alone?

CREUSA. I was all alone in the cave where he coupled with me.

OLD MAN. And where is the boy, to put an end to your childless state?

CREUSA. He's dead, old man, abandoned to the wild animals.

OLD MAN. Dead? Was cruel Apollo no good at all?

CREUSA. No, my son's childhood is being spent in Hades' halls.*

OLD MAN. Who put him out to die? Surely not you?

CREUSA. Yes, it was I, after dressing him in baby clothes in the darkness.

OLD MAN. But did no one else know about the child's being exposed?

CREUSA. No, catastrophe and concealment were my only companions.

OLD MAN. How did you harden your heart enough to abandon your son in the cave?

CREUSA. How? With many expressions of grief falling from my lips.

OLD MAN. Oh, what misery this act of cruelty has brought you! But your cruelty was less than Apollo's.

CREUSA. Yes, if you had seen my son with arms held out towards me!

OLD MAN. Seeking your breast, I suppose, or wanting perhaps to lie in your arms.

CREUSA. And by depriving him of them I have caused him undeserved suffering.

OLD MAN. When you chose to expose your child, what did you hope for?

CREUSA. That the god would rescue his own offspring, at least.

OLD MAN. Oh, what storms assail your house and its prosperity!

In distress, he pulls a fold of his khiton over his head.

CREUSA. Why have you covered your head, old man?* Why these tears?

OLD MAN. Because I see misfortune oppressing you and your father.

CREUSA. That's what it is to be human: there's no such thing as security.

OLD MAN. It's time now for us to turn from weeping, daughter.

He uncovers his head.

CREUSA. Why? What can I do? Misery is helpless.

OLD MAN. Pay back the god who first wronged you.

CREUSA. And how can I, a mere mortal, get the better of higher powers?

OLD MAN. Set fire to the holy shrine where Loxias delivers his oracles.

CREUSA. I fear to. I've suffered enough as it is.

OLD MAN. All right, then, find the courage to do what is within your power: kill your husband.

CREUSA. But there was a time when he was good, so I still honour our marriage.

OLD MAN. At least you can kill the boy who has come to supplant you.

CREUSA. If only it were possible! That would be my choice! But how?

OLD MAN. By equipping your slaves as swordsmen.

CREUSA. I'd go for that! But where is this to happen?

OLD MAN. In the consecrated tent where he's entertaining his friends.

CREUSA. Slaughter is hard to conceal, and slaves lack determination.

OLD MAN. Ah, I see you lack the courage for it. You come up with a plan, then.

CREUSA. In fact, I do have a plan—one which is both cunning and practicable.

OLD MAN. It will have my assistance in both respects.

CREUSA. Let me tell you it, then. You know the battle fought by Earth's offspring?

OLD MAN. Yes, when the giants took on the gods at Phlegra.*

CREUSA. That was when Earth gave birth to that hideous monster, the Gorgon.

OLD MAN. As an ally for her children, wasn't it? And to make things difficult for the gods?

CREUSA. Yes, and the goddess Pallas, Zeus' daughter, killed the Gorgon . . .

OLD MAN. Isn't the story you're telling the one with which I've long been familiar?

CREUSA. That Athena wears on her breast the Gorgon's skin.

OLD MAN. You mean Pallas' armour—the 'aegis', as it's called.

CREUSA. A name it acquired when she rushed to join the ranks of the gods.*

OLD MAN. What does the aegis look like? What has been made from the savage thing?

CREUSA. A breastplate equipped with a viper's coils.

OLD MAN. So how will this harm your enemies, daughter?

CREUSA. Do you know who I mean by Erichthonius, or not? But of course you do, old man.

OLD MAN. Yes, your first ancestor, who arose out of the earth.

CREUSA. Just after his birth Pallas gave him . . .

OLD MAN. What? Go on. Don't hesitate to tell me.

CREUSA. . . . two drops of blood from the Gorgon.

OLD MAN. And what effect do they have on humans?

CREUSA. One is fatal, while the other cures illness.

OLD MAN. What container did she use to attach them to the child's body?

CREUSA. A golden bracelet, which Erichthonius gave to my father.

OLD MAN. And when he died it came down to you?

CREUSA. Yes, and I wear it on my wrist.

She shows him it.

OLD MAN. So what use is ordained of the twofold gift of the goddess?

CREUSA. The blood which dripped from the hollow vein . . .*

OLD MAN. What does one do with it? What effect does it have?

CREUSA. . . . wards off illness and sustains life.

OLD MAN. And the second one you mentioned? What does it do?

CREUSA. It causes death, for it is poison from the Gorgon's snakes.

OLD MAN. Do you keep the poison apart, or do you carry it mixed with the other?

CREUSA. I keep them separate, since good and bad don't blend.

OLD MAN. My dearest child, you have everything you need.

CREUSA. That's how the boy will meet his death. And you shall be the assassin.

OLD MAN. Where and how shall I go about it? It's your job to explain, mine to find the courage.

CREUSA. In Athens, once he's come to my house.

OLD MAN. That's not a good idea. Well, you did criticize my suggestion.

CREUSA. What do you mean? Do you have the same worry that occurs to me?

OLD MAN. People will think you killed the boy, even if you didn't.

CREUSA. You're right, because of the notion that stepmothers resent children.*

OLD MAN. So kill him here, where you can deny any part in the murder.

CREUSA. That brings it so close that I can taste the sweetness already.

OLD MAN. And you'll hide from your husband what he's been trying to keep from you.*

CREUSA. So you know what to do. Take this antique golden bauble of Athena's from my wrist, (*she gives him the bracelet*) and go to where my husband has gone, without telling me, to sacrifice an ox.* When they've finished eating and are about to pour libations to the gods, with the bracelet hidden in your clothes quickly drip the poison into the drink of the young man who would be master of my house.† Having swallowed the drink, he will never come to illustrious Athens, but will remain here, the place of his death.

OLD MAN. You had better go inside the guest-house now, while I carry out my assignment. Come, old foot, even though time has robbed you of your youth, be youthful now in what you do! Proceed against your enemy on behalf of your mistress. Kill him, rid the house of him! You act with her blessing. In fortunate circumstances it's all very well to value piety, but when one intends to harm enemies no law stands in one's way.

Exeunt CREUSA *and* OLD MAN, *by separate exits.*

CHORUS (*sings*). O Lady of the Crossroads, daughter of Demeter!*
You rule over assaults carried out by night, but guide too
the fatal content of this day-time bowl against those whom my mistress
—ah, my mistress!—sends it, the poison formed from blood-drops
that fell from the severed throat of the earth-born Gorgon
against him who would seize the house of the children of Erechtheus.
Never may another come and rule over the city,
usurping the place of the noble children of Erechtheus!

If the murder comes to naught, and my mistress's efforts fail,
and the time slips by for the bold attempt which just now
caused a glimmer of hope to arise, she will take
either a whetted sword or a neck-encircling noose to her throat,
and, making a sorrowful end to all her sorrows, she will descend
to an alternative form of life. For never would one
as noble-born as she endure to live in the brilliant sunlight
and see strangers from abroad holding sway in the house.

I could not bear to face the god, celebrated in many a hymn,

if by the streams of Callichorus the usurper were to gaze in vigil,
a witness to the night-long torch of the twentieth day.*
Why, even the star-studded heavens of Zeus began the dance,
and the moon dances and the fifty Nereids,*
who by the sea and the tireless, eddying rivers
dance for the golden-crowned maiden and her reverend mother.*
That is where he hopes to rule, having inserted himself
into the hard-won achievements of others,
this rootless vagabond of Phoebus.

I call on all whose Muse takes you down the path
of singing raucous songs of the liaisons and unholy unions
to which law-breaking Cypris subjects us women
to see how far we surpass in piety men and their immoral coupling.
May a song and a raucous Muse with the opposite theme
be let loose against men, to sing of their unions!
For the descendant of Zeus displays his forgetfulness.*
When he could not father on my mistress the shared happiness
of children, he gratified his lust with another woman
and got himself a bastard son.

Enter SLAVE.

SLAVE. Women, where may I find our mistress, the illustrious daughter of Erechtheus? I've been looking for her all over the place. I've completed ⟨every possible journey throughout⟩† the city, but I haven't been able to find her.

CHORUS. What's up, my friend? Why are you in such a hurry? What news do you bring?

SLAVE. They're after us. The local rulers of the land are looking for her and want to stone her to death.

CHORUS. Oh, I dread what you're going to say! Surely we can't have been caught in our secret attempt to murder the boy?

SLAVE. You've guessed it. And punishment will be meted out first to you.

CHORUS. But our intrigues were secret. How did they come to be disclosed?

SLAVE. The god exposed them, since he had no desire to incur pollution.

CHORUS. How? I beg and beseech you to tell us all. For if we are to die, we will die happier for having heard your news—and the same goes if we are to live.

SLAVE. When Creusa's husband Xuthus left the oracular shrine with his new-found son and went to attend to the feast and the sacrifices he was preparing for the gods, he went to the place where the Bacchants' fire prances in honour of their god, to drench the two cliffs* of Dionysus with the blood of sacrifice in gratitude for the first sight of his son. Before going, he said: 'Son, you stay here and make use of the industry of labourers to erect a tent as an enclosure. If sacrificing to the gods of birth takes me a long time, please start the feast with those of your friends who are present.'

Once Xuthus had taken some heifers and left, the young man set about his task with due solemnity. He used upright poles to fix in place the surrounding framework, paying careful attention to the sun's rays to ensure that the tent would be open towards the sun neither at the heat of midday nor when it was going down. He measured out each side to be a plethron* in length and shaped the whole into a square enclosing an area of ten thousand feet, to use technical language, because he was intending to invite the whole population of Delphi to the feast. He borrowed from the treasuries* some wonderfully decorated tapestries that had been offered as sacred dedications and used them to provide shade. First, to form a wing-shaped roof, he threw over pieces of material which had been dedicated by Zeus' son Heracles, given by him to the god from the spoils he took from the Amazons.* Among them were tapestries woven with the following designs: with Heaven mustering the stars in the vault of the sky, the Sun-god was guiding his horses to the point of his flame's extinction, pulling in his wake the bright light of Hesperus.* Meanwhile, dark-cloaked Night, with stars in attendance, was urging on her pair-drawn, traceless chariot.* Through the centre of the sky were journeying the Pleiades and sword-bearing Orion, and above them went the Bear,* pivoting around the pole on his golden tail. The orb of the mid-month's full moon was shooting her darts upwards, and you could see the Hyades,* the clearest of signs for sailors, and light-bringing Dawn putting the stars to flight. The sides he covered with other eastern tapestries, showing ships well equipped with oars drawn up opposite Greek vessels,* hybrid semi-human creatures,* the horseback hunting of deer, and the pursuit of fierce lions. At the entrance to the tent he placed the dedication of an Athenian, depicting Cecrops with intertwining coils and daughters near by,* and in the middle of the dining-area he set up mixing-bowls of gold.

A town-crier then strutted around, announcing that any of the local inhabitants who wanted to could come to the feast. When the tent was full they put garlands on their heads and feasted on the plentiful food to their heart's content. Afterwards, when they were happily full,† an old man entered and stood in the middle, and afforded plenty of amusement to the diners with his officious behaviour. For he brought water in jugs for them to wash their hands, burnt the resin of myrrh for its fragrance, and took charge of the golden cups, with no one else's authority for undertaking these tasks than his own. When it was time for the pipe-players and the shared bowl, the old man said: 'The small wine cups are to be removed and large ones brought in, so that these guests may more quickly reach a state of happiness.'* And so slaves busied themselves with bringing in cups of hammered silver and gold. Then the old man took hold of a special cup and, under the guise of doing a favour to his new master, he filled it and gave it to him, once he had dropped into the wine the lethal poison which, I've been told, our mistress gave him, to bring about the death of the new son. No one was aware of what the old man had done, but just as the boy, the newcomer, was holding the libation in his hands, with the rest of the company holding theirs too, one of the slaves spoke an ill-omened word. Now, the newcomer had been brought up in a temple among respectable diviners, so he counted this as a portent and ordered a fresh bowl to be filled. The ground received the libation formerly intended for the god, and he ordered everyone else to pour theirs away as well. The company fell silent, and we filled the consecrated mixing-bowls with water and wine from Biblos.* As we were engaged in this task a flock of doves, which dwell fearlessly in Loxias' temple,* clattered into the tent. Since they were thirsty they dipped their beaks into the wine that had been poured away and sucked it up into their fair throats. No harm came to any of the birds from the libation offered to the god, except to the one which settled where the newly discovered son had poured his away. No sooner had this bird tasted the drink than its fair body was shaken with convulsions, and it emitted an unearthly shriek of pain. The whole assembled company watched its struggles in amazement, until it died, gasping for breath, and its red legs went limp. The boy—the son promised by the oracle—leapt over the table, with his legs exposed from his cloak, and yelled: 'Who has designs upon my life?* Tell me, old man. You were the one who took charge and I accepted the cup from your hand.' So saying, he seized the old man's arm and began to search him, hoping to catch him red-handed in possession of ⟨. . .⟩†. Eventually the truth was wrung out of him, and he denounced Creusa's bold endeavour and the trick with the drink.

As soon as he heard this, the young man named in Loxias' oracle ran outside, taking the guests with him. He presented himself before the leaders of Pythia* and said: 'I call this holy land to witness that the foreign woman, the daughter of Erechtheus, tried to poison me to death.' The lords of Delphi unanimously decreed death by stoning for my mistress,* for attempting to kill the consecrated young man and commit murder within the sacred precinct. The whole city is looking for her, who in her misery too quickly chose a miserable path to follow. For having got her desire for children from Phoebus, it is due to him that she has lost her life and any chance of children.

Exit SLAVE.

CHORUS (*sings*). There's no escape, no escape from death for wretched me.
The truth of this business is clear now, clear for all to see—
the truth of the libations from Dionysus' clusters*
mixed with the blood of the swift-acting viper.†
Clear too are the sacrifices to the gods below—
the ending of my life and the death by stoning of my mistress.
To what regions may I flee on wings,

or down into the dark recesses of the earth,
to escape the disfigurement of death by stoning?
What chariot, drawn by swift-hoofed steeds, may I mount?
On the stern of what ship may I embark?
Concealment is impossible, unless it pleases a god to steal us away.
O wretched mistress, what pain awaits you now in your life?
Are we too to feel pain, ordained by justice,
for desiring to harm those close to us?

Enter CREUSA, agitated.

CREUSA. Slave-women, they're hunting me down to put me to death. The people of Pythia voted to condemn me, and I have been betrayed.

CHORUS. Oh, you poor woman, we know the disastrous way things have turned out for you.

CREUSA. So where shall I run? I only just got out of the house in time to escape death, and it took stealth for me to escape my enemies and make my way here.

CHORUS. You can only go to the altar.

CREUSA. What shall I gain by doing that?

CHORUS. Killing a suppliant is forbidden by divine law.*

CREUSA. But it's human law that condemns me to death!

CHORUS. Yes, but only if you're taken prisoner.

CREUSA. But look! Here they are now, my bitter enemies, running with swords in their hands!

CHORUS. Seat yourself at the altar. If you're killed there, you will at least infect your killers with blood that calls for vengeance. But you must endure whatever happens.

Enter ION, running, with armed attendants. CREUSA crouches by the altar.

ION. Cephisus, bull-headed Cephisus,* what a viper you fathered in this woman! Or perhaps she's one of those snakes whose fiery eyes shoot out deadly flames.* There are no limits to what she can bring herself to do; she's just as virulent as the drops from the Gorgon with which she was planning to kill me. Seize her! I want to see her hair with its perfect braids scoured well by the slabs of Parnassus, from where she will be hurled into flight on to the rocks below. A good deity has seen to it that I got the measure of your mind and saw how hostile and malignant you are towards me while I was still among friends, before I went to Athens and fell under a stepmother's spell. Once you had me trapped inside your house, you'd have sent me all at once on my way to Hades! See, there she is, the wicked woman, who wove a many-layered web of deceit! She has crouched at the god's altar to avoid punishment for her crimes.

CREUSA. I command you, not just for my sake but for that of the god: you cannot kill me here, where we have taken our stand.

ION. What do you and Phoebus have in common?*

CREUSA. I hereby consecrate my body to the god.

ION. And yet you tried to poison the god's slave?

CREUSA. But by then you belonged to your father rather than to Loxias.

ION. But I had been his—in the absence of my father, I mean.†

CREUSA. But you weren't at that time. And now I am his, while you no longer are.*

ION. But your actions are irreligious, whereas at the time I acted with due piety.

CREUSA. My attempt on your life was prompted by your hostility towards my house.

ION. Look, I made no armed incursion into your land.

CREUSA. Yes, you did, and you set fire to the house of Erechtheus.*

ION. With what torches? Where's the fiery brand I used?

CREUSA. You were planning to seize what's mine and take control of it.

ION. So it was fear of these 'plans' of mine that made you try to kill me?

CREUSA. Yes, to save my life, if in fact you were doing more than just planning.

ION. You are childless: do you resent the fact that my father has found me?

CREUSA. And are you, then, going to deprive a childless person of house and home?

ION. Yes, since my father owns the land and gives it to me.

CREUSA. What have the descendants of Aeolus to do with the land of Pallas?

ION. He kept it safe—and did so by military prowess, not by mere skill with words.

CREUSA. Yes, but a mercenary has no true rights to the land.*

ION. Well, can't I at least make the same claim as my father?

CREUSA. Only as much as shield and spear can claim: that is the sum total of your property.

ION. Leave the altar and the temple built for the god.

CREUSA. Go and tell your mother what to do, if you can find her.

ION. Aren't you going to submit to punishment for your attempt on my life?

CREUSA. Yes—if you're prepared to kill me inside this shrine.

ION. How will a death surrounded by the god's wreaths make you happy?

CREUSA. Because I shall make unhappy someone who has made me unhappy.

ION. Oh, no! These stupid, wrong-headed laws imposed by the god on men are terrible! Rather than finding a place of refuge at altars, criminals should be driven from them. Sinners should keep their hands off what belongs to the gods, and leave them to the righteous. A victim of injustice should be able to find sanctuary in sacred places, but it should not be the case that the gods dispense the same treatment to all men, good or bad, just because they resort to the same expedient.

Enter the PRIESTESS *of the shrine, carrying a wicker crib.*

PRIESTESS. Wait, child, while I just leave the oracular shrine with its tripod and step over this wall here.* I am the priestess of Phoebus, chosen from among all the women of Delphi; I preserve the ancient custom of the tripod.

ION. Welcome, mother—as you are to me, even though you did not give birth to me.*

PRIESTESS. Yes, that's what you call me, and I've never found the title distasteful.

ION. Have you heard that this woman here made a deliberate attempt on my life?

PRIESTESS. Yes, I have. But your savage rage is a mistake.

ION. It's wrong for me to try to repay killers with death?

PRIESTESS. Wives are always hostile to stepchildren.

ION. As we are to our stepmothers, when they treat us badly.

PRIESTESS. Enough! You must leave this sacred place, go to your native country . . .

ION. What's this you're telling me to do?

PRIESTESS. . . . and enter Athens untainted and with good omens.

ION. Everyone who kills enemies is free of taint.

He threatens CREUSA.

PRIESTESS. No, stop! Hear what I have to say!

ION. Go on, then. I know that whatever you say will be spoken by someone who has my best interests at heart.

PRIESTESS. You see this basket in my arms?

ION. I see an old crib wrapped in garlands.

PRIESTESS. This is what you were in when I found you, when you were just a new-born baby.

ION. What do you mean? You've never told me this before.

PRIESTESS. Yes, I kept quiet about it. But I'm showing you the crib now.

ION. Why did you keep it secret for so long after you found me?

PRIESTESS. The god wanted to keep you in the temple as his servant.

ION. And now he's changed his mind? How can I be sure of this?

PRIESTESS. He's sending you away from here, now that he's revealed who your father is.

ION. Why did you keep these things to yourself? Were you acting on instructions?

PRIESTESS. Loxias put the idea into my mind at the time.

ION. For what purpose? Do finish what you have to say.

PRIESTESS. To keep this crib I found hidden until the time that is now here.

ION. And how will it help me or harm me?

PRIESTESS. Inside it are the baby clothes you wore.

ION. They could lead me to my mother. Is that why you're showing them to me?

PRIESTESS. Yes, since that's what the god wants. He didn't earlier, though.

ION. What a day! These revelations make it a really happy one for me!*

PRIESTESS. So take these things and go in search of your mother.

She gives him the crib.

ION. Yes, throughout Asia and the furthest limits of Europe.

PRIESTESS. That's up to you. As far as the god's will is concerned, however, my child, it was that I should bring you up and pass these things on to you. Although I received no express command, he wanted me to take them and keep them, but I can't say why.† No one knew that I had them, and no one knew their hiding-place either. Goodbye—I embrace you just as if I were your mother.

Exit PRIESTESS.

ION. Ah, how my eyes overflow with tears when I look back to the time when my mother was secretly bedded and then stealthily tried to dispose of me instead of offering me her breast. And so I lived without a name, a slave in the god's temple—not that I'm criticizing the god at all: no, but fate gave me a heavy load to bear. At the time when I should have been pampered in a mother's arms and have found some pleasure in life, I was deprived of a mother's intimate care. And the woman who bore me is no better off. Her experience has been identical, in that she never knew the pleasures a child brings. But now I'll take this crib and dedicate it to the god,* with a prayer that what I find may conform to what I want. For if it turns out that it was some slave woman who bore me, finding my mother will be worse than leaving well alone.

Phoebus, in your temple I dedicate this crib. (*He hesitates*) But what's wrong with me? Am I going against the will of the god, since he has preserved for me these clues to my mother's identity? I'd better summon up my courage and open the crib. After all, I could never evade my destiny. Sacred garlands, what has lain hidden inside you? What things, precious to me, have been guarded within these wrappings? It's remarkable how, thanks to the providence of some god, the covering of the rounded crib has not aged—how the wickerwork is free of mould—in spite of all the time that has passed since these treasures were laid down!

CREUSA (*standing up*). What's this? Something I never expected to see!

ION. You be quiet! You've caused me enough trouble already!

CREUSA. No, I cannot keep quiet. Don't tell me what to do! For here before my eyes is the basket in which once I abandoned—*you*, my child, when you were a new-born baby, in Cecrops' cave roofed by the Long Rocks. I'm going to leave this altar, even if it means death for me.

She leaves the altar.

ION. Seize her! Driven out of her wits by some god she has sprung away from the altar and its images. Bind her arms!

The attendants seize her. She struggles.

CREUSA. Go ahead, kill me! But I *will* embrace you, along with this crib and its hidden contents.

ION. Oh, this is awful! This is a lie, an attempt to steal me, by one who has no right to me!*

CREUSA. No, it isn't. You're being found and claimed as kin by kin!

ION. I your kin? And yet you surreptitiously tried to kill me?

CREUSA. Yes, not just kin, but son, and there is nothing dearer to parents!

ION. Enough of this web of deceit! I shall get you myself!

CREUSA. And I shall get you too! That's what I am aiming for, my child!

ION. Is this basket empty, or is there something hidden inside?

CREUSA. Yes, it contains the clothes you were wearing when I abandoned you.

ION. And can you describe them before seeing them?

CREUSA. Yes, and if I fail to do so, I shall submit to death.

ION. Go on, then. There's something formidable about your boldness.

CREUSA. Look for a piece of weaving I did when I was young.

ION. What's it like? There are plenty of pieces woven by young women.

CREUSA. It's unfinished, as if it were a test-piece taken from the loom.

ION. What design does it have? I don't want you to catch me out with this.

CREUSA. There's a Gorgon in the middle panels of the cloth . . .

ION. O Zeus, what fate is this that hunts me down?

CREUSA. . . . and it's fringed with snakes, like an aegis.*

ION (*holding it up*). Look! Here is the sampler! A miraculous discovery!†

CREUSA. The long-lost product of my maidenly work at the loom!

ION. Is there anything else as well, or does your luck end with just this piece?

CREUSA. Two snakes gleam with jaws of solid gold. This piece is a gift of Athena, in accordance with her instruction that children are to grow up with them, in imitation of their ancestor, Erichthonius.

ION. What did she require them to do with the piece? Tell me. What use were they to make of it?

CREUSA. Her instructions were that a new-born baby was to wear them as a necklace, my child.

ION. Here they are, in the crib. But I need you to tell me about the third thing.

CREUSA. All those years ago I put on your head a garland made from the original olive tree that grew on Athena's rock.* If it is genuine, the colour of this wreath never fades, but stays fresh, since the tree from which it comes is pure.

ION. O mother, O my dearest mother, here you are before my eyes! I'm so happy! Let me embrace you, cheek to happy cheek!

The attendants release her and they embrace.

CREUSA. O my son! The god will forgive me if I say that you light up your mother's life more gloriously than the sun. I'm holding you in my arms, when I never expected to find you. I thought you were dwelling with the dead below the earth, in Persephone's realm.*

ION. No, here I am, mother, in your arms, as you can see. The dead one is not dead!

CREUSA. Ah, vast vault of the bright sky, what words, what cries shall I utter? How did this unexpected bliss happen to me? How did I receive this joy?

ION. This was the last thing I could have expected, mother—that I should be yours.

CREUSA. I shiver still with fear.

ION. In case you do not hold me, though you do?

CREUSA. Yes, because I had abandoned all hope. Ah, woman,* how did my baby find himself in your arms? By whose hand did he come to Loxias' temple?

ION. It was a miracle. But may our future be as happy as our past was miserable!

CREUSA. My child, many a tear was shed at your birth, and with cries were you parted from your mother's arms. But now my breath caresses your cheeks and I am blessed with the greatest happiness.

ION. These words of yours express my feelings as well as yours.

CREUSA. No longer am I childless, no longer are children denied me. The house is secure in its hearth, the land has its rulers, Erechtheus is young again. No longer does night cover the eyes of the house of the earth-born, but its sight is restored in the brilliant rays of the sun.

The embrace ends.

ION. Mother, I'd like my father to be here too, to share in the joy I have given you both.

CREUSA. Oh, child, what are you saying? How you . . . how you test me!

ION. What do you mean?

CREUSA. Your parentage is not what you think—no, not what you think at all.

ION. Oh, no! So was I a bastard, born before you were married?

CREUSA. The union that resulted in your birth, my child, was not accompanied by the torches and dances of marriage.

ION. Ah, woe! Then is my lineage base, mother? What are my origins?

CREUSA. I invoke the Gorgon-slaying goddess to be my witness . . .

ION. What's this you're saying?

CREUSA. . . . she whose seat is the olive-bearing hill on the cliffs of my native city . . .

ION. Your words seem evasive and obscure to me.

CREUSA. . . . that by the rock of the nightingales* Phoebus . . .

ION. Why do you mention Phoebus?

CREUSA. . . . took me to be his secret lover . . .

ION. Go on! It looks as though you're going to bring me good and fortunate news.

CREUSA. ... and in the cycle of the tenth month,* in secret labour I bore you for Phoebus.

ION. How I love to hear this! It is the truth, isn't it?

CREUSA. Here are the baby clothes in which I dressed you, the uncertain work of my loom, made by your mother† in the days of her maidenhood. I offered you no maternal nourishment—no milk from my breast—nor washed you with my hands, but in a deserted cavern you were cast out into Hades, a victim for the beaks of birds to feast upon.

ION. What terrible things you brought yourself to do, mother!

CREUSA. Bound fast by fear, my child, I threw away your life. I killed you, though it was not of my choosing.

ION. And, in an act of sacrilege, you were all but killed by me.

CREUSA. Oh, how awful my fortune was in the past, and how awful were these acts of yours too! We spin to and fro between misery and happiness, with the winds changing. May they hold steady! We have suffered enough already. I pray that a fair wind may now take the place of our troubles, my son.

CHORUS. Bearing in mind what is happening here, no one should ever regard anything as beyond hope.

ION. How fickle is fortune! Thousands upon thousands of people in the past have moved from misery to success under her influence! I came within a hair's-breadth in my life of killing my mother and suffering undeserved pain. But does a day ever pass without our hearing a whole catalogue of such horrors as we go about within the sun's bright embrace? Anyway, mother, I am so glad to have found you, and, in my opinion, my lineage leaves little to be desired! But I'd like to have a few words with you in private. Come here, so that I can whisper what I have to say in your ear and shroud the matter in darkness. (*She comes close to him*) Are you sure, mother, that you weren't tempted into a secret affair (a recurrent problem among young women) and then blamed the god? You're not attempting to evade the disgrace of my birth by claiming that Phoebus is my father, when really no god is?*

CREUSA. I swear by Athena-Victory, who bore her shield alongside Zeus' chariots against the earth-born giants, that no mortal man is your father, my child, but the lord Loxias, who brought you up.

ION. So why did he give his own son to another father? Why did he say I was the son of Xuthus?

CREUSA. He didn't say you were Xuthus' son; he just gave you to him, since you were his, just as a man might give his son to his friend, for the friend to be the guardian of his house.*

ION. But was the god's oracle true or false? I find this a disturbing question, mother, as well I might.

CREUSA. Well, I'll tell you what's occurred to me, my child. Loxias is trying to do you good in settling you on a noble house. If you were known as the god's son, you would never have inherited a house or gained a father's name. And how could anyone know who you were, when I myself concealed the liaison and surreptitiously tried to kill you? No, in giving you to another father, Loxias was doing you a favour.

ION. I need to go deeper into the matter than this. I shall go into the temple and enquire of Phoebus whether he or a mortal man was my father.

But oh! Which god is this we see rising over the sacrificial temple with a face as glorious as the sun? Let's flee, mother! Unless it is appropriate for us to see them, the gods are not for us to see.

ATHENA appears above the backdrop in a chariot.

ATHENA. Stop! You are running from one who is not your enemy but is well disposed towards you, whether you are here or in Athens. I am Pallas, she who gave her name to your land, and I have sped here from Apollo, who chose not to come to meet you himself, in case his past deeds should provoke you to open criticism.* Instead he sent me to deliver his message: this woman is your mother, and Apollo is your father; he gave you to that man not because he is your natural father, but so that you might be received into a house of the highest nobility. But once the whole business had been revealed, he was afraid that you might be killed as a result of your mother's plotting, and that she might die at your hands, and so he saw to it that you were rescued. Despite his long silence, however, it was his intention that in Athens she would be made known to you and that you would discover that she was your mother and Phoebus your father.

But now listen to what I have to say, so that I may bring this business to an end and fulfil the god's oracles, which were the reason I harnessed my chariot.* Creusa, you are to take this child with you to Cecrops' land and establish him on the royal throne. As a descendant of Erechtheus, he has a right to rule over my land, and his fame will spread throughout Greece. For his sons—four from the one root—will give their names to the land and to the native tribes of the land, the inhabitants of my cliff.* The first-born will be Geleon, then the second ⟨. . .⟩† the Hopletes and the Argades, and the Aegicores,* named after my aegis, will constitute a single tribe. Then in due course of time the children of these four will found communities on the islands of the Cyclades* and the coastal mainland, whose might will support my land. They will also colonize the opposite sides of the straits on the two continents, Asia and Europe. They will be named Ionians, after your son here, and they will win great renown.

Moreover, Xuthus and you will have offspring between you: Dorus, who will give his name to the Dorian city,* famed in song, in the land of Pelops; and secondly Achaeus, who will rule the coastlands near Rhium,* and a people named after him shall bear his name as their distinguishing mark.

Everything was well arranged by Apollo. First, he made sure that your pregnancy was free of illness, so that your friends and family should not realize what was going on. Then, after you had given birth to your son and had abandoned him in his baby clothes, he told Hermes to take the baby in his arms and carry him here; and he brought the child up and saw to it that he didn't die. So now don't tell anyone that this boy is your son, so that Xuthus can remain in blissful ignorance* and so that you too, woman, may be well off in your journey through life. And so farewell. I assure you both that a happy future will follow from this cessation of your troubles.

ION. O Pallas, daughter of almighty Zeus, your words have fallen on receptive ears, and I now believe that Loxias is my father and this woman here my mother. Even before you spoke, I was prepared to entertain the idea.

CREUSA. I must tell you what I think too. I am pleased with Phoebus, although I wasn't before, because he has restored to me the child he previously neglected. The doors of the temple here, and the god's oracular shrine, are agreeable to me now, although earlier they were hateful. But now I am glad to cling to the knocker and bid farewell to the doors.

ATHENA. It pleases me that you have changed your mind for the better† and speak well of the god. The gods may be thought to take their time, but in the end they are not without power.

CREUSA. My child, let's go home.

ATHENA. Yes, go, and I shall go with you.

ION. You will make a worthy companion for us.

CREUSA. Yes, and one who cares for our city.

ATHENA. Take up your place upon the ancient throne.

ION. It is mine by right.

Exeunt ION, CREUSA, *and* ATHENA

CHORUS. Farewell, Apollo, son of Zeus and Leto. Anyone whose house is beset by disaster should keep worshipping the gods and not lose heart. For in the end good men receive their deserts, while the very nature of a bad man ensures that he will never prosper.

ORESTES

Characters

ELECTRA, *daughter of Agamemnon and Clytemnestra*
ORESTES, *son of Agamemnon and Clytemnestra*
HELEN, *daughter of Tyndareus and wife of Menelaus*
MENELAUS, *brother of Agamemnon*
TYNDAREUS, *king of Sparta*
PYLADES, *loyal friend of Orestes*
MESSENGER, *an old peasant, retainer of Agamemnon*
HERMIONE, *daughter of Menelaus and Helen*
PHRYGIAN, *slave of Helen*
APOLLO

CHORUS *of Argive women*

Scene: In front of Agamemnon's palace in Argos. ORESTES *is lying on a couch,* ELECTRA *sitting on the ground by his side.*

ELECTRA. It is scarcely an exaggeration to say that there is nothing terrible—no pain or god-given disaster—the burden of which human nature is not liable to endure. For instance, that happy man Tantalus (and I don't mean to slight his fate), said to be the offspring of Zeus, flies through the air in constant terror of the rock looming over his head.* This is his punishment—or so they say—because, a mortal man among gods, with equal honour at their shared table, he contracted the worst of diseases, an unbridled tongue. He was the father of Pelops, whose son was Atreus, and Atreus was the victim of designs spun by the goddess Strife, who made him engage in hostilities against his brother Thyestes.* But what need is there for me to rehearse these obscenities? Suffice it to say that Atreus killed Thyestes' children and gave them to him to eat.† I pass in silence over what happened next,* and move on to Atreus' sons: glorious Agamemnon (if glorious he was) and Menelaus, children of Aerope of Crete.* Of these Menelaus married Helen, who was loathed by the gods,* and lord Agamemnon wedded Clytemnestra—a notable alliance in

Greek eyes. To him she bore the three of us girls—Chrysothemis, Iphigenia, and me, Electra—and one boy, Orestes, children of the same mother, a woman so far gone in iniquity that she trapped her husband in the coils of an endless cloth* and killed him. Her motives it would be improper for a young woman like myself to mention;* I leave them veiled and forebear to go into them in public. Next, Phoebus—it is hard to accuse a god of injustice, but he persuaded Orestes to murder his mother, the woman who bore him.* Despite the fact that some would count the deed infamous, Orestes obeyed the god and killed her, and I did what a woman could to help him commit the murder.

The upshot is that poor Orestes lies here sick, ravaged by a fierce disease, prostrate on his bed,† his mother's blood goading him with fits of insanity. I shrink, as you see, from naming the divine Eumenides,* who are striving to encompass his downfall with this horror. This is now the sixth day since our mother's corpse was purified with fire, following her slaughter, and in all this time he has neither taken food into his stomach nor bathed his body.* Hidden inside his robes, he weeps when his body gains some respite from its disease and he is in his right mind; but sometimes he leaps up from his bed and runs around like a colt freed from the yoke.

By a decree of this city of Argos no one is to take us into hearth and home, nor speak to us, since we are matricides. And this is the decisive day on which the citizens of Argos will cast their vote for or against the proposal that we two are to be stoned to death.* But our hopes of avoiding death have been raised by the arrival of Menelaus here from Troy. On his way back from Troy he was driven well off course and strayed for a long time, but now he lies at anchor by the coast, filling the harbour of Nauplia* with his fleet. As for the mass-murderer Helen,* he waited for nightfall, in case any of those whose sons died at Troy should see her making her way there in the daytime and should take to hurling stones, and sent her on ahead to our palace. She is indoors, weeping for her sister and her family's misfortunes. But she does have something to alleviate her grief, because Hermione, the daughter Menelaus brought from Sparta and left at home in my mother's care when he sailed for Troy, gives her great pleasure and helps her to forget her woes.

I am looking in every direction, watching for Menelaus' arrival. We are in an extremely precarious situation, and he offers our only chance of safety. A house plagued by misfortune is a thing without resources.

Enter HELEN *from the palace, carrying libation jugs and a lock of her hair.*

HELEN. Electra, still unwed after all these years,* how are you, you poor thing? And how is your brother? I incur no pollution in addressing you,* because the fault lies with Phoebus, in my opinion. And yet I mourn the fate of my sister Clytemnestra. The last time I saw her was before I made that voyage of mine to Troy, driven in a fit of supernatural insanity by my destiny, and so in my bereavement I grieve for what has happened.

ELECTRA. Helen, why should I tell you what you can see with your very own eyes? Here I sit, keeping vigil beside a wretched corpse—I don't mean to slight his troubles, but his breath is so faint now that he might as well be a corpse. You and your husband, a happy couple, have arrived to find us in a miserable state.

HELEN. How long has he been lying here on his bed?*

ELECTRA. Ever since he carried out the slaughter of his mother.

HELEN. I feel sorry for him, and also for his mother. Look at the way she died!

ELECTRA. What's happened is that he has been overwhelmed by his woes.

HELEN. Electra, please may I ask you to do something for me?

ELECTRA. Yes, but I *am* busy keeping watch by my brother's bed.

HELEN. Would you go to my sister's tomb for me . . .

ELECTRA. You want me to go to my mother's tomb? What for?

HELEN. . . . and take these hair-trimmings of mine,* and some libations?

ELECTRA. Is it forbidden for you to go to the family tomb?

HELEN. I would be embarrassed to be seen by the Argives.

ELECTRA. Proper behaviour at last, but you had no sense of shame when you left your home that time.

HELEN. What you say is correct, even if unkind.

ELECTRA. But what is it about the Mycenaeans that makes you hold back?

HELEN. I'm afraid of the fathers of those who died at Troy.

ELECTRA. Yes, there's certainly something frightening about the way voices are raised about you in Argos.

HELEN. So you can free me of fear by doing me this favour.

ELECTRA. I couldn't bear to look on my mother's tomb.

HELEN. But it would be wrong for slaves to take these offerings there.

ELECTRA. Why don't you send your daughter Hermione?

HELEN. It's not right for young women to go about in public.

ELECTRA. But she would be repaying the dead woman for looking after her.

HELEN. Yes, that makes sense: I'll send my daughter. (*She calls out*) Hermione, dear, come out here to the front of the palace.

Enter HERMIONE *from the palace.*

Take these libations and trimmings from my hair, and go and pour out the honeyed milk and the frothy wine around Clytemnestra's tomb. Then stand on top of the mound* and say, 'These libations are a gift from your sister Helen, though fear of the people of Argos makes her too nervous to approach your tomb herself.' Ask her to look kindly upon me and you, and my husband, and this wretched pair here, brought low by a god, and assure her that I shall certainly be providing her with all the gifts it is appropriate for me to offer a dead sister. Quickly, child, off you go, and once you've poured the libations at the tomb see that you hurry back again.

Exit HERMIONE, *with the jugs and hair.*
Exit HELEN *back into the palace.*

ELECTRA. What a terrible thing a person's nature is! Did you see* how she has trimmed just the ends of her hair, to preserve her beauty? She's the same woman she always was. You have ruined not just my life and that of my brother, but the whole of Greece, and I pray that the gods may hate you for it!

Enter CHORUS.

Oh, no! Here come my friends again, who share my sorrow. Their singing will soon wake my brother here from his peaceful sleep, and start the tears flowing from my eyes when I see him raving. Good friends, come on tiptoes! No loud or harsh noises! I appreciate your friendship, but please be quiet all the same.

CHORUS (*softly, while approaching* ORESTES). Quietly!* Quietly now! Tread lightly on the ground! Make no harsh noise!

ELECTRA. No, over there, please! Keep well away from his bed!

CHORUS (*moving away, but compensating by speaking louder*). There. I'm doing as you wish.

ELECTRA. No, no, my dear! Please keep your voice down, as soft as the breath of a gently blown pipe.

CHORUS (*very softly*). How about this? I'm singing as low as I would indoors.*

ELECTRA. Yes, that's perfect! Now come closer, closer—but quietly! Come quietly up to me, and tell me what brings you here. For at last he has lain down and fallen asleep.

CHORUS. How is he? Do tell me, dear. How am I to describe his condition?

ELECTRA. He breathes still, but it's very ragged and shallow.

CHORUS. Really? The poor boy!

ELECTRA. I'll be so upset if you make his eyelids flutter open, now that he's succumbed to the sweet boon of sleep!

CHORUS. The poor boy! I feel sorry for him. Look at the appalling deeds he has done, thanks to the gods.

ELECTRA. Oh, what he has had to endure! There was no justice in the god, no justice in the oracles he uttered that day, when on Themis' tripod Loxias decreed that murder should be paid for by the murder of my mother!*

ORESTES stirs restlessly.

CHORUS. Do you see how he tosses in his robes?

ELECTRA. Yes, for you've disturbed his sleep with your shouting, you wretch!

CHORUS. But I thought he was asleep.

ELECTRA. Why don't you leave us, leave the palace? Retrace your steps back to where you came from—but without making any noise.

CHORUS. He's asleep.

ELECTRA. I'm glad to hear it. Lady Night, you who give sleep to long-suffering mortals, come from Erebus!* Come, lady, come on wings to Agamemnon's palace! For overcome by grief and disaster we perish, we perish! Oh, no! You made a noise! Quietly, quietly! Take care not to raise your voice! Stay away from the bed, and afford him the gentle boon of sleep, please, my dear!

CHORUS. Tell me how he will find an end to his troubles.

ELECTRA. Through death, only through death! He has no desire even for food.

CHORUS. There's no doubt, then, what the future holds for him.

ELECTRA. We are the victims of Phoebus, for he sanctioned the piteous, unnatural murder of our mother, in retaliation for her murder of our father.

CHORUS. Justice demanded it . . .

ELECTRA (*forcefully*). But it was not right. Mother, who gave me life, you killed and died, and in destroying our father you destroyed these your children, born of your blood. We are lost, ruined, as good as dead! For my brother here is among the dead, and the greater part of my life has been spent on weeping and wailing and tears in the night, as without husband* or children I draw my pitiable life out into an interminable future.

CHORUS. Electra, since you're close beside him, please check whether your brother has died without your noticing it. The complete slackness of his body worries me.

ELECTRA inspects ORESTES. He stirs and struggles to sit up.

ORESTES. O Sleep, precious enchantment and ally against sickness! You came just when I needed you and your visit was so welcome! O lady Oblivion, through whom we forget our troubles, what skill you wield! You are indeed a goddess to whom those in distress should pray. (*He looks about in surprise*) But where have I come from? How did I get here? I can't remember: I have no recollection of the past.

ELECTRA. Darling, I was so glad that you fell asleep. Can you bear me to touch you? Shall I prop you up?

ORESTES. By all means, yes, please go ahead, and also wipe the sticky crust from my poor mouth and eyes.

She attends to him.

ELECTRA. There. I welcome the menial task and am glad to look after my brother's body with a sisterly hand.

ORESTES. Let me lean on you. And please brush the lank hair from my face, because I can't see clearly.

ELECTRA. Your poor head with its greasy hair! It's been so long since you've washed that you look quite savage!

ORESTES. Help me lie back down on my bed. When the madness subsides my body is limp and drained.

ELECTRA. There. The possession of a bed is like a friend to a sick person: a necessary pest.

ORESTES. Now lift me up again and turn me over on to my other side. Invalids are so helpless that it's hard to please them.

ELECTRA. Would you also like me to settle your feet on the ground? It's been a long while since the earth received their imprint, and everyone enjoys a change.

ORESTES. Yes, please. At least I'll be imitating health that way, and an imitation isn't too bad, even if it falls short of reality.

ELECTRA makes ORESTES sit up.

ELECTRA. Now, listen to me, brother, since at the moment the demons of destruction aren't robbing you of your wits.

ORESTES. You have some news to tell me. I welcome it if it's good, but if its outcome is likely to be painful, I already have more than my share of unhappiness.

ELECTRA. Your uncle Menelaus has arrived, and his ship is riding at anchor in Nauplia.

ORESTES. What's that? Someone has arrived to dispel the gloom of the troubles darkening my life and yours? A kinsman who is in debt to us for our father's various kindnesses to him?*

ELECTRA. Yes, he's here, and you can take my word for this too, that he's brought Helen from the walls of Troy.

ORESTES. I would congratulate him if he had been the only one to be saved, but if he's brought his wife with him, he has come with a heap of troubles.

ELECTRA. What a remarkable brood of daughters Tyndareus fathered—remarkable for the hostility they arouse, and notorious throughout Greece!*

ORESTES. Well, you had better prove yourself different from them, since it is within your power to do so; and the difference should come from your heart, not just your words.

ORESTES starts to display signs of madness.

ELECTRA. Oh, no! Brother, there is a wildness in your eye. Your madness has returned so quickly: just a moment ago you were in your right mind.

ORESTES makes as if to ward off the Eumenides.

ORESTES. Mother, I implore you, don't set them on to me! They come! They come, those women with their eyes of blood and serpent forms!* They're bounding towards me!

ELECTRA. Ah, how you suffer! Stay! Lie quietly on your bed! This is a hallucination, not as real as you think.

ORESTES. Phoebus, the hound-faced, savage-eyed, dread goddesses who slaughter victims for the dead—they're killing me!

ORESTES goes into convulsions.

ELECTRA. I won't let go of you. I'll entwine my arms in yours and check these horrid spasms.

ORESTES. Let go! You're one of the demons who are after me! You want to hurl me into Tartarus*—that's why you've got a grip on my waist!

ORESTES breaks free of her grip and jumps to his feet.

ELECTRA. Oh, this is too much for me! I need help—but from where shall I get it, when the gods are against us?

ELECTRA covers her head with a fold of her khiton in distress.

ORESTES. Pass me my horn-tipped bow! Loxias gave it to me* and told me to defend myself with it against the goddesses if I was terrified by the fits of insanity with which they plague me. A missile, released by mortal hand, will strike an immortal in a moment, if she remains within my sight! Do you hear me? (*He notches an arrow on the invisible bow and shoots*) Don't you see the feathered shafts of my far-shooting bow hurtling towards you? Aaah! So what are you waiting for? Scale the highest heaven with your wings! Guilt lies not with me but with Phoebus and his oracles. (*He comes to himself*)

Oh! What's happening? I'm so confused and short of breath. Where . . . where was I off to, leaping up from my bed? The storm is over and again I see calm waters.* Sister, why are you weeping? Why have you covered your head with your robes? I feel so ashamed for involving you in my pain and burdening a young woman with my sickness. Please don't let my troubles grieve you. It's true that you agreed to the business, but it was I who carried out our mother's murder. I blame Loxias, because it was he who prompted me to perform such an abominable deed, though his encouragement took the form of words not deeds. But suppose it had been my father I had consulted, eye to eye, about whether I should kill my mother: I think he would have taken my face in his hands and pleaded with me,* over and over again, not to drive a sword into a mother's throat, since it wouldn't bring him back to life, and I would be afflicted with these terrible torments. So uncover your head now, sister, and dry your eyes, however pitiful our situation. When you see me sunk in despair, you must reduce the terror and chaos of my mind and raise my morale; and when you are despondent, I should be by your side, telling you kindly what to do. This is the right kind of help for people who love each other to give. You poor thing! Why don't you go inside the palace, lie down, let sleep close your sleepless eyes, and then find your appetite for food and bathe yourself?* I'll be lost if you let me down or get ill from sitting by my side. For you are the only person I can rely on for help; as you can see I have no one else.

ELECTRA. No. I shall stay with you whether this choice means life or death. It makes no difference to me, because if you die, what can I, as a woman, do? How shall I be safe, when I shall be all alone, without brother, father, friends? If that's what you want, though, I shall do as you suggest. (*She smoothes his bed*) But lie down to rest and try to resist whatever it is that startles you in terror from your bed. Rest quietly on your bed, which I've tidied up for you. After all, even if illness is imaginary rather than real, we mortals feel exhausted and helpless.

Exit ELECTRA *into the palace.*

ORESTES *lies down again on the couch.*

CHORUS (*sings*). Ah, woe! O fast, furious, winged goddesses,
who form a joyless coven amid tears and lamentation,
you dark-featured Eumenides, who scour the high heavens

exacting the penalty due for bloodshed, the penalty due for murder,
I beg you, I beseech you, let Agamemnon's son be free
of the raving bewilderment of madness. Ah, wretched man,
overwhelmed by trouble! What a terrible deed you attempted,
to your undoing, when you accepted the oracle,
the oracle spoken by Phoebus from the tripod
on the floor said to house the recess of the navel of the world.*

O Zeus, what pitiful, murderous contest urges you on,
miserable Orestes? Some ruthless demon, haunting the house,
is piling tears on tears for you, driving you insane
in revenge for your mother's blood.
I grieve for you, mourn for you. Here on earth
great success is insecure. As if he were shaking the sail
of a swift boat, some god overwhelms great success
in the violent, deadly waves of a sea of terrible suffering.
For which house should I yet sooner revere than
that of Tantalus, descended thanks to that first union from the gods?*

Enter MENELAUS. The CHORUS stop singing and the Chorus-leader continues alone.

But here comes the king, lord Menelaus, in all his might and luxury, an obvious descendant of Tantalid blood. Prime mover of the thousand-shipped invasion of Asia,* I bid you welcome. That you are personally attended by good fortune is shown by the fact that the gods have answered your prayers.

MENELAUS. Royal palace, though I am surely pleased to have got back from Troy and to be seeing you, yet the sight of you makes me grieve, because I have never seen a house more beset on all sides by appalling troubles. For I learnt what happened to Agamemnon when I put in at Malea.* Glaucus, the prophet of Nereus, who is the sailors' seer and a soothsaying god, appeared from the waves and told me the news. He came before me and said: 'Menelaus, your brother lies dead. His wife made sure that the bath she gave him was his last.' I and my companions shed many tears at the news, and then, when I came ashore at Nauplia, with the intention of enfolding in a kinsman's arms my brother's son Orestes and his mother, on the assumption that good fortune attended them both, I heard from one of the harbour salts of the foul murder of Tyndareus' daughter. So, young women, tell me where I may find Agamemnon's son, who brought himself to commit such a terrible deed. For when I left the palace and went to Troy he was just a baby in Clytemnestra's arms, so I wouldn't recognize him if I saw him.

ORESTES runs forward and adopts the suppliant position, clasping MENELAUS' knees.

ORESTES. Here's the person you're asking about, Menelaus. I am Orestes. I shall not hesitate to inform against myself and tell you of my crimes, and the first act I perform as a suppliant is to clasp your knees, though the prayers I utter lack a suppliant's leafy boughs.* Save me from my troubles! You have come at just the right time.

MENELAUS. Ye gods, what am I seeing? Is this one of the dead?*

ORESTES (*standing up*). You're right: alive I may be, but my troubles have killed me.

MENELAUS. You poor thing! And how savage your lank hair makes you look!

ORESTES. What disfigures me is not my looks but what I've done.

MENELAUS. Your gaze is terrifying, your eyes harsh.

ORESTES. My body has gone. All I have left is my name.

MENELAUS. O hideous! Inconceivably hideous to look at!

ORESTES. Yes, that's me, the killer of my poor mother!

MENELAUS. I've already heard the news. Restrain yourself: evil does not bear repetition.

ORESTES. I am restraining myself, but fortune is generous in sending evil my way.

MENELAUS. What exactly are you suffering from? What illness is destroying you?

ORESTES. Awareness—because I know that I have done terrible things.

MENELAUS. What do you mean? Clarity, not vagueness, is a sign of knowledge.

ORESTES. What is destroying me above all is grief . . .

MENELAUS. Yes, Grief is a fierce spirit, but she can be allayed.

ORESTES. . . . and then there are fits of insanity, in retribution for my mother's murder.

MENELAUS. And when did this madness begin? On what day?

ORESTES. It was the day when I was heaping the earth over my wretched mother's tomb.

MENELAUS. And were you at home when it began, or still sitting beside the funeral pyre?

ORESTES. I was outside, waiting for the bones to be collected for burial.*

MENELAUS. Was anyone with you, to stop you falling down?

ORESTES. Yes, Pylades,* my accomplice in the bloody murder of my mother.

MENELAUS. And what kind of apparitions do you see in your times of sickness?

ORESTES. I seemed to see three maidens, as dark as night.

MENELAUS. I know whom you mean, but I would rather not name them.

ORESTES. No, for they are formidable. It was tactful of you to avoid mentioning them.

MENELAUS. They are the ones who are driving you out of your wits for murdering a member of your family.

ORESTES. Oh, they hunt me, they hound me, miserable wretch that I am!

MENELAUS. There's nothing terrible in the terrible suffering of those who have committed terrible deeds.

ORESTES. But I do have a means of settling disaster . . .

MENELAUS. Don't talk of dying. That's just stupid.

ORESTES. . . . on to Phoebus, on whose orders I carried out my mother's murder.

MENELAUS. Yes, proving himself rather ignorant of propriety and justice.

ORESTES. We are slaves to the gods, whatever the gods may be.

MENELAUS. And yet does Loxias do anything to protect you from your troubles?

ORESTES. He's biding his time, in typically divine fashion.

MENELAUS. How long is it since your mother breathed her last?

ORESTES. It was five days ago. Her funeral pyre is still warm.

MENELAUS. It didn't take long for the goddesses to come after you for your mother's murder!

ORESTES. The god may be ignorant, but he is true to his own.†*

MENELAUS. Does it help you at all that you were avenging your father?

ORESTES. Not yet—and there's no difference, in my opinion, between 'not yet' and 'not at all'.

MENELAUS. How do the citizens treat you as a result of what you've done?

ORESTES. They hate us so much that they refuse to talk to us.

MENELAUS. And haven't you even purified the blood on your hands in the customary way?*

ORESTES. No, because I am barred from people's houses wherever I go.

MENELAUS. Which of the citizens are striving to drive you from the land?

ORESTES. Oeax, who blames my father for the antagonism towards Troy.

MENELAUS. I understand: he's punishing you for the murder of Palamedes.*

ORESTES. Which was nothing to do with me. But there are three reasons for my destruction.

MENELAUS. Who else, then? Some of Aegisthus' friends, I suppose.

ORESTES. Yes, they abuse me, and they have the ears of the citizens at the moment.

MENELAUS. But don't they let you hold Agamemnon's sceptre?

ORESTES. Of course not, since they don't even let me continue my life.

MENELAUS. What are they doing? Can you tell me exactly?

ORESTES. They are going to condemn us today.

MENELAUS. And yet you aren't fleeing across the border?

ORESTES. No, because we are surrounded on all sides by fully armed men.

MENELAUS. Were these men mustered by your enemies on their own, or are they official Argive forces?

ORESTES. The entire citizen body is involved. They want to see me die. That's all there is to say.

MENELAUS. I feel for you. Your situation is as bad as it could get.

ORESTES. You are my hope, the safe haven from the troubles that afflict me. Success attends your arrival here, so please share your good fortune with those dear to you who are in a desperate plight. Don't take the good and keep it for yourself, but play your part and share some of our trials too. In this way you will recompense those you should for my father's favours to you. People are friends in no more than name if their friendship fails in times of adversity.

CHORUS. Here comes Tyndareus of Sparta, his aged legs rivalling each other for haste. He is wearing dark clothes and he has cut his hair short in mourning for his daughter.

ORESTES. Menelaus, I am lost! Look, Tyndareus is coming up to us, and there's no one I scruple more to meet because of what I've done. For he brought me up when I was young and showered me with kindnesses. For instance, he used to carry 'Agamemnon's son' around in his arms, and Leda did as well. They treated me with as much respect as they did Castor and Polydeuces.* And—I feel it in my wretched heart, and in my soul—I have not repaid them well. What darkness can I find to cover my face? Where is the cloud I can hide behind, to stay out of the old man's sight?

Enter TYNDAREUS *with attendants.*

TYNDAREUS (*to his attendants*). Where is he? Where may I find Menelaus, my daughter's husband? While I was pouring libations at Clytemnestra's tomb,* I heard that he had arrived at Nauplia with his wife, safe after all these years. Take me to him. I want to stand by him and clasp him by the right hand. It's been so long since I saw my dear friend.

MENELAUS. You are very welcome, sir, whose wife was also loved by Zeus.*

TYNDAREUS. And greetings to you too, Menelaus, my son-in-law. (*He catches sight of* ORESTES) But what's this? The serpent who killed his mother is here in front of the palace, noisome lightning gleaming from his eyes. How I loathe him! Are you talking to the foul creature, Menelaus?

MENELAUS. So what if am? His father meant a lot to me.

TYNDAREUS. Could such a creature really be Agamemnon's son?

MENELAUS. He is, and I am obliged to honour him in his misfortune.

TYNDAREUS. You've spent so much time among foreigners that you've taken up foreign ways.

MENELAUS. But it is Greek practice to honour one's kith and kin under all circumstances.

TYNDAREUS. And also not to want to subordinate the laws to oneself.

MENELAUS. Wise men say that anything which is the result of compulsion is servile.

TYNDAREUS. *You* may have accepted that idea, but *I* won't.

MENELAUS. That's because two things are making you stupid: your anger and your old age.

TYNDAREUS. Yes, a debate on stupidity is relevant to this man's case.† When everyone knows what is and what is not acceptable behaviour, was there ever a more stupid person than him? He gave no thought to justice, nor did he have recourse to standard Greek practice. After Agamemnon had died from the blow to the head he received from my daughter—a shocking action, which I shall never condone—he ought to have punished her for murder, while keeping religious propriety in mind: that is, he should have expelled his mother from the palace. Instead of facing disaster, he would have gained a reputation for good sense, he would have kept within the law, and he would have shown himself to be a man of religious sensibility. As things are, however, he has made himself liable to the same fate as his mother. For although he was right to regard her as bad, in killing his mother he proved himself even worse.

I've only one question for you, Menelaus. Suppose Orestes' wife were to kill him: next his son will kill his mother, and then this son's son will avenge blood with blood—how long will these horrors go on?* When will they end? Our forefathers arranged things well: they would not allow anyone tainted with blood to meet or encounter anyone else, but rather than seeing a life taken in exchange for a life, they had him purify himself with exile. Otherwise there would always be a single individual involved in bloodshed, his hands polluted by the most recent act. Speaking for myself, I loathe women who ignore religious propriety, and my daughter above all, for killing her husband. And not only will your wife Helen never meet my approval, but I shall refuse to speak to her. In fact, I don't admire you for having gone to the land of Troy for the sake of a vile woman. But I shall do my utmost to defend the law and to end this murderous savagery, which never fails to destroy a land and its communities.

(*To* ORESTES) For what did you feel, you wretch, when your mother bared her breast and begged you for mercy? Although I was not a witness to the horrors that happened there, tears flow from my poor old eyes. And one thing certainly confirms what I've been saying: these fits of insanity and terror show that you have incurred the hatred of the gods and are paying the penalty for your crime against your mother. I have no need to hear the truth from other witnesses when I can see the evidence myself. So just to make sure you understand, Menelaus: if you choose to help this man, you will be acting contrary to the will of the gods. Don't do it; let him be stoned to death by the citizens. My daughter's death was what she deserved, but it was wrong of him to kill her. My daughters have been the only blight on my otherwise fortunate life, the only respect in which my happiness is marred.

CHORUS. Enviable is the man who has met with good fortune in his children and has avoided notable disaster in this respect.

ORESTES. Sir, if I respond to you I am bound to upset you,† and that makes me hesitate. If we can keep your old age, which is what makes me worried about speaking, from being a factor in our argument, then I shall go ahead, even though in fact I am anxiously aware of your grey hair. What should I have done? Set the pairs of factors opposite one another. On the one hand, there was my father, who planted his seed; on the other, your daughter, the field which received the seed from someone else. In killing my mother I committed an immoral act, but from another point of view you could call it moral, in that I was avenging my father. And your daughter (I shrink from calling her my mother) was carrying on an unsanctioned, licentious affair with another man. In slandering her I blacken my own reputation, but I shall speak out all the same. I killed this other man too, and slaughtered my mother, which was an immoral act, but performed to avenge my father.

The acts for which you say I deserve to be stoned actually make me the benefactor of all Greece. Here is my argument for this. If women are going to be so brazen that they murder their husbands and then find protection from their children by using their breasts to seek mercy, they'd be making little of killing their husbands for any old grievance. Although what I did was terrible, as you insist, I did put an end to this practice.

I can justify the hatred which led me to kill my mother. When her husband was abroad on armed service, commanding an army on behalf of all Greece, she betrayed him by failing to preserve the purity of her marriage-bed. Aware of her sins, she did not punish herself, but, in order to avoid retribution from her husband, she punished him, my father, instead, and put him to death. Sir, in fathering a wicked daughter, you have proved my undoing; thanks to her brazen behaviour I have lost my father and killed my mother. By the gods—even though it may be inappropriate to mention the gods who judge guilt in cases of murder—if I had tacitly approved what my mother had done, what would the murdered man have done to me? Out of hatred for me, wouldn't he be goading me into madness with his demons? Or could it be that my mother has deities on her side while he does not, even though the wrong committed against him was greater?

Let's turn now to Apollo, who resides at the central navel of the world and speaks to mortal men with supreme reliability. It was in obedience to him that I killed my mother. It is him you people should regard as immoral and put to death; the sin is his, not mine. What should I have done? Or does the god not carry enough weight for me to be cleared of pollution by referring matters to him? If not, then where else might one flee for safety, if the one who issued the order will not save me from death? You should not say, then, that the deed was wrong, but only that it has been the ruin of me, the person who did it.

CHORUS. When they involve themselves in the affairs of men, women always make things worse.

TYNDAREUS. Your brazen and unbridled words, and the deliberately upsetting nature of your response, will only kindle all the more enthusiasm in me to encompass your death. I actually came here only to arrange my daughter's tomb, but I shall consider your death an excellent bonus to this task. I shall go before the assembled Argives and, whether or not they want it, I shall set the citizens on to you and your sister, and make sure that your punishment is death by stoning.

Your sister deserves death even more than you do, because she aroused your anger against your mother by constantly filling your ears with stories designed to increase your hatred. She went on proclaiming as scandalous the business with Agamemnon and the love-affair with Aegisthus (which I pray the gods below may find appalling, just as the gods of this world found it vile), until she set the palace ablaze—though not with fire.*

(*He turns to* MENELAUS) Menelaus, I should warn you—and this is no idle threat—if you are taking no account of my hatred and our kinship,* not to go against the will of the gods and protect this man from death. If you do, you had better not set foot on Spartan soil. I won't say anything more about this, but you mark my words: don't side with impious men and reject the friendship of those with greater piety. But now, slaves, take me away from this palace.

Exeunt TYNDAREUS *and attendants.*

MENELAUS *paces in distress.*

ORESTES. Yes, go. I'd like my next remarks to reach Menelaus here without being interrupted and without being restricted by your old age. Menelaus, what's the matter? Why are you pacing to and fro, marking out the double path that indicates a divided mind?

MENELAUS. Leave me alone. I'm turning something over in my mind, since I don't know what to do in the present circumstances.

ORESTES. Well, don't come to any conclusions yet. First hear what I have to say, and then do your deliberating.

MENELAUS *stops pacing.*

MENELAUS. Go on, then. You're right: although silence is sometimes preferable to speech, the opposite may also be true.

ORESTES. Here I go, then. Long speeches are better than short ones and make their points more clearly. Menelaus, I'm not asking you to give me anything that belongs to you, but only to give me back what was not originally yours, what you gained from my father. I have done wrong, and the evil I have done requires from you some wrong in return. After all, even my father Agamemnon did wrong when he formed the

Greeks into an army and went to Troy, when he had committed no crime himself, but because he wanted to remedy the crime and wrong committed by your wife. As men should in response to an appeal from those who are dear to them, he gave genuinely of himself and fought alongside you, so that you could retrieve your wife. All I'm asking, then, is that you repay me in exactly the same way as you were repaid then. Nor will it take ten years: I want you to help us out just for one day by standing firm and protecting us. You should do this single thing for us in repayment for the single thing that was done for you. As for the sacrifice of my sister at Aulis,* I shall let you have that: you don't need to kill Hermione. Given my current situation, you're bound to come off better and I'm bound to make concessions. But make my life your repayment to my poor father, because my death will leave my father's house with no means of perpetuating itself.

'Impossible,' you may say. But the point is this: it's when those dear to us are afflicted by troubles that we have to help them. When the gods grant success, what need have we of friends? The gods themselves are enough, when they're prepared to help us.

It is generally held throughout Greece that you love your wife, and I say this not out of any desire to flatter my way under your guard. But I implore you in her name. (*To himself*) I hate this! Look at the depths to which I have sunk! But so what? I have to abase myself. If this appeal of mine succeeds, the whole house will benefit. (*He again takes up the suppliant position at* MENELAUS' *knees*) Uncle, imagine that your brother, though dead and buried, is listening, with his soul hovering over you, and is saying what I am saying. I have said what I wanted to say; I have made my request. All I want to do is survive, and that is something everyone desires, not just I.

CHORUS. For all that I am a woman, I too implore you to help those in need. It is within your power to do so.

MENELAUS. Orestes, I respect you, and I'd like to assist you in your time of trouble. By means of such assistance we should help our kin to rid themselves of their troubles (if, thanks to the gods, we have the power) by killing or being killed by their enemies. But on the other hand I do need to get the power from the gods, because I have come here poorly equipped with military support; after all the countless trials I encountered on my wanderings, I am left with few friends and have little in the way of military might to offer. So it would be impossible for us to overcome the Pelasgian Argives* in battle, but if we could make use of soft words—this is a hopeful situation for us to find ourselves in. For when the populace of a city becomes angry and passionate, it is like trying to extinguish a furious fire. But if one gently yields and gives way while the energy is running high, while watching out for the opportune moment, it may well blow itself out. If it does die down, you can easily get everything you want. I'll go and try to persuade Tyndareus and the city to make good use of their excessive zeal. For a violently taut sheet makes even a ship go under, but it rights itself again if one slackens the sheet.† The gods hate excessive displays of enthusiasm—a hatred shared by the common people of a city. If I am to save you from superior forces—and what I say is true— I must use cunning rather than force. You might perhaps be thinking that I could use force of arms to save you, but that is not so: it's no easy matter for a single spear to win through against the troubles that are besetting you.*

Exit MENELAUS.

ORESTES *sits down on his couch.*

ORESTES. You coward! You're no help to your friends at all! All you can do is go to war for the sake of a woman! Do you turn from me and run away? Are Agamemnon's claims on you forgotten? And so it turns out, father, that you have been abandoned to your misfortune by your friends. Oh, I have been betrayed! My last hopes of finding a way to escape death at the hands of the Argives have been dashed! For he was my safe haven, my best chance of survival. But I can see my closest friend Pylades running here! He's come from Phocis.* What a sweet sight! In times of trouble a man welcomes the sight of a true friend more than sailors do calm water.

Enter PYLADES, *running.*

PYLADES. Here I am! I made my way with excessive haste through the city, because I heard that a general assembly was taking place (and in fact I saw it clearly with my own eyes) with a view to killing you and your sister before long.† What's going on? How are things with you? How are you, my dearest companion, friend, and relative? For you are all this to me.

ORESTES. To explain my troubles to you in a nutshell—it's all over with me.*

PYLADES. Your ruin would mean mine too, since friends share everything.

ORESTES. Menelaus has behaved in a despicable fashion towards me and my sister.

PYLADES. Of course, since bad women make their husbands bad.

ORESTES. As far as getting anything from him is concerned, he might as well not have come.

PYLADES. So he really has come here to this land?

ORESTES. He took his time getting here, but it didn't take long for the hollowness of his friendship to be exposed.

PYLADES. And did he ship that awful wife of his here too?

ORESTES. It wasn't he who brought her here, but she who brought him.

PYLADES. Where is she, this woman who singlehandedly destroyed so many Greeks?

ORESTES. In my palace, if you can call this palace here mine.

PYLADES. And what did you say to your uncle?

ORESTES. I asked him not to stand idly by while my sister and I were put to death by the Argives.

PYLADES. And tell me: how did he respond to that? I'd really like to know.

ORESTES. He gave the kind of circumspect reply you'd expect from a false friend.

PYLADES. And what reason did he give for his caution? When I understand this I'll have the whole picture.

ORESTES. It was the arrival of our friend, (*sarcastically*) the one with such noble daughters.

PYLADES. You mean Tyndareus. I suppose he was angry with you about his daughter.

ORESTES. You've got it. And Menelaus gave more weight to his connection with him than to his connection with me.

PYLADES. And he lacked the courage to step up and take on some of the burden of your trials?

ORESTES. Yes, because he lacks martial spirit. It's only when he's surrounded by women that he displays any valour.

PYLADES. So your situation could hardly be worse. Is there no way for you to avoid death?

ORESTES. The citizens have to cast their votes about us on the charge of murder.

PYLADES. I'm frightened to ask, but what will be decided by the vote?

ORESTES. Whether we live or die. A simple answer about a complex matter.

PYLADES. So leave this place and run away with your sister.

ORESTES. Can't you see? There are guards watching us on all sides.

PYLADES. I did see armed men barricading the streets.

ORESTES. Our bodies are as beleaguered as a city by a hostile army.

PYLADES. And what about me? It's time for you to consider my situation. For it's all over with me too.

ORESTES. Thanks to whom? This would be another disaster to add to my troubles.

PYLADES. My father Strophius has turned me out of his house in anger and banished me.

ORESTES. On what grounds? Was it a private quarrel, or did he and your fellow citizens bring a public suit against you?

PYLADES. The charge was that I helped you murder your mother, which he claims is an act of impiety.

ORESTES. You poor wretch! It looks as though my troubles are going to afflict you too.

PYLADES. But I'm no Menelaus. I shall endure the burden.

ORESTES. Aren't you afraid that the Argives might want to kill you as well as me?

PYLADES. It's the Phocians' job to punish me, not theirs.

ORESTES. But the masses can be terrifying when they gain unscrupulous leaders.*

PYLADES. But with good leaders they always make good decisions.

ORESTES. Anyway, we had better share our thoughts.

PYLADES. What do we have to do?

ORESTES. Suppose I were to go before the Argives and say . . .

PYLADES. . . . that your actions were justified?

ORESTES. Because I was avenging my father.

PYLADES. But beware: they may just welcome the opportunity to arrest you.

ORESTES. But shall I cower and die in silence?

PYLADES. That would be a cowardly option.

ORESTES. What should I do, then?

PYLADES. Is there any way for you to survive if you stay put?

ORESTES. No.

PYLADES. But if you go there's some hope of your finding a safe way out of your troubles?

ORESTES. Yes, that might perhaps happen.

PYLADES. Isn't it better than staying put?

ORESTES. So shall I go, then?

PYLADES. At any rate, if you die your death will be more honourable this way.

ORESTES. You're right. I avoid cowardice this way.

PYLADES. More so than you do by staying.

ORESTES. Yes, and my cause is just.

PYLADES. But all that's important is for you to make sure it *appears* just.

ORESTES. And I might make people feel sorry for me . . .

PYLADES. Your noble birth is an important factor.

ORESTES. . . . out of anger at my father's death.

PYLADES. All this depends on how they see it.

ORESTES. I had better go. An inglorious death isn't fitting for a man.

PYLADES. I approve of your decision.

ORESTES. So shall we tell my sister?

PYLADES. No, definitely not.

ORESTES. There would certainly be tears.

PYLADES. And wouldn't that be a significant omen?*

ORESTES. So it's clearly preferable not to say anything.

PYLADES. Yes, you'll be saving time.

ORESTES. The only thing stopping me is . . .

PYLADES. What new point are you raising now?

ORESTES. . . . the worry that I might be overcome by the goddesses' madness.

PYLADES. But I'll look after you.

ORESTES. It's distasteful to touch a sick man.

PYLADES. Not to me, when the sick man is you.

ORESTES. Beware of catching my insanity.

PYLADES. No, never mind about that.

ORESTES. So you won't hesitate?

PYLADES. No, because it's terrible for friends to hesitate.

ORESTES. Come, then, steer my feet . . .

ORESTES struggles to his feet.

PYLADES. Yes, for I hold dear the bond of friendship.

ORESTES. . . . and take me to my father's tomb.

PYLADES. What for?

ORESTES. So that I can beg him to save me.

PYLADES. That would be the right thing for him to do.

ORESTES. I hope I don't catch sight of my mother's tomb.

PYLADES. Quite: she was your enemy. But hurry up: you don't want to be overtaken by the Argives' vote. Let me support you, since you have been enfeebled by illness. You should know that I'll bear you through the city without the least embarrassment, and taking little notice of people. How am I to demonstrate my affection for you if I'm not there for you when your situation is disastrous?

ORESTES. That's it! Make your companions, not just your family, your friends! The friendship of a man whose character melds with yours, even if he doesn't belong to your immediate family, is worth more to a man than countless thousands of relatives.

Exeunt ORESTES and PYLADES, who is supporting his friend.

CHORUS (*sings*). The great prosperity and prowess that held high its head
throughout Greece and beside Simois' streams* have receded
once more away from good fortune for Atreus' line—
yes, once more receded as a result of the ancient doom of the house,
when the dispute over the golden lamb* came to the Tantalids†
with hideous, pitiful feasting and the slaughter of high-born children.
Since then woe succeeding woe achieved through blood
never abandons the twofold house of Atreus.*

It's wrong, not right, to cut parent's flesh with fire-forged steel,
and to display to sun's light the sword in its black sheath of gore.
To do a 'good' crime is nothing but the tortuous impiety
and muddled thinking of wrong-headed men.
In fear of death Tyndareus' wretched daughter screamed:
'My child, this is an impious undertaking, to kill your mother.
Beware, lest in honouring your father's kindness
you bind to yourself an undying name for infamy!'

Can there be in the world a greater sickness—
or a greater source of tears and sadness—
than tainting one's hand with matricidal blood?
For this crime the son of Agamemnon
is being goaded with fits of insanity,
hunted down by the Eumenides, his eyes rolling with fear.
How I pity him! When from his mother's robes,
threaded with gold, he saw her breast appear,
he made his mother his victim,
in exchange for his father's fate.

Enter ELECTRA. *She looks for* ORESTES.

ELECTRA. Women, would I be right in thinking that poor Orestes' god-given madness overwhelmed him and drove him from this place?

CHORUS. Not at all: he has gone to face the people of Argos.

ELECTRA. Oh, no! What has he done? Who persuaded him to go there?

CHORUS. Pylades. But here comes a messenger, who will presumably soon give you news of your brother and tell you what happened there.

Enter MESSENGER.

MESSENGER. My lady Electra, Agamemnon's daughter, I bring bad news. What I have to tell you is . . .

ELECTRA. Ah, woe! We are finished! That's clear from what you say.

MESSENGER. . . . that the Pelasgians have voted today to put you and your brother to death.

ELECTRA. Oh, no! This is what I was afraid of. The prospect that has been making me weep for a long time has now arrived! But what happened in the trial? What were the arguments used before the Argives which convicted us and condemned us to death? Tell me, old man. Am I to breathe my last as a result of being stoned to death or put to the sword? And is my fate to be the same as my brother's?

MESSENGER. It so happened that I was on my way into the city from the countryside because I wanted to find out what was going on with you and Orestes. In the past I was always loyal to your father, and I depended on your household for my daily bread; I am poor, but that doesn't stop me being a true friend. I saw a crowd hurrying up to the hill where they say Danaus was the first to muster and assemble the people, when he wanted to grant Aegyptus a legal hearing.* When I saw that the townspeople were assembling I asked one of them, 'What's new in Argos? Has a declaration of war stirred the city of the Argives?' In reply he said, 'Don't you see Orestes? There he is, approaching us over there. He's come to enter the lists in a trial for his life!'

I saw a sight I hoped never to see, and wish I never had. Pylades and your brother were walking together, the one drooping and enfeebled by illness, the other, like a brother, just as distressed as his friend, conscientiously tending his illness. With the Argives packed into their assembly-place, a town-crier stood up and said: 'Who wants to speak on the question whether Orestes should or should not be put to death for matricide?' At this Talthybius* got to his feet. Now, he was with your father at the sack of Troy, but since he is always influenced by those in power, his speech was ambivalent. On the one hand, he expressed great admiration for your father, but on the other hand, twining bad arguments into good, he criticized your brother for establishing unsound rules in respect of parents. And at the same time he was constantly giving a bright look to Aegisthus' friends. This is typical of his kind: heralds always run over to a successful man and side with whoever has political influence and authority.†

Next lord Diomedes* addressed the people. He was against killing either you or your brother, but recommended banishment as the penalty that would satisfy religious sensibilities. His speech met with shouts of both approval and disapproval, and then an outspoken, arrogantly self-assured fellow stood up. He spoke in favour of stoning you and Orestes to death, but his proposals were really made by Tyndareus. Then someone else got to his feet and argued the contrary point of view. He's not an attractive man, physically, but he's brave; he rarely makes his presence felt in the city or the main square. He's a smallholder—and these men alone are the salvation of the land—but prepared to confront the issues intelligently,† and with self-discipline acquired in the course of an incorruptible and blameless life. He spoke in favour of rewarding Orestes, Agamemnon's son, for having been prepared to avenge his father by killing an evil, godless woman, who would have made it impossible for a man ever to take up arms and campaign abroad, if those left behind were going to subvert his domestic situation and corrupt his marriage. These arguments struck all decent men, at any rate, as valid.

No one else spoke after that, so your brother stepped up and said: 'Gentlemen, inhabitants of the land of Inachus,* when I killed my mother I was defending you just as much as my father. For if murdering men is to be legitimate for women, your deaths will soon follow, or you must be the slaves of women.' But the assembled people failed to find his argument convincing, even though he seemed to have a point, and when it came to a show of hands the majority gave victory to the bad man I spoke of, who argued in favour of killing you and your brother. It was only with difficulty that poor Orestes persuaded them not to stone him to death. Instead he promised that he and you would commit suicide today. Pylades, with tears in his eyes, is bringing him here from the assembly, and they are accompanied by their supporters, who are weeping in sorrow. A bitter sight, a wretched spectacle, is on its way. Anyway, you had better start preparing a sword, or a noose for your neck, since you have to end your life. No advantage has come to you from your high birth, nor from Phoebus and his Pythian tripod;* in fact, it is he who has destroyed you.

Exit MESSENGER.

CHORUS (*sings*). O Pelasgia,* I start the lamentation, with cheeks raked
in bloody disfigurement by pale fingernail,
with head beaten, as is the due of the fair maiden goddess
Persephone, queen† of the dead below the ground.*
Let the Cyclopian land* resound with the woes of the house,
as we take iron to shear our heads.
I see pity drawing nigh, pity for those about to die,
who once led Greece to war.*

For gone, lost and gone, is the entire line of Pelops' children
and the success that once crowned his blessed house.
The gods' envy has doomed it, and the bloody vote,
cast in hatred by the citizens of this place.*
O fleeting race of mortals, whose life is naught but tears and trials,
see how fate comes, confounding expectations!
As the long years pass men exchange one woe for another,
and the whole of human life is unfathomable.

ELECTRA (*sings*). Suspended midway between heaven and earth
on golden chains floats a rock,
a fragment torn from Olympus,*
driven along by the cosmic whirl.
Would that I could go there now
and in tears sob out to old father Tantalus,
the ancestor, the forebear of my line,
the tragedies I have seen befall his house.
First there were winged colts giving chase,
when on his four-horse-drawn chariot
Pelops rode over the open sea
and as he drove over the sea's surge
by Geraestus' surf-beaten shores
hurled Myrtilus to his death in the swell of the waves.*
Next there came to my house a much-mourned curse,
when among the flocks of horse-farming Atreus†
there arose that fatal prodigy,
the lamb with the golden fleece.
Then Strife took the Sun's winged chariot
and changed its route, fitting the one-horse car
of Dawn to the westward path of heaven,

and Zeus altered the running course
of the Pleiades with their seven tracks.†*
And for that death†* Strife added further death—
the banquet that bears the name of Thyestes,*
and the marriage-bed of Cretan Aerope,*
traitress in a treacherous union.
And now the final end has come
to me and my father
in the tragic doom of our house.

CHORUS. But here come your brother, now condemned to death, and that most loyal of friends, Pylades, who, brother-like, is guiding his infirm footsteps here,† carefully keeping pace with him and sticking close to his side.

Enter ORESTES *and* PYLADES, *who supports him as before, and seats him on his couch.*

ELECTRA. Alas! Brother, the sight of you before your tomb, before the pyre of the dead, stirs me to grief. Again I cry alas! This final sight of you has scattered my wits.

ORESTES. Hush, now! No more of this womanish wailing! Try to submit to what is fated to happen. It's a hard fate, but you must try to accept it.

ELECTRA. How can I keep quiet? This is the last chance we poor wretches have to see the Sun-god's light.

ORESTES. Stop! Don't you kill me too! Isn't it enough that I've been put to death by the Argives? Don't go on about the troubles that beset us!

ELECTRA. I feel sorry for you, Orestes—so young, and doomed to untimely death! You are dead when you should be alive!

ORESTES. Please, I beg you, don't unman me! By reminding me of our troubles you'll reduce me to tears.

ELECTRA. We're going to die! It's impossible not to weep for our plight! Everyone holds life so dear that its loss is grievous.

ORESTES. This is the decisive day for us. We must either tie a rope around our necks as a noose or sharpen a sword to wield.

ELECTRA. I want you to kill me, brother. It would be an insult to Agamemnon's house were one of the Argives to do it.

ORESTES. Having my mother's blood on my hands is enough for me. I won't kill you. You must kill yourself, in a manner of your own choosing.

ELECTRA. All right. You'll find me your equal with a sword. But now I'd like to put my arms around your neck.

ORESTES. Enjoy the empty pleasure, if pleasure it is for those near death to embrace.

They embrace.

ELECTRA. My darling! There's nothing more precious and sweet to your sister than you.† Our lives are one.

ORESTES (*weeping*). See! You've made me break down and cry. And now I'd like to hug you in return. Why should I in my wretchedness hold back any more?

ELECTRA. Oh, if it were right, how I wish that the same sword might kill us both, and that a single coffin, wrought of cedar, could receive us both!

ORESTES. Nothing would be sweeter than that! But you can see how few members of our family remain, to bury us together.

End of embrace.

ELECTRA. Didn't Menelaus make an effort in his speech to save you from death? Oh, the wicked man, the betrayer of my father!

ORESTES. He wasn't even anywhere to be seen.* With his hopes set on the throne, he was careful not to protect his family. But come now! Let's make sure we die in a noble fashion,* worthy of Agamemnon. I plan to demonstrate my high birth to the city with a sword-thrust to my vitals, and you should match the boldness of my action. Pylades, please would you oversee our suicides, and when we are dead array our bodies well, take us to our father's tomb, and bury us together. (*He gets to his feet*) And now farewell. As you see, I am off to do the deed.

PYLADES. Wait! Apart from anything else, I take exception to one aspect of your plans. Did you really think that I would want to live after you're dead?

ORESTES. Why is it your business to die along with me?

PYLADES. I can't believe you had to ask that question. What sense does it make for me to live without your friendship?

ORESTES. You didn't kill a mother, as I did, to my misfortune.

PYLADES. Yes, I did, along with you. So I ought to suffer the same fate.

ORESTES. No, don't die with me. Go back to your father. For you have a city, while I have none, and you have your father's palace and the refuge of great wealth. As for marriage, it's true that you have lost my poor sister, whom I betrothed to you in honour of our friendship, but you can find someone else to wed and bear your children. We no longer have any relationship to bind us. And now, my dear friend, farewell—as you can and we cannot, since faring well is what we dead relinquish.

ORESTES again makes as if to leave.

PYLADES. You could hardly be further from understanding what I have in mind. May the fertile ground not receive my blood, nor the bright air my soul, if ever I treacherously abandon you while ensuring my own freedom. I shall not seek to deny that I was your accomplice in the murder you committed, and I helped you plan everything for which you are now being punished. So I too should die along with you and Electra here, whom I consider to be my wife, in so far as marrying her found favour with me. For how could I ever go to Delphi, the citadel of the Phocians,* and explain myself with honour, if I supported you as your friend before your downfall, but deserted you now that your luck has changed? Impossible. I am just as involved in this as you. But since we are to die, let's put our heads together and try to find a way to make Menelaus suffer too.

ORESTES. My dearest friend, if only I could see that before I die!*

PYLADES. Do as I say, then, and delay the cutting thrust of your sword.

ORESTES. I shall, if I am to find some measure of revenge on my enemy.

PYLADES (*lowering his voice*). Be quiet. I have little trust in women.

ORESTES. You needn't worry about these ones here. They're on our side.

PYLADES. Let's kill Helen.* That will cause Menelaus bitter grief.

ORESTES. How? I commend† your readiness, provided the outcome is good.

PYLADES. Put her to the sword. She's hiding in your palace.

ORESTES. So she is. In fact she's putting her seal on all my property.*

PYLADES. Not any more she isn't, now that she has Hades* as her bridegroom.

ORESTES. But how do we do it? She has her foreign attendants.

PYLADES. Who are they? No Phrygian* would cause me fear.

ORESTES. They tend to things like her mirrors and perfumes.

PYLADES. So she's come here with all her Trojan luxuries?

ORESTES. Yes, Greece was always too small an abode for her.

PYLADES. Slaves stand no chance against non-slaves.

ORESTES. If I could see this through, I would not hesitate to die twice over.

PYLADES. The same goes for me too, since I'll be helping you.

ORESTES. Explain what we have to do. Finish telling me what you have in mind.

PYLADES. We'll go into the palace making out that we intend to commit suicide there.

ORESTES. That's clear, but I still don't understand how we manage all the rest.

PYLADES. We'll go up to her, complaining of our plight.

ORESTES. At this she will be all tears on the surface, but happy inside.

PYLADES. Just as we shall too; we'll be no different from her.

ORESTES. And then how shall we go about our assignment?

PYLADES. We'll have swords hidden in these clothes of ours.

ORESTES. But first how will we encompass the death of her attendants?

PYLADES. We'll lock them out in various parts of the palace.

ORESTES. Yes, and we'd better kill anyone who tries to raise the alarm.

PYLADES. After that the deed itself will make clear how we have to proceed.

ORESTES. To murder Helen. I understand your implication.

PYLADES. You're right. But now listen to the beauty of my plan. If the woman we were killing were a more upright person, there would be no glory in murdering her. But as things are, we shall be punishing her on behalf of all Greece, for the fathers she killed, the children she destroyed, the brides she robbed of husbands. There will be cries of joy, and people will burn thanks-offerings for the gods, as they pray for us to be showered with rewards, because we exacted retribution in blood from an evil woman. Once you've killed her, you won't be called 'the matricide' any longer. That will be a thing of the past, and your reputation will improve, because you'll be known as the killer of the mass-murderer Helen. It's quite unthinkable that Menelaus should prosper while you, your father, and your sister all die, and your mother . . . but in common decency I refrain from mentioning her case. Anyway, it's unthinkable that Menelaus should recover his wife and occupy your palace thanks to Agamemnon's prowess. I would certainly deserve to die right now if my dark sword remains in its sheath and is not used against her. And should we fail to encompass her murder, we'll set fire to this palace here* before killing ourselves. One of these two endeavours will succeed, and we shall be applauded either for the manner of our deaths or for the way in which we saved our lives.

CHORUS. Tyndareus' daughter is a disgrace to her kind and every woman should find her hateful.

ORESTES. Oh, there's nothing better than a reliable friend—not even wealth or kingship. A true friend is worth as much as an incalculable number of people. For instance, not only did you devise the mischief we made against Aegisthus* and stand by me when danger threatened, but now you've found a way for me to be revenged on my enemies and again you remain by my side. But I'll stop singing your praises, because even that—even being praised to the skies—is somewhat oppressive. Since I am in any case on the point of death, I would like to do something to my enemies before I die, to repay those who betrayed me and to ruin the lives of those who ruined mine. I am, remember, the son of Agamemnon, who became the leader of Greece on his merits,* not as a result of autocratic authority—though he did, in fact, have a certain godlike power. I am not about to disgrace him by dying a servile death. No, I shall depart this life as a free man should, and I shall be avenged on Menelaus. There's only one thing we need for complete success: if somehow we could remain alive, unlikely though it seems, and kill without being killed—well, that's what I pray for. I'm glad even to give my mind the easy satisfaction of voicing this desire of mine in fleeting words.

ELECTRA. Brother, I think I know how to achieve exactly that—safety for all three of us, you, me, and Pylades here.

ORESTES. Your plan needs divine providence. But where will we find it? I know that intelligence is a strong component of your mind, so tell us what you mean.

ELECTRA. Listen, then, to what I have to say. And the same goes for you, Pylades: pay attention to me.*

ORESTES. Go on. For what pleasure is there in the postponement of good things?

ELECTRA. You know Helen's daughter? But that's an unecessary question.

ORESTES. Yes, of course: Hermione, whom my mother brought up.

ELECTRA. She's gone to Clytemnestra's tomb . . .

ORESTES. What for? What prospect are you holding out?

ELECTRA. . . . to pour libations for her mother at the tomb.

ORESTES. And why are you telling me this? What has it to do with our safety?

ELECTRA. You must take her hostage when she returns.

ORESTES. In what respect will that remedy things for us three companions?

ELECTRA. Once Helen has been killed, if Menelaus makes an attempt against you—or indeed against Pylades and me, since we're all united in this—you must tell him you will kill Hermione. You should have your sword drawn and close to the girl's throat. Now, if he removes the threat against your life because he doesn't want Hermione to die, let the girl go into her father's keeping. But he's an irascible man, and if he loses his temper and moves to kill you, then you make as if to cut the girl's throat. I think that for all his initial bravado he'll eventually soften his resolve. After all, he's not temperamentally bold or warlike. This is the strategy I have for securing our safety. That's what I wanted to say.

ORESTES. You may be physically as womanly as any of your sex, but you have the mind of a man! Indeed, you deserve to live rather than die. Pylades, you will rue the day you lose such a woman—but if you live, you will be lucky to have her as your wife.

PYLADES. That's what I pray for—that she may come to the city of the Phocians the worthy subject of fine wedding-songs.

ORESTES. But when will Hermione reach the palace? After all, the undoubted excellence of your plan depends on our success in capturing this whelp* of an unholy father.

ELECTRA. I would think she's close to home now. She's been away as long as one might expect.

ORESTES. Good. So, Electra, you had better stay in front of the palace so as to be here for the girl when she arrives, and also to keep an eye out in case anyone enters the palace too soon, before the murder has been carried out. If anyone does come, let us know within the palace, either by banging on the door or by sending word to us inside. As for us, let's go inside and equip ourselves with swords for the final ordeal.

Father, from the halls of dark Night you now inhabit, hear your son Orestes as he calls on you to come to his aid!

ELECTRA. Yes, father, come, if from within the earth you hear the cries of your children, who are dying for your sake.

PYLADES. Agamemnon, close kin of my father,* hear my prayers too: keep your children safe.

ORESTES. I killed my mother . . .

ELECTRA. I put my hand to the sword . . .

PYLADES. And I offered my encouragement and banished doubts.

ORESTES. . . . to proffer aid to you, father.

ELECTRA. . . . and never let you down.

PYLADES. Will what you're hearing not shock you into rescuing your children?

ORESTES. My tears are my libation to you.

ELECTRA. And mine are my laments.

PYLADES: Enough. Let's set about the task. For if prayers penetrate inside the earth, he can hear you. May Zeus our ancestor and Justice in all her glory grant success to this man, this woman, and me—three companions sharing one ordeal, one trial.

Exeunt ORESTES and PYLADES into the palace.

ELECTRA. Women of Mycenae,* my friends, noble women of Argos, the Pelasgian seat . . .

CHORUS. What orders would you give us, my lady? For you are still entitled to be addressed as such in the city of the Argives.

ELECTRA. Let some of you stand on the carriageway here,

while the rest of you take up positions there on the other path. You will serve as the palace's garrison.

CHORUS. Why are you setting us this task? Tell me, dear.

ELECTRA. I don't want anyone to make our troubles worse by catching sight of my brother as he sets his hand to bloody murder.

The CHORUS divides according to ELECTRA's instructions.

SEMICHORUS A. Come on, hurry up. I shall watch over this road here, the eastward one.

SEMICHORUS B. And I this one here, which tends west.

ELECTRA. Cast your eyes to and fro.

CHORUS. From here to there and back again we keep our watch, just as you told us to.

ELECTRA. Keep those eyes moving around. Cast your glance from side to side in all directions.

SEMICHORUS A (*excited*). There's someone on the road. Who is it?† Who's this peasant walking by your palace?

ELECTRA. We're lost, it seems, my friends! Before long he will reveal the secret hunting of our swordsmen to our enemies.

SEMICHORUS A. Don't be alarmed, my dear: there's no one on the path as you thought.

ELECTRA. What? Can I still rely on you? Tell me truly: is the road up to the forecourt clear?

SEMICHORUS A. Yes, all's well in this direction. But keep an eye out on your side, because none of the citizens is approaching this way.

SEMICHORUS B. It's the same here as with you: there are no people to be seen here either.

ELECTRA. Wait, now, while I listen at the doors.

CHORUS. Why the hushed delay? What's keeping you people inside the palace from sprinkling the victim with her blood?

ELECTRA. They're not listening. Oh, no! As if I didn't have enough to suffer! Can it be that their swords have been blunted when faced with her beauty?

CHORUS. Soon an armed Argive will sprint up to the palace in his haste to come to her rescue.

ELECTRA. Keep a sharper eye out, please! This is not a contest of idleness. You lot look here, you lot there.

CHORUS. I patrol the path, watching in all directions.

HELEN (*from within*). Alas! Citizens of Pelasgian Argos, I am foully murdered!

ELECTRA. Did you hear that? The men have set about the murder! That was Helen screaming, I suppose.

CHORUS. O Zeus, O Zeus of never-failing might, come in earnest and help those dear to me!

HELEN (*from within*). Menelaus, I am dying! Where are you when I need you?

ELECTRA AND CHORUS (*sing*).
Murder her, slay her, smite her, kill her!
Strike at close range with your two two-edged swords!
Strike her who abandoned father and husband,
and caused the death of countless Greeks,
slain beside the river by hostile spears,
where thanks to weapons of iron tears fell on tears
by the eddying waters of Scamander.*

CHORUS. Quiet, quiet! I can hear the sound of someone on the path by the palace!

ELECTRA. My dearest friends, it's Hermione! She has arrived in the middle of the murder! (*Lowering her voice*) Let's keep our voices down. She's going to blunder into the coils of our net! If we capture her, she'll make a fine catch. Take up your posts once more with a calm look and a complexion that doesn't betray what's happened. I'll keep my eyes resentful, to pretend I have no knowledge of what has happened.

Enter HERMIONE. *She carries the empty libation jugs.*

So here you are, girl! Have you finished making offerings at Clytemnestra's tomb and pouring libations for the dead?

HERMIONE. Once I secured her favour, I came straight back. But at the moment I'm feeling somewhat afraid, because while I was still a long way off I heard a cry from inside the palace, but I don't know what it was.

ELECTRA. Well, you'd expect us to be upset, given what's happening to us.*

HERMIONE. No words of ill omen, please. But what do you mean? What new trouble has arisen?

ELECTRA. The city has condemned Orestes and me to death.

HERMIONE. Oh, no! That this should happen to members of my family!

ELECTRA. Their minds are made up; the yoke of necessity is upon us.

HERMIONE. So is this the reason for the shouting inside the palace?

ELECTRA. Yes, the cries come from a suppliant on the ground at Helen's knees.

HERMIONE. Who? Tell me. I don't want to remain in ignorance.

ELECTRA. Poor Orestes, who is begging her to save his life, and mine too.

HERMIONE. Then the house certainly has a good excuse for tears.

ELECTRA. Yes, what better reason could there be for an outcry? But since we're all members of the same family, why don't you come and join us in our supplication? Why not fall to the ground before your mother, in all her high prosperity, and beg her not to let Menelaus stand by and watch us die? Come. Remembering how my mother cradled you in her arms, take pity on us and relieve us of our troubles. Come and join us here in our endeavour; I'll show you the way. You're the only one who can guarantee us complete safety.

HERMIONE. There, I'm entering the palace as quickly as I can. In so far as it is up to me, you will be safe.

ELECTRA escorts HERMIONE to the door and calls inside.

ELECTRA. You swordsmen of mine there inside the palace, here is our quarry for you to seize. Hold her! Hold her! Once your swords are at her throat, calm down, so that Menelaus may know that he is up against no cowardly Phrygians, but real men, and that he's being treated exactly as cowards should be treated.

Exeunt ELECTRA and HERMIONE into the palace.

CHORUS (*sings*). Ah! Ah, my friends! Make a noise, a loud
noise,
and raise a cry here in front of the palace,
lest the murder that has been committed
might make the Argives so fiercely afraid
that they run to offer assistance

to the royal palace before I have certain sight
of Helen's bloodied corpse lying within,
or else hear word from one of her attendants.
For though clear about some aspects of these events,
there are others of which I am less certain.
In full justice has divine wrath
come to Helen. For she filled all Greece with tears
thanks to that pernicious, baneful man from Ida,
Paris,* who brought Greece to Troy.

Enter PHRYGIAN* *from palace, running and agitated.*

PHRYGIAN (*sings*). I have fled for my life from Argive sword
in eastern slippers over the cedar-wood beams
of the colonnade and the Doric triglyphs*—
O Earth! O Earth, it's all past, past!—
running scared like the easterner I am.
Oh, woe! Where can I flee, ladies?
Would that I could fly to the bright sky
or to the sea which bull-headed Oceanus*
winds in his arms as he encircles the earth!

CHORUS. Tell me, Trojan, Helen's slave from Ida: what's the matter?

PHRYGIAN (*sings*). Troy, alas! Alas, Troy! O city of the Phrygians,
O fruitful soil of sacred mount Ida,
in eastern grief I raise my voice for your fall,
brought about by the beauty of that bird-born,
swan-feathered whelp of Leda,*
Helen of ill fame, ill-famed Helen,
wrath descending on the hewn towers
of Pergamum, built by Apollo.
Aaaah! The dirges, the dirges!
O Dardanus' wretched land!*
O horseman Ganymede,* bed-mate of Zeus!

CHORUS. Tell us clearly and in detail exactly what happened indoors.

PHRYGIAN (*sings*). Sorrow! Sorrow!
That is how with Asian voice in the east
they start the plaint—oh, woe!—when on the ground

is shed by Hades' iron swords the blood of kings.
So from me you want exact details?
Into the palace there came with matching gait
a matched pair of Greek lions.
The one named by his father the war-leader;
the other, the son of Strophius, is like Odysseus*
an evil-scheming man, devising tricks in silence,
but loyal to his friends, courageous under threat,
skilled in the arts of war, and a deadly serpent.
Damn him for his evil ways and his quiet cunning!
Inside, their eyes marred with tears,
they drew near the seat of the wife of the archer, Paris.*
They abased themselves, one on either side,
and, each clasping her from his own side,
they threw suppliant arms,
threw them around the knees of Helen.
Back they leapt at a run, the Phrygian attendants,
back they leapt, speaking one to another
in abject fear of a trick. Some thought not,
but it seemed to others that Tyndareus' daughter
was being enmeshed in a device of nets
by the matricidal serpent.

CHORUS. But where were you at this time? Or were you so afraid
that you were long gone?

PHRYGIAN (*sings*). Following the Phrygian custom, the
Phrygian way,
with rapid movement of firm, feathered fan
before her cheek I was wafting a breeze,*
a breeze past Helen's hair, Helen's locks,
while her hands wound the thread,
the thread on the distaff,
and the finished yarn fell to the floor.*
With the thread she wanted to sew
from Phrygian spoils offerings for the tomb,
purple-dyed clothing, a gift for Clytemnestra.
Said Orestes to the bride from Sparta:
'O daughter of Zeus, come away from your chair,
walk over here to the ancient hearth-seat
of my forefather Pelops, to hear my words.'

And so he took her—he took her and she followed,
with no foresight of what the future held.
Meanwhile his accomplice, the foul Phocian,
was about other business. 'Out of the way!
Begone,† you Phrygian cowards!' said he.
Each of us he shut in a different part of the palace,
some in the stables, some in the porches,
some here, some there, dividing us up,
and keeping us far from our mistress.

CHORUS. What happened next?

PHRYGIAN (*sings*). O great mother, mighty Idaean mother,
mighty goddess Antaea!* O the blood and the pain,
the foul crimes I saw there, saw in the royal palace!
Holding swords drawn from the darkness
of purple-bordered clothes, they whirled from side to side
their eyes, checking that no one was there.
As firm as mountain-dwelling boars,
they stood facing the woman and said:
'Now you are going to die, to die!
Blame your death on the coward you married,
who betrayed to death, here in Argos,
the children of his brother.' She screamed.
She screamed 'Alas! Alas for me!',
and her pale arm smote her breast and head†
with piteous blows. She was trying to run away,
trying to flee, to flee on gold-sandaled foot,
when past her in Mycenaean boots ran Orestes.
His hand shot into her hair; he bent her neck
on to his left shoulder and was poised
to plunge his dark sword into her throat.

CHORUS. And where were you Phrygian house-slaves? What were you doing to defend her?

PHRYGIAN (*sings*). With a shout and with crowbars
we ripped out the frames and the posts
from the doors of the buildings where we were held,
and ran to help from the various parts of the palace,
bearing stones, or hooks, or drawn sword.
But we were opposed by Pylades,
as irresistible as . . . as Phrygian Hector,

or as Ajax* in his three-plumed helmet,
whom once I saw, saw there in the gates of Priam's city.
Sword clashed with sword, and that was when . . .
yes, that was when we Phrygians made it clear
how far our martial skill and prowess† fall short
of Greek weaponry. One turned and fled,
another was killed, another was wounded,
while a fourth took to begging to protect his life.
They were dying, or about to die, or already dead,
and so we fled into the shadows.
Then poor Hermione entered the palace,
to see her wretched mother, who gave her life,
sprawled on the ground at the point of death.
They ran and seized her as if they were two Bacchants,*
freed from their coven, and she a mountain cub.
Then once more they turned their attention
to the slaughter of the daughter of Zeus.
But she was nowhere to be seen in the palace!
I swear by Zeus, by Earth, by Light, by Night,
whether drugs were involved or magic craft,
or whether the gods had stolen her away,
she had vanished! I have no knowledge
of what happened next, for out of the palace
I was stealing, making good my escape.
But after enduring so much, so many trials
and ordeals, Menelaus has gained nothing, nothing,
by rescuing his wife Helen from Troy.

Enter ORESTES, running with a sword in his hand.

CHORUS. Here comes something strange, on top of the strange news we've just heard. For I can see Orestes, sword in hand, running out to the front of the palace in a high state of agitation.

ORESTES. Where's the man who fled from the palace to avoid my sword?*

The PHRYGIAN throws himself at ORESTES' feet.

PHRYGIAN. Lord, I prostrate myself before you on the ground, as is the eastern fashion.

ORESTES. This place is not in Troy, but in Argive territory.

PHRYGIAN. But the wise prefer life to death wherever they are.

ORESTES. You didn't call out for Menelaus to come and help, did you?

PHRYGIAN. For my part I would summon help for *you*, since you deserve it more.

ORESTES. So the death of Tyndareus' daughter was justified, then?

PHRYGIAN. Perfectly justified, even if she had three throats for striking.

ORESTES. You flatter with a coward's tongue, but you weren't of this opinion indoors.

PHRYGIAN. No? When she brought ruin to Troy as well as Greece?

ORESTES. Swear that you're not just trying to flatter me—swear it, or I'll kill you!

PHRYGIAN. I swear on my life, and I'm not likely to swear falsely on that!

ORESTES. Was it like this in Troy too? Did bare steel terrify every Phrygian there?

PHRYGIAN. Remove your sword. From close at hand it glints with grim death.

ORESTES. Are you afraid of turning into stone, as if you'd seen the Gorgon?

PHRYGIAN. No, of turning into a corpse. I am aware of no Gorgon's head here.

ORESTES. Are you afraid of Hades, though he will release your from the hardship of your slavery?

PHRYGIAN. Every man, even if he be a slave, enjoys life on earth.

ORESTES. You're right—and your intelligence saves you. Now, go inside the palace.

ORESTES removes his sword from the PHRYGIAN's neck and steps back. The PHRYGIAN gets to his feet.

PHRYGIAN. You're not going to kill me, then?

ORESTES. Your life is spared.

PHRYGIAN. That is good news indeed.

ORESTES. But I'm about to change my mind.

PHRYGIAN. That is *not* good news.

ORESTES. You're an idiot if you think that I would bring myself to slit *your* throat, when although you're not a woman, you're no man either.* The reason I came out of the palace was to stop you raising the alarm. For when it hears a cry, Argos is quick to respond. But I'm not worried about getting Menelaus back within range of my sword—just let him come, flaunting his yellow hair on his shoulders.*

Exeunt the PHRYGIAN *to one side, and* ORESTES *into the palace.*

CHORUS (*sings*). Ah! Ah, Fortune! Another conflict,
another terrible conflict faces the house,
affecting the line of Atreus. What shall we do?
Inform the city or keep it to ourselves?
In silence lies greater safety, my friends.
But look! There, in front of the palace! Look!
This smoke hastening up into the air tells us
they are lighting torches to burn Tantalus' house,*
and there is no end yet to the killing.
The end of things for mortals is in the hands
and at the whim of the gods. But mighty too
is the power of the demons of revenge.
This house has fallen, fallen through bloodshed,
because of the fall of Myrtilus from the chariot.*

The CHORUS *stop singing and the Chorus-leader continues alone.*

But now I can see Menelaus too approaching the palace at a run. I suppose he's heard of recent events here. Hurry! Lock and bar the doors, you members of Atreus' line inside the palace. A man at the height of success is a formidable foe to those who are doing badly, as you are now, Orestes.

Enter MENELAUS, *armed, with attendants.*

MENELAUS. I've come in response to news of the appalling deeds of violence committed by the two lions—I can't call them men. Someone open the house! Slaves, put your shoulders to these doors here, so that we may at least rescue my daughter from the bloodstained hands of those murderers!

ORESTES, PYLADES, *and* HERMIONE *appear on the roof.* ORESTES *has his sword held close to* HERMIONE*'s throat, and is holding a slab of masonry in his other hand.* PYLADES *is holding burning torches.*

ORESTES. You there! Keep your hands off the doors! They're locked! I'm talking to you, Menelaus, in all your towering audacity! Do as I say, or I'll smash your head with this slab I've broken off the roof, the work of builders long dead and gone. The doors are barred: they'll stop this hurried rescue attempt of yours and keep you out of the house.

MENELAUS. Oh, what's this? I see the light of torches on the roof where they're beleaguered, and I see a sword guarding my daughter's neck.

ORESTES. Are there questions you want to put to me, or do you want to listen to what I have to say?*

MENELAUS. I don't want to do either, but it looks as though I have no choice but to listen to you.

ORESTES. You might like to know that I'm going to kill your daughter.

MENELAUS. You've already murdered Helen, and now you're committing another murder as well?

ORESTES. If only I'd managed that and hadn't been robbed of success by the gods.

MENELAUS. Are you denying that you killed her? Is this some kind of high-handed joke?

ORESTES. It hurts me to deny it. If only I had . . .

MENELAUS. . . . done what? Tell me, because you're making me afraid.

ORESTES. . . . sent the polluter of Greece hurtling to Hades.

MENELAUS. Give me my wife's body, so that I can bury her.

ORESTES. Ask the gods for her body, but I shall kill your child.

MENELAUS. Your mother's blood is already on your hands. Isn't that enough for you?

ORESTES. I'll never tire of killing evil women.

MENELAUS. What about you, Pylades? Are you going to help him commit this murder?

ORESTES (*after looking at* PYLADES). His silence is agreement.* There's no need for him to speak as well as me.

MENELAUS. But you won't get away with it, unless you can fly away.

ORESTES. We have no intention of escaping. We'll set fire to the palace.

MENELAUS. You'll destroy this house, your family home?

ORESTES. Yes, to stop it falling into your hands. And I'll slaughter this girl over the flames.

MENELAUS. Go ahead, then: kill her—but rest assured that then I'll make you pay for what you've done.

ORESTES. Be quiet, then, and face the fact that your misery is justified.

MENELAUS. Put up your sword! Keep it away from my daughter!

ORESTES. But you're a liar.†

MENELAUS. Are you really going to kill my daughter?

ORESTES. Now you're telling the truth.

MENELAUS. Oh, no! What am I to do?†

ORESTES. Go to the Argives and persuade them . . .

MENELAUS. . . . to do what?

ORESTES. Ask the citizens to spare our lives.

MENELAUS. Otherwise you'll murder my child?

ORESTES. That's right.

MENELAUS. What? Do you deserve to live?

ORESTES. Yes, and to rule.

MENELAUS. Where?

ORESTES. Here, in Pelasgian Argos.

MENELAUS (*sarcastically*). Oh, yes, you're just the person to handle the sacred basins . . .

ORESTES. And why not?

MENELAUS. . . . and to slaughter victims before battle.

ORESTES. Would *you* be the right man for the job?

MENELAUS. Yes, because my hands are free from pollution.

ORESTES. Your hands, maybe, but not your heart.

MENELAUS. But who would talk to you?

ORESTES. Anyone who respects his father.

MENELAUS. And what about those who respect their mothers?

ORESTES. They are lucky.

MENELAUS. As you are not.

ORESTES. Because I have no liking for evil women.

MENELAUS. O Helen, poor Helen . . .

ORESTES. What about poor me?

MENELAUS. . . . I brought you back from Troy just to be a victim . . .

ORESTES. If only that were true.

MENELAUS. . . . after all my trials and tribulations.

ORESTES. None of which effort was spent on me.

MENELAUS. I suffered terribly.

ORESTES. Yes, when you proved to be no friend in need.

MENELAUS. I am in your power.

ORESTES. Your own villainy put you there. (*He calls down inside the palace*) Hey, Electra! Set fire to the palace there! (*Quieter, to* PYLADES) And Pylades, truest of my friends, put the roof here to the torch!*

MENELAUS. O land of the Danaans and inhabitants of horse-rearing Argos! Come on, now! Aren't you going to arm yourselves and run to help? For this man is forcing the whole of your city to let him live, when he has committed the abominable crime of matricide.

*APOLLO appears above the backdrop with HELEN.**

APOLLO. Enough, Menelaus! Enough of this whetted passion! It is I, Phoebus, son of Leto, who address you from close at hand! And you, Orestes: remove the threat of your sword from the girl, so that you may hear the message I bear. First, Helen, whom you failed to kill, for all the determination your anger at Menelaus gave you: acting on Zeus' orders, I rescued her and snatched her from under your sword. As Zeus' daughter, she is to have eternal life, and she will sit enthroned with Castor and Polydeuces in heaven's hollows, a saviour to sailors.†*

That is how things stand with Helen. As for you, Orestes, you must depart beyond the borders of this land and live for a full year in a place in Parrhasia, which will be named after the fact that you passed your exile there.* From there you must go to Athens and submit to judgement by the three Eumenides for the crime of murdering your mother. The gods will supervise the trial on the Areopagus and will cast their votes in accordance with full righteousness, and you are fated to win there.

As for Hermione, against whose neck you hold your sword, Orestes, she is destined to be your wife.* Neoptolemus, who thinks he is to marry her, will never do so, because he is fated to be killed by Delphic sword when he comes to ask me for compensation for the death of his father Achilles.* You have already agreed to the marriage between Pylades and your sister, so give her to him, and the life that awaits them in the future will be happy.

As for Argos, let Orestes rule it,* Menelaus, while you go to Sparta and take up the throne there, the dowry left you by your wife. Hitherto she always caused you countless troubles, but that is over now. You must find another wife to take into your house. For Helen's beauty was merely the instrument used by the gods to bring about the encounter between Greeks and Phrygians, and to cause enough deaths to relieve the earth of the foul burden of a vast swarm of humans. And I shall put right the relations between the city and Orestes, since it was I who compelled him to murder his mother.

ORESTES. O Loxias, god of prophecy! It turns out after all that your oracles were true and contained no deceit. There were times when I was afraid, though, that when I thought I was hearing your voice I was actually hearing some vengeful demon. But all's well that ends well, and I shall do as you say. There! I release Hermione from slaughter, and I agree to marry her when I have her father's permission.

MENELAUS. Farewell, Helen, daughter of Zeus! Soon you will join the gods in their blessed palace, and I congratulate you on that. Orestes, I betroth my daughter to you, as Phoebus commands. As you are noble and from noble stock, I pray that you may do well from this marriage—and that I may too, who give this woman to you.

APOLLO. Go, then, each of you, to the places I have assigned you, and let there be no more discord between you.

MENELAUS. It shall be as you command.

ORESTES. I agree. I have no more quarrel with events, Menelaus, or with your oracles, Loxias.

Exeunt severally ORESTES, PYLADES, HERMIONE, and MENELAUS, along with his attendants.

APOLLO. Be on your way, then, and respect Peace, the fairest of the gods. Right across the bright starry vault of heaven I shall take Helen to Zeus' palace, where a throne alongside Hera and Hebe, Heracles' wife,* awaits her, and men will honour her as a goddess for ever with libations. Along with Castor and Polydeuces, sons of Zeus, her domain will be the safety of sailors on the waves of the sea.

Exit APOLLO.

PHOENICIAN WOMEN

Characters

JOCASTA, *mother—and wife—of Oedipus*
POLYNICES, *exiled son of Oedipus and Jocasta*
ETEOCLES, *son of Oedipus and Jocasta, king of Thebes*
ANTIGONE, *daughter of Oedipus and Jocasta*
SLAVE, *Antigone's aged tutor*
CREON, *Jocasta's brother*
MENOECEUS, *Creon's son*
TIRESIAS, *Theban prophet*
MESSENGER, *a soldier in Eteocles' company*
SECOND MESSENGER, *a slave of Eteocles*
OEDIPUS, *former king of Thebes*

CHORUS *of young Phoenician women*

Scene: In front of the royal palace on the acropolis of Thebes. JOCASTA enters from the palace, wearing black and with her hair cut short in mourning.*

JOCASTA. O Sun, you who trace a fiery circuit in the sky with your swift steeds,* how unlucky was the light you shed on Thebes that distant day when Cadmus reached this land from his coastal home of Phoenicia!* For it was Cadmus long ago who fathered Polydorus by his wife Harmonia, the daughter of Cypris,* and Polydorus, we hear, was the father of Labdacus, who in turn was the father of Laius. As for me, I am known as the daughter of Menoeceus, and they call me Jocasta, the name given me by my father. I became Laius' wife, but our marriage proved childless, and after I had been living with him for many years he went and asked Phoebus* about it, and at the same time requested that the two of us may produce male children for the good of the house. 'Lord of horse-rich Thebes,' the god replied, 'you should not be trying to seed the child-bearing furrow against the will of the gods. If you beget a child, the offspring will kill you and the future course of your whole house will be one of blood.' But Laius succumbed to pleasure and in a moment of drunken madness planted a child in me. Having done so, he recognized his mistake and called to mind what the god had said. He went to Hera's meadow by the cliffs of Cithaeron* and gave the child to herdsmen, with instructions that they were to expose him, once they had driven iron spikes through the middle of his ankles (hence he is known in Greece as Oedipus*).† But the herdsmen of Polybus* took the baby home and handed him over to their mistress, who put the child of my labour to her breast and convinced her husband that she had given birth to him.

So my son grew up and reached the age where reddish down covered his cheeks. At this point, either because he had guessed the truth or been told by someone, he went to Phoebus' temple to find out who his parents were—and so did my husband Laius, to enquire whether or not the exposed child was still alive. The two of them met at Split Way in Phocis, and Laius' driver said to my son in a high-handed manner: 'Sir, make way for a king.' In his pride, the young man carried on without saying a word, but the colts wounded him with their hoofs on the tendons of his feet.* Then—to keep strictly to the heart of the tragedy—son killed father. He took the chariot and gave it to Polybus, who had brought him up.

With the Sphinx preying savagely on the city,* and my husband dead, my brother Creon made a public offer of my bed, saying that he would marry me to whoever managed to solve the cunning maiden's riddle. It so happened that for some reason it was my son Oedipus who understood the meaning of the verses, and unwittingly married his mother, the wretch, while she in her ignorance slept with her son. I bore my child two sons, Eteocles and the glorious warrior Polynices, and two daughters, one of whom her father named Ismene, while I gave the elder of the two the name Antigone. When he found out that in marrying me he had married his mother, Oedipus—as if he hadn't suffered enough—in an act of gruesome, bloody violence stabbed golden pins into his own eyes.

When my sons reached the age where their cheeks were darkened by beards, they locked their father away, to stop people talking about what had happened to him, although this required a lot of cunning and trickery. He's still alive, here in the palace. Driven mad by this turn of events he called terrible curses down on his sons, praying that they would resort to sharpened steel to divide their inheritance, this palace, between themselves. They were terrified by the thought that if they lived together the gods might fulfil this curse, and so the two of them came to an agreement whereby the younger one, Polynices, should be the first to go into voluntary exile from this land, while Eteocles remained behind as its ruler, and that they should exchange places year by year. But once Eteocles had taken up the helm of kingship he refused to relinquish the throne, and he banished Polynices from here. Polynices went to Argos, where he married into the family of Adrastus* and mustered a huge army of Argives, which he led right here to the walls with their seven gates,* to demand the rule that is his inheritance, and a portion of the land.

In order to try to reconcile them, I have persuaded one son to meet the other under a truce before resorting to force of arms. The man who delivered the message says he will come. O Zeus, you who dwell in the hollows of the bright sky, keep us safe, I pray you, and grant my sons an agreement. If you see things aright, you should not allow the same person* constantly to be in a state of misery.

Exit JOCASTA *into the palace.*

Enter SLAVE *above the backdrop.**

SLAVE. Antigone, child who brings glory to your father's house, your mother has given you permission* (after you pleaded with her) to leave the girls' quarters and come to the palace's upper storey and its edge to see the Argive army, but wait, please! I need to look over the road first, to check whether it is empty, because one of your fellow citizens might be petty enough to criticize me, as a slave, and you, as my mistress, for what we're doing.* I am in full possession of the facts, and I'll tell you what I saw and was told by the Argives when I went there and back again to your brother with the truce offer. (*He looks around*) No, there's no one near the palace, so climb up to the top of the old cedar-wood ladder and gaze out on the plain, where you can see how large the enemy army is, beside the rivers Ismenus and Dirce.*

ANTIGONE joins the SLAVE.

ANTIGONE (*breathless*). Reach out ... reach out your aged hand for my young one, and help me lift my feet up from the ladder.

SLAVE. Here you are: take my hand, my dear. You've come at just the right time, since the Pelasgian* army is on the move: they are dividing themselves into companies.

ANTIGONE. O lady Hecate, daughter of Leto,* the whole plain is flashing with bronze!

SLAVE. Yes, it's no trivial force that Polynices has invaded with. Listen to the din all his horsemen and the countless foot soldiers make!

ANTIGONE. Are the gates barred? Have the bronze-covered bolts been shot into the stones of the wall, built by Amphion?*

SLAVE. Don't worry. The city is safe—or at any rate all is secure inside the walls.

ANTIGONE. Who's the man with the white crest on his helmet, who is leading the way in front of the army, making little of the shield of solid bronze on his arm?

SLAVE. That's the lord Hippomedon, who is said to be from Mycenae, but lives by the waters of Lerna.*

ANTIGONE. Oh, what a splendid, fearsome sight! He looks like one of those earth-born giants you see in paintings, with a dazzling face, rather than a mortal human being.

SLAVE. But can you not see the man crossing the river Dirce?

ANTIGONE. Yes, who is he?

SLAVE. He is Tydeus, the son of Oeneus, and he has the warlike spirit of Aetolia in his breast.

ANTIGONE. Old man, is he the one who's married to the sister of Polynices' new wife?* His weaponry is strange, almost foreign in appearance.

SLAVE. Aetolians always carry shields, child, and are very accurate marksmen with their spears.

ANTIGONE. And what about the one who's crossing by Zethus' tomb?* The young man with thick hair and a wild look in his eyes? I assume he's one of the commanders, since a mass of armed men are following behind him.

SLAVE. That's Parthenopaeus,* the child of Atalanta.

ANTIGONE. Well, I hope that Artemis, who races in the mountains with his mother, kills him with her arrows, since he has come to sack my city.

SLAVE. I hope so too, child. But their invasion is justified, and that's exactly what makes me afraid: I think the gods may approve their cause.

ANTIGONE. Where is the one who was born from the same mother as me—born to a grievous destiny? Tell me, old man, as I love you dearly, where is Polynices?

SLAVE. He's standing by the tomb of Niobe's seven daughters,* near Adrastus. Can you see him?

ANTIGONE. Yes, I can, but not very well. I can just make out something that looks like the outline of his form and his chest. Would that I could race through the air to my brother as fast as the wind-swift clouds and throw my arms around his beloved neck at last, the poor exile! But see how glorious he looks in his golden armour, old man, gleaming like the sun's first rays in the morning.

SLAVE. He's going to come here to the palace under a truce, so that will make you happy.

ANTIGONE. And who's that, old man, the one steering the white chariot on which he is mounted?

SLAVE. That's the diviner, Amphiaraus,* mistress. He has his sacrificial victims with him, which will soon stream blood on the thirsty earth.

ANTIGONE. O Moon, daughter of bright-girdled Sun! O goddess of golden, circling light!* How steadily and calmly he guides his chariot, goading now this horse, now that! But where is Capaneus, the one who made those terrible and abusive threats against the city?

SLAVE. There he is, working out how to make an assault on the fortifications, measuring the walls from top to bottom.*

ANTIGONE. Ah! O Retribution, O Zeus' loud-rumbling thunder,* O thunderbolt with your blazing light! It's your job to quell arrogance and boasting. Here is the man who claims that he will by force of arms make Theban women prisoners of war and will give them to Mycenaean women and to the Lernaean Trident, by imposing on them slavery to the Poseidonian waters of Amymone.* I call on the lady Artemis, golden-haired daughter of Zeus, to ensure that I never have to endure such slavery—never!

SLAVE. Child, now that you've gratified your longing and seen everything you wanted to see, you had better go indoors, inside the palace, and stay in your quarters. For the city is gripped by panic, and a crowd of women is approaching the royal palace. Women are a critical lot, and at the slightest excuse for telling tales they bring up more and more. It affords women a peculiar pleasure to speak ill of one another.

Exeunt SLAVE and ANTIGONE.

*Enter the CHORUS, in plainly non-Greek costume.**

CHORUS (*sings*). Leaving the surge of the sea at Tyre, I have come
as an offering to Loxias* from the Phoenician island,
a slave for Phoebus' temple, in the place where
he has made his dwelling under Parnassus' snow-girt ridges.*
By ship I came across the Ionian Sea,* as with the sweetest soughing
Zephyrus* rode on his breezes in the sky high above
the barren plains of the sea that washes the shores of Sicily.

Selected from my city as a fair offering to Loxias,
I have come to Cadmus' land, escorted here
to the fortress of Laius, where dwell my kin,
the glorious race of Agenor's descendants.*
Just as Phoebus receives golden gifts, so now I am his servant.
The Castalian waters* await me yet, to drench my hair,
the pride of my young womanhood, in service to Phoebus.

You crag, shining with the gleam of Bacchic fire
above the twin peaks of Dionysus,* and you vine,
ripening day by day, on which the fruitful cluster
grows daily from the bloom, and you sacred caves,
the serpent's lair,* and you peaks where the gods keep watch,
and you holy snow-girt mountain, I wish we were a chorus,
sacred to the god, dancing for the immortals, free from fear,
in Phoebus' valley at the centre of the earth, far from Dirce.

But in fact I see fierce Ares* assaulting the walls,

and—may the gods forbid it!—kindling deadly bloodshed for this city.
Friends share their woes, and so any suffering endured
by this seven-towered place will be shared by the Phoenician land.
Alas, alas! Shared blood flows in our veins, we share the same children
in common descent from horned Io,* and so their troubles are mine too.

Around the city flares a thick cloud of shields, a portent
of the bloody battle soon to be witnessed by Ares,
as he brings to the sons of Oedipus the woe of the Erinyes.*
O Pelasgic Argos, I fear your might and the plans of the gods.
For the son who, armed for his effort, has brought his pursuit
of his heritage to battle has justice on his side.*

Enter POLYNICES, *circumspectly, with drawn sword.*

POLYNICES. The gatekeepers readily unbarred their gates and let me into the city—and that is exactly what makes me afraid. They might capture me in their nets and not let my body out again unbloodied. That's why I have to keep looking here and there, all around me, for fear of ambush. But this sword in my hand will bolster my courage. (*He suddenly wheels round*) Hey, who's there? Or was it just a noise that startled me? Walking through enemy territory is risky and makes everything seem frightening. But I trust my mother, who persuaded me to come here under a truce—though at the same time I don't entirely trust her. But help is at hand, since I've reached the altars, and the palace is not deserted. So let me just make my sword invisible in its sheath, and then ask these women who are standing by the palace who they are. You foreigners there, tell me: how is it that you come to be here at a palace in Greece? Which country have you come from?

CHORUS. Phoenicia is where I was brought up, and Agenor's descendants sent me here as an offering in thanks for victory in war. But just as Oedipus' glorious son was going to send me to the oracular shrine and the altars sacred to Loxias, the Argives assaulted the city. But now I have a question for you in your turn. Who are you that have come to the seven-gated fortress of the land of Thebes?

POLYNICES. My father is Oedipus, son of Laius, and my mother Jocasta, the daughter of Menoeceus. The Theban people know me as Polynices.

CHORUS (*prostrating themselves*). I fall to my knees in supplication before you, lord, in observance of my native custom. Oh, at last you are here, back in the land of your birth! (*Calling out*) Ah, my lady! My lady, come quickly! Open the doors! Can you hear me? The son you bore is here. What's taking you so long? Hurry through the palace rooms so that you can take your son in your arms!

Enter JOCASTA from the palace.

JOCASTA (*sings*). I heard you calling, young women, heard your Phoenician cries,
but I am old and no longer steady on my feet as I walk.
Ah, my child, at last, after days beyond number, I see your face.
Take in your arms the mother who gave you suck!
Reach your cheek down to mine, and your hair—
let your hair's dark locks shadow my neck.
Oh, you have come at last, when I had lost all hope, all faith,
but now you are here in your mother's arms.

She releases him and steps back to look at him.

What words shall I use for you? How can I recover,
in its entirety, the long-lost pleasure and joy? With my hands?
With speech? By delighted dancing to and fro in complex steps?
Ah, child, you left your family home empty
when in an act of violence your brother banished you.
You have been missed by your friends, missed by Thebes.
And so I have cut my white hair and I let fall tears of grief,
dressed no longer in robes of white, but instead, my child,
in these night-black, gloomy rags. And the old man,
eyeless in the palace, clings to his tearful longing
for the team of brothers which has been unyoked from the house,
and starts up for the suicidal slaughter of the sword

and the roof-beam noose, groaning out curses against his sons.
He is hidden, along with his constant cries of woe, in darkness.
And as for you, my child, I hear that now you are wedded,
and find the pleasure of fatherhood in a foreign house,
and in an act which brings inconsolable grief to your mother here
and to the house of long-dead Laius, that you cherish
the bane of foreign marriage, an alliance with strangers.
Nor did I kindle for you the torch customary at weddings
for the happy mother.† Ismenus* was brought into the marriage bond,
but no wedding-songs were heard, no water was borne in celebration,
and Thebes resounded with no noise at the entry of your bride.
I pray for an end to it all, whether the sword is to blame, or Strife,
or your father, or whether the gods made deadly revel in Oedipus' house.
For the grief that these troubles bring has descended on to me.

CHORUS. The pains of childbirth have a powerful effect on women, and it is a universal trait in them to love their children.

POLYNICES. Mother, in an act both sensible and foolish, I have come to meet my enemies. Still, everyone is bound to love the country of their birth, and anyone who says he doesn't is playing verbal games while his heart tends in that direction. I am so anxious† and afraid in case my brother is treacherously planning to kill me that as I walked through the town I had my sword in my hand and kept looking all around. The only thing that sustains me is the truce and the pledge you have given, which is what induced me to enter the city of my birth. But my visit has cost me plenty of tears, as I saw after so long the shrines and altars of the gods, the training-schools* where I was brought up, and the river Dirce. It was wrong for me to be expelled from here to live, as I do now, in a foreign city, with the tears constantly flowing from my eyes. But further grief is piled on grief, for I see you with your hair cut short and wearing dark clothes. Alas for my plight! What a terrible thing hostility is between members of the same family, mother!

JOCASTA. One of the gods is destroying Oedipus' family in misery, and this is how he began: I gave birth unlawfully, your father's marriage was wicked, and so was your birth. But so what? One must endure what the gods give. But I'm concerned about how I can ask the questions I want without causing you anguish. All the same, I do feel a strong need to ask them.

POLYNICES. Go ahead, ask your questions, and leave nothing out. For your wishes, mother, are my desires too.

JOCASTA. What is it to be deprived of your country? It must be a terrible thing.*

POLYNICES. There's nothing worse—but the reality of it is worse than talking about it.

JOCASTA. What's it like? What is it that exiles find so ghastly?

POLYNICES. The worst thing of all is not having freedom of speech.*

JOCASTA. This is the lot of a slave, to be unable to speak what is on his mind.

POLYNICES. One has to put up with the stupidities of the powers that be.

JOCASTA. That's horrible too, to be caught up in the idiocy of idiots.

POLYNICES. In order to get anywhere you have to be servile, however much it goes against the grain.

JOCASTA. But it's said that those in exile feed on hopes.

POLYNICES. Yes, hopes flirt with us, but never go all the way.

JOCASTA. Doesn't time in fact show up their emptiness?

POLYNICES. But they have a certain attraction, which serves to relieve one's troubles.

JOCASTA. Where did you get food from before you found sustenance through marriage?

POLYNICES. Sometimes my daily needs were fulfilled, sometimes they weren't.

JOCASTA. Did your father's friends and guest-friends not come to your assistance?

POLYNICES. I pray that you do well, because friends are worthless when one is badly off.

JOCASTA. Didn't even your noble birth raise you on high and make you great?

POLYNICES. Destitution is a wretched state. My high birth failed to feed me.

JOCASTA. It seems, then, that there is nothing more dear to people than the country of their birth.

POLYNICES. You couldn't even express how dear it is.

JOCASTA. How did you end up in Argos? What was your plan?

POLYNICES. Loxias gave Adrastus a certain oracle . . .

JOCASTA. Saying what? Why have you mentioned it? I don't understand.

POLYNICES. . . . to the effect that he would marry his daughters to a boar and a lion.*

JOCASTA. And what did this naming of beasts have to do with you, my child?

POLYNICES. I've no idea. The god summoned me to my fate.

JOCASTA. The god is clever. But how did you come to get married?

POLYNICES. It was night when I came to Adrastus' door.

JOCASTA. Looking for a place to sleep, as a homeless exile must?

POLYNICES. Exactly. And then a second refugee arrived.

JOCASTA. Who? To judge by what you've told me, he must have been in a sorry state too.

POLYNICES. It was Tydeus, the one who is called the son of Oeneus.

JOCASTA. So why did Adrastus think you were like wild beasts?

POLYNICES. Because we came to blows over the bed.

JOCASTA. And that was when the son of Talaus* understood the oracle?

POLYNICES. Yes, and gave the two of us his two daughters in marriage.

JOCASTA. Well, was it a fortunate or unfortunate marriage for you?

POLYNICES. To this day I have no complaints about it.

JOCASTA. How did you persuade the army to come here with you?

POLYNICES. Adrastus solemnly promised his two sons-in-law that he would restore us both to our native lands, but me first; and many leading Argives and Mycenaeans have come, doing me a service which is upsetting to me, for all that I have no choice in the matter. For I am marching against my own city. I swear by heaven that it was not by my choice that I took up arms against my kin: it was they who chose it. But the resolution of this evil—an end to the troubles that beset you, me, and the whole city—depends on you.

CHORUS. Look! Here comes Eteocles, ready to negotiate. Jocasta, it is up to you to find the words to reconcile your sons with each other.

Enter ETEOCLES *with attendants.* POLYNICES *turns his back on his brother.*

ETEOCLES (*abruptly*). Here I am, mother, out of deference to your wishes. What would you have me do? Let the negotiations begin.

JOCASTA. Wait! Haste and fair play do not go together; the wise find leisurely discussion the most productive. Enough of your fierce gaze and angry breathing. You're not looking at the Gorgon's decapitated head,* but at your brother, who has come to see you. And for your part, Polynices, turn and face your brother. For if you look him in the eye, the give and take of discussion will go better. Now, I've got a piece of good advice for you both: when a man who is angry with someone close to him meets that person and they look each other in the eye, the only thing that should be on his mind is the reason for the meeting; he should forget all about the bad things that have happened in the past. (POLYNICES *turns to face* ETEOCLES*, but their body language continues to express hostility*) Anyway, you had better open the discussion, Polynices, since you've come at the head of an Argive army, claiming that you have been wronged. I pray that one of the gods may judge and resolve this evil situation.

POLYNICES (*addressing* JOCASTA *rather than his brother*). To tell the truth is perfectly straightforward; just claims require no complex interpretations, since their point is perfectly clear. It is an unjust argument which needs sophisms to remedy its inherent unsoundness. Where our father's estate is concerned, I looked out not just for my interests, but for his as well, because I wanted us to avoid the curses Oedipus called down on us. And so I left this land of my own accord, and let him rule the country for the period of a year. For all that he approved of what I had done, and swore an oath by the gods, he has carried out none of his promises, but has retained the kingship and my portion of the estate. So now I am ready, if I get what's mine, to send the army away from this land, to take my turn in managing my own estate, and then to give it up again to him for an equal period of time, without ravaging the country or assaulting the fortifications with our sturdy scaling-ladders. But if I don't get justice, that is exactly what I shall try to do. And I call on the gods to witness that although I am acting with justice I am being unjustly denied access to my country, an act of gross impiety. In stating the facts of the case like this, mother, I haven't stitched together a subtle argument, but what I've said must strike both sophisticated and unsophisticated alike as fair, I think.

CHORUS. For my part, even though I wasn't brought up in Greece, I think what you say is reasonable.

ETEOCLES (*also addressing* JOCASTA). If everyone found the same things acceptable and sensible, there would be no disputes. But as things are, nothing is similar or the same for people except at the verbal level, which does not correspond to reality. For instance—and I shall speak with complete candour, mother—I would travel to where the stars rise in the sky† and I would go beneath the earth (supposing such things to be possible), if by doing so I would gain Sovereignty, the greatest of the gods. I am therefore reluctant to hand this boon over to someone else; I would rather keep it for myself. It is nothing but cowardice to lose more and accept less. Moreover, it would shame me were he to come here with an army, lay waste to the land, and get what he wants. Thebes would be an object of scorn if fear of Mycenaean weaponry caused me to yield my throne to him. He should not be relying on armed force to bring about a reconciliation, mother, because everything that hostile weaponry can achieve can be gained by speech. If he's prepared to live here on other terms, that can happen, but kingship is something I shall not willingly surrender. (*Turning to* POLYNICES) As far as that is concerned, bring on fire, bring on swords, yoke your horses and fill the plain with chariots—but be assured that I shall not yield this kingship to you. Given that one is bound to do wrong, the best course of action is to do wrong where kingship is concerned and to honour the laws in all other respects.

CHORUS. One ought not to argue well except in defence of rightful deeds, because this is not right, but an offence against justice.

JOCASTA. Eteocles, there are few good things about old age, but one of them is that experience enables one to argue with rather more wisdom than young people. Why, my son, do you pursue the worst of the gods, Ambition? Don't: she is a goddess without justice. Often in the past she has entered prosperous houses and communities, and left after destroying those who cling to her. Yet this is the goddess with whom you are infatuated. Equality is more deserving of your devotion, child, for she never fails to join friends with friends, communities with communities, allies with allies. Equality is a source of legality for men, whereas the lesser is always constitutionally hostile to the greater and institutes a state of enmity. For Equality organized measures and units of weight for men, and distinguished numbers from one another; the dark eye of night and the light of the sun equally share the path of the yearly cycle, and neither of them comes off worse and feels resentment. So sun and night are subject to due measure, and yet you refuse to put up with an equal share of the estate? Why are you so excessively devoted to the blessed injustice of kingship? Why do you rate it so highly? Do you value being an object of admiration? But that is empty. Or do you want plenty of worries when you already have plenty of wealth in your halls? What is this 'more'? No more than a word. After all, anyone with any sense finds sufficiency enough. All right, suppose I set two choices before you, side by side, and ask whether you want to be king or to keep the city safe, will you choose kingship? But if Polynices here defeats you and Argive troops overwhelm the Theban army, then this wealth which you seek to possess will come at a high cost for Thebes, and yet you persist in your ambition.†

So much for what I want to say to you. Now I turn to you, Polynices. It was foolish of Adrastus to commit himself to this service for you, and you acted thoughtlessly too, in coming to destroy Thebes. Look at it this way: if you conquer Thebes (which I pray will never happen), tell me, please, how are you going to erect a victory trophy, sacred to Zeus? How will you, the conqueror of his own country, initiate sacrificial rituals? What will you inscribe on your spoils by the river Inachus?* 'Having put Thebes to the torch Polynices dedicates these shields to the gods'? I hope you never become famous in Greece for that, my son. Or suppose you lose and Eteocles' forces overwhelm you: what sort of a reception will you have back in Argos, when you'll have left countless corpses here? People will berate Adrastus for burdening them with a baneful betrothal. 'We have been ruined,' they'll say, 'and all for the marriage of just one girl!' You're chasing two evils, my son; you fall in between them and lose either way.

You should both put an end to your extreme behaviour. Give it up! When two people have the same aim, their folly is the worst of evils.

CHORUS. I pray that the gods may avert this evil and reconcile the sons of Oedipus.

ETEOCLES. Mother, the time for talking has passed. From now until battle is joined the hours spent on any other activity are wasted, and all your effort is futile. For there is no way that we shall be reconciled, except on the terms I have stated: that I retain the throne and rule this land of Thebes. Let's hear no more of your long-winded censure! Leave me be! And you, Polynices, had better take yourself outside the city walls, on pain of death.

POLYNICES (*putting his hand to his sword-hilt*). And who will kill me? Who is so immune to wounds that he might stab me with his sword without earning himself the same fate?

ETEOCLES. He is close by, not far away. Do you see these hands of mine?*

POLYNICES. Yes, I can see them, but wealth breeds cowardice and an abject fondness for life.

ETEOCLES. So you brought all these troops to engage a nonentity in battle?

POLYNICES. Yes, for a cautious commander is better than one who takes risks.

ETEOCLES. This boasting of yours is born from your confidence in the truce, which is the only thing stopping you from dying.

POLYNICES. The same goes for you. But I repeat my demand for rulership and a portion of the land.

ETEOCLES. I refuse to accept your demand. The royal house is mine, and I shall live there.

POLYNICES. With more than your fair share?

ETEOCLES. Yes. Now leave this land.

POLYNICES. O altars of my ancestral gods . . .

ETEOCLES. . . . which you came to destroy . . .

POLYNICES. . . . hear me, I pray . . .

ETEOCLES. What sort of a hearing do you expect to get as an invader of your own country?

POLYNICES. . . . and temple of the white-horsed gods . . .*

ETEOCLES. . . . who find you abhorrent . . .

POLYNICES. . . . see how I am being driven out of the land of my birth . . .

ETEOCLES. Yes, and you came to drive me out.

POLYNICES. . . . in an act of injustice. O gods . . .

ETEOCLES. Go and call on the gods in Mycenae, not here!

POLYNICES. You act with impiety . . .

ETEOCLES. But at least I'm no enemy of my country, as you are.

POLYNICES. . . . in banishing me and refusing me my fair share.

ETEOCLES. Yes, and I shall kill you too.

POLYNICES. Father, can you hear what I have to put up with?

ETEOCLES. Yes, because he can also hear what you've been up to.

POLYNICES. Mother, can you hear him too?

ETEOCLES. How dare you mention our mother!

POLYNICES. O city of Thebes . . .

ETEOCLES. Go to Argos and call on the waters of Lerna.

POLYNICES. Don't worry, I'll go. But thank you, mother.

ETEOCLES. Leave the land!

POLYNICES. I will! But just let me see my father.

ETEOCLES. You won't get your way in this.

POLYNICES. My young sisters, then.

ETEOCLES. You'll never see them either.

POLYNICES. Sisters . . .

ETEOCLES. Why do you appeal to them, when you are their worst enemy?

POLYNICES. Mother, I only hope you may be happy.

JOCASTA (*bitterly*). Oh, yes, I feel such happiness, child!

POLYNICES. You are losing your son.

JOCASTA. I was born to a life full of misery.

POLYNICES. Yes, because Eteocles here is treating us foully.

ETEOCLES. I give no more than I get in return.

POLYNICES. Where will you take your stand in defence of the fortress?

ETEOCLES. Why do you ask?

POLYNICES. Because I shall position myself opposite you, to kill you.

ETEOCLES. That's exactly what I long to do to you too.

JOCASTA. Oh, alas! What are you going to do, my sons?

POLYNICES.† Time will tell.

JOCASTA. Won't you try to escape the demons brought down by your father's curse?*

ETEOCLES. The whole house can go to hell.

POLYNICES. You can be sure that soon my sword will no longer rest unbloodied. And I call on the land and the gods that nurtured me to witness how despicably I am being treated in being deprived of my rights and driven into exile, as if I were his slave and not his brother, with Oedipus as our common father. Whatever happens to you, Thebes, blame him, not me. And so farewell, Phoebus Agyieus.* Farewell, palace and friends and sacrificial altars. I have no idea whether I shall ever be able to speak to you again, but my hopes are still awake, and if they are anything to go by I shall, with the gods' help, kill this man and rule here in Thebes.

ETEOCLES. Go, leave the land! Our father was right to call you Polynices;* it was divine foresight on his part to name you after strife.

Exit POLYNICES. *Exit* JOCASTA *into the palace.*

CHORUS (*sings*). Here to this land came Cadmus of Tyre, and down for him
the four-legged beast, the untamed heifer,* threw herself,
bringing fulfilment to the oracle, at the place where
the god's voice told him to settle the fertile plains
for his home, and where water in the form of fine rivers
reaches the pastures of ⟨. . .⟩ Dirce,†
which bear fresh green shoots in their deeply sown soil.
There after union with Zeus his mother gave birth to Bromius,*
whom even in infancy twining arms of ivy wrapped

in fresh green shoots in abundance, and protected
his back from the sun—he for whom Theban maidens
and ecstatic women would dance the Bacchic dance.

There was Ares' bloody dragon, a savage guardian,
overseeing the watery streams and the green rivers
with restless, glancing eyes. In search of lustral water
came Cadmus, and crushed the dragon's bloody head
with a rock, hurled by the force of his death-dealing arms.
On the orders of Pallas, the motherless goddess,*
he cast the teeth into the soil of the fertile pastures,
and then there arose from the earth fully armed men,
appearing over the topmost limits of the ground,
till steely slaughter rejoined them with the dear earth,
and drenched with blood the earth which had first
displayed them to the sunlit breezes of the upper air.

And you, Epaphus, offspring long ago of foremother Io,
child of Zeus,* I call on you, call with foreign voice—
ah, yes!—raised in foreign prayers. Come, come to this place,
which your descendants first founded and which was
occupied
by the goddesses who are invoked together as a pair,
Persephone and her loving mother Demeter,
queen of all and as Earth nurse of all.
Escort them, the fire-bearing goddesses,*
defend this land. For all things are easy for gods.

Enter CREON.

CREON. I've gone to a great deal of effort† in my desire to see you, lord Eteocles. I've done the rounds of the gateways and the guards of the city in search of you.

ETEOCLES. Well, I've been wanting to see you too, Creon. I met with Polynices and we talked things through, but I found the terms he was offering highly unsatisfactory.

CREON. I've heard that his confidence in Adrastus and his troops has made his attitude towards Thebes rather too arrogant. But we had better leave this in the hands of the gods; meanwhile, I have come to inform you of the most pressing matter.

ETEOCLES. What? I don't know what news you bring.*

CREON. An escaped prisoner has come from the Argives.

ETEOCLES. What news does he bring of the situation there?

CREON. He said that the Argive army is shortly going to surround Thebes and its fortifications with their weaponry.

ETEOCLES. Then Thebes must deploy her weapons outside the city walls.

CREON. Where? Are you too young to see what you should see?

ETEOCLES (*pointing*). Beyond the trench there, so that battle may soon be joined.

CREON. But our Theban numbers are small, while they have an enormous army.

ETEOCLES. I know they *talk* bravely.

CREON. Argos does have a certain reputation for bravery in Greece.

ETEOCLES. Don't worry: it won't take long for me to fill the plain with their dead.

CREON. I hope you're right, but it looks to me as though this will cause a great deal of grief.

ETEOCLES. You should know that I shall not keep my army cooped up inside the city.

CREON. But victory depends entirely on sound judgement.

ETEOCLES. Would you rather I followed some other course of action?

CREON. Yes, anything, before plunging straight into danger.

ETEOCLES. What if we were to creep up on them at night and attack?

CREON. Yes, provided you could get back here safely if things went wrong.

ETEOCLES. Night brings equality, but favours the bold.

CREON. But failure in the dark of night is terrifying.

ETEOCLES. Shall I launch an attack on them while they are eating?*

CREON. That would take them by surprise, but victory is what we need.

ETEOCLES. Well, deep water would hinder their retreat across the Dirce.

CREON. There's nothing as good as sound circumspection.

ETEOCLES. Suppose we had our cavalry charge the Argive army?

CREON. Their troops are barricaded behind a ring of chariots against just that eventuality.

ETEOCLES. So what shall I do? Am I just to surrender the city to the enemy?

CREON. No, of course not. Think—you're a clever man.

ETEOCLES. Well, what plan proves to be more clever than mine?

CREON. The information I have is that seven of their men . . .

ETEOCLES. Have been assigned to do what? There's not much strength in seven men.

CREON. . . . are leading detachments in assaults on the seven gates.

ETEOCLES. What are we to do, then? I won't abide indecision.

CREON. You must choose seven men too, to face them at the gates.

ETEOCLES. In charge of companies or in single combat?

CREON. In charge of companies—and pick your very best fighters.

ETEOCLES. I understand. They have to stop the wall being scaled.

CREON. Yes, and they should share command with you. One man cannot see everything.

ETEOCLES. Should I choose them for their courage or for their sound judgement?

CREON. For both, because either quality is useless if the other is lacking.*

ETEOCLES. All right, I shall go down to the seven-towered city and deploy my captains at the gates, as you suggest, one for each of the enemy they are to face. It would take too long to mention each of their names,* with the enemy in position under the very walls. And so I'm off, to avoid further inactivity. But there is one thing yet to do, and that is to find out from the diviner Tiresias if there's any oracle he should tell us about. I shall send your son Menoeceus, Creon, who has the same name as your father, to fetch Tiresias here, because he'll gladly come to talk to you, but I once criticized divination in front of him, and so he's not best pleased with me. (*To his attendants*) Bring out my weapons and armour for the conflict which now faces us. And we pray that Circumspection, that most useful deity, will keep our city safe.

Exeunt ETEOCLES *and attendants.*

CHORUS (*sings*). O Ares,* bringer of toil, why are you in the grip
of blood and death,

and so dissonant with Bromius'* celebrations? Why not toss your hair
at dances performed by garlanded youth in its bloom and sing
to the blowing of the pipes a song full of the dancing Graces?
Why instead do you inspire the Argive army to slaughter of Thebes
and lead a dance of joyless revelry in the company of armed men?
Where is the thyrsus-goading god, where are the fawnskins,*
as you whirl your hoofed colt† amid chariots rigged for four steeds
and at the waters of Ismenus race forward on horseback,
having inspired against the Argives the offspring† of the Sown Men,*
having decked with bronze your band bearing shields and armour
in hostility along the walls of stone. A grim goddess indeed is Strife,
for she has contrived these woes for the kings of the land.

O Cithaeron of sacred foliage, glade teeming with beasts,
snow-nurturing delight of Artemis,* once he had been laid out for death
would that you had never nurtured Oedipus, new-born child of Jocasta,
a baby cast out from his home, with his distinctive golden pins.
And would that the winged maiden Sphinx,* the omen from the mountain,
had never come with her discordant strains, bringing grief to the land—
she who used to approach the walls and with her four claws bear off
to the inaccessible light of the sky the offspring of Cadmus—
she whom underworld Hades* sent as the bane of Thebes.
Now another ill-fated strife flourishes in the palace and the city
of the sons of Oedipus. No good can ever come from bad,
nor from the unlawful children, their mother's brood, their father's taint;

for the bed to which she came was the bed of a member of her own family.†

O Earth, the story I heard from abroad, heard once at home, tells
how you gave birth, long ago gave birth, to the teeth-sown race
of the savage red-crested dragon, to be the glory and the shame of Thebes;
and how long ago the children of heaven came to Harmonia's wedding;*
and how the walls of Thebes arose to the sound of the harp,
the fortifications to Amphion's lyre,* filling the space between the two rivers,
where in front of Ismenus the fresh green of the plain is watered by Dirce*
and where our horned foremother Io bore the line of Theban kings.*
And now after years of blessings, piled on countless blessings,
this city has taken its stand on its topmost towers, Ares' adornments.

Enter MENOECEUS *and* TIRESIAS, *who is led by his daughter.**

TIRESIAS. You go in front of me, daughter. You are the eye for my blind feet, as a star is for seamen. Place my foot here, on level ground, and then lead the way, so that we don't stumble. You have a feeble father. Hold carefully for me in your girlish hand the lots* which I took and brought with me after studying the omens produced by birds from the sacred seat where I practise divination. And young Menoeceus, Creon's son,* tell me how far there remains for us to go through the town to your father. For my knees are tired, and the number of steps I take makes it hard to go on.

CREON. Don't worry, Tiresias, there are friends near whom you can anchor your feet. Give him a helping hand, son. For a fledgling child and an old man tend to wait for the relief that someone else's arm can offer their feet.

TIRESIAS. All right, here we are. Why the urgent summons, Creon?

CREON. As if I would have forgotten already! But why don't you first gather your strength and get your breath back, after your steep climb here.

TIRESIAS. It's true that I'm exhausted. I got back here only yesterday from Athens, since there was a war there too, against Eumolpus and his army,* in which I arranged victory for the Athenians. As you can see, I'm wearing this golden chaplet, which I was given as the first fruit of the booty they took from the enemy.

CREON. I take your victory wreath to be a good omen. For, as you know, we are beset by a storm of Argive spears, and Thebes is involved in a fierce struggle. The king, Eteocles, has already armed himself and gone to face the Mycenaean forces, but he has instructed me to find out from you what we should do to keep the city safe.

TIRESIAS. For Eteocles I would have shut my mouth and withheld my oracles. But since it's you asking, I'll tell you. This land has been sick for a long time, Creon, ever since Laius became a father against the will of the gods and gave birth to poor Oedipus, to be a husband to his mother.† Losses will be high, with corpses fallen near corpses in a tangle of Argive and Theban limbs, arousing bitter grief in Thebes. And you, wretched city, will be razed to the ground, unless someone hearkens to my words. But it's not only unsafe for me to say this, but also bitter for those whose fortune it is to provide for the city its remedy of salvation, and so I'm off. Farewell. I am just one man among many, and I shall suffer what the future brings, if I must. For what other choice do I have?

He starts to leave, but CREON *detains him.*

CREON. Wait there, old man!*

TIRESIAS. Take your hands off me!

CREON. Stay here! What are you running from?

TIRESIAS. It may look like me, but actually it is the gift of fortune that is trying to keep away from you.

CREON. Tell me how safety may be won for the city and my fellow citizens.

TIRESIAS. You want to know now, but soon you'll want not to know.

CREON. How could I not want to save my native land?

TIRESIAS. So you really want me to tell you? It's a burning need in you?

CREON. There's nothing one could desire more.

TIRESIAS (*lowering his voice*). I'd like first to know where Menoeceus is, who brought me here.

CREON. He's not far off—close to you, in fact.

TIRESIAS. Send him far enough away so that he can't hear my oracle.

CREON. He's my son; he won't let slip anything he's supposed to keep to himself.

TIRESIAS. So do you want me to speak in front of him?

CREON. Yes. He'll be pleased to hear how safety may be won.

TIRESIAS. Hear, then, the course of my oracle: for the sake of your country you must slaughter Menoeceus here, your son. You did insist on hearing what fortune had in store for you.

CREON. What are you saying? What have you said, old man?

TIRESIAS. I have said what has been revealed, and you have to carry it out.

CREON. Oh, how little time it took you to speak so much evil!

TIRESIAS. Yes, my words spell evil for you, but for your country they are portentous words, spelling safety.

CREON. I wasn't listening, I didn't hear what you said. The city can look after itself.*

TIRESIAS. This man here has changed: he's pulling back from the brink.

CREON. Go away. I have no need of your oracles.

TIRESIAS. Is the truth destroyed by your misfortune?

CREON (*falling to his knees*). I implore you by your knees and your venerable white hair.*

TIRESIAS. Why are you kneeling before me? You must accept this evil, since it is hard to avoid.

CREON. Be quiet. Please don't let my fellow citizens hear what you're saying.

TIRESIAS. You're telling me to do wrong. I refuse to remain silent.

CREON. What will you do to me, then? Are you going to kill my son?

TIRESIAS. That will be up to others, but I shall speak what I must.

CREON. Why has this evil come to me and my son?

TIRESIAS. The boy must be sacrificed in the lair where the earth-born dragon arose, the guardian of Dirce's waters, and the blood of his slaughter must be spilled on the earth. The reason is the ancient wrath of Ares against Cadmus, for Ares seeks to avenge the slaughter of the earth-born dragon; by doing this you will gain him as your ally. And once Earth has received fruit in recompense for her fruit, human blood for the blood of her offspring, you will find that she, who once produced the gold-helmed crop of Sown Men, will look kindly upon you. One of this race has to die, a child born from the dragon's jaw; and you are the last of the line of the Sown Men here, a pure descendant on both your mother's and your father's side.* This young colt has been allowed to roam free* for Thebes, and in death he will save his native land. He will give Adrastus and the Argives a bitter journey home by casting black doom on their eyes, and he will bring glory to Thebes.

You must choose one or the other of two fates: save either your son or your city. That is the long and short of what I have to say. (*To his daughter*) Now take me home, child. Anyone who practises seercraft labours in vain: if he brings bitter news he incurs the hostility of the people whose diviner he is, and if he tells lies out of pity for those who consult him he transgresses against the gods and their business. Phoebus should be the only one to speak oracles for mankind, because he fears no one.

Exeunt TIRESIAS *and his daughter.*

CHORUS. Why are you silent, Creon? Why do you remain speechless with your mouth hanging open? I am just as shocked as you.

CREON. What is there to say? It's obvious what I have to say: my circumstances will never be so terrible that I sacrifice my son and yield him up to the city. Love of children is part of human existence; no one would give his own son to be killed.* I would not have myself and my actions praised by someone who intends to kill my child. I am getting on in years; I am ready to die myself to free my country from danger. Anyway, my son, you should ignore the undisciplined utterances of diviners, and before the whole city hears about this make your way as quickly as possible out of the country. If we get you away before Tiresias has told everyone else, you'll be safe; but if you delay, we are lost: you will die.

MENOECEUS. Where shall I go? To which city? To which of our guest-friends?*

CREON. Wherever you'll be furthest away from this land.

MENOECEUS. Isn't it your job to tell me, and mine to see it through?

CREON. Go past Delphi . . .

MENOECEUS. Where should I go, father?

CREON. . . . into Aetolia . . .

MENOECEUS. And then where?

CREON. To the land of Thesprotia . . .

MENOECEUS. To the sacred site of Dodona?*

CREON. You've got it.

MENOECEUS. How will this protect me?

CREON. The god will be by your side.

MENOECEUS. And what will I do for money?

CREON. I'll give you gold.

MENOECEUS. Thank you, father. You had better leave now. I'm off to your sister, at whose breast I first suckled when I was a motherless, lonely waif—Jocasta, I mean. After I've spoken to her, I shall go and save my life. Come on, you must leave; don't let your concerns prevent you from going.

Exit CREON.

Women, do you see how cleverly I allayed my father's fears? I lied to him, in order to get my way. He's trying to get me out of the country, which would deprive the city of its chance of safety, and burden me with a reputation for cowardice. This is pardonable behaviour in an old man, but there would be no excuse for me if I were to betray the land of my birth. For your information, then, I shall go and save the city. I shall give my life on behalf of this land. The alternative is disgraceful. Others, who are not constrained by oracles and are not facing a fate ordained by the gods, will stand in the ranks and not hesitate to die fighting in defence of their country in front of the fortifications. Shall I, then, betray father, brother, and my own city, flee the land like a coward, and be known wherever I live as a man of no worth? No—I swear it by Zeus who dwells among the stars, and by bloody Ares, who once settled the earth-arisen Sown Men as lords of this land. Instead, I shall go and stand at the highest point of the battlements, and kill myself there, so that my blood flows into the dark depths of the dragon's lair, according to the diviner's instructions. I shall free the land. There's no more to be said.

Exit MENOECEUS.

CHORUS (*sings*). You came, you came, O winged one,
offspring of Earth and underworld Echidna,*
preying on Thebes, spreading far and wide
death and grief, half-woman, fierce omen,
on roving wings and with claws
for gripping your food, raw flesh.
From Dirce's region you used to snatch up
young men, chanting your grim song,
a demon of destruction, and you brought—
yes, you brought bloody woe to the land.
And bloody is the god whose work this was.*
The lamentation of mothers,
the lamentation of young girls,
filled the houses with weeping.
Now one, now another keened forth
the mournful cry, the mournful strain,
in succession throughout the city.
As loud as the thunder clap
was the sound of mourning
whenever the winged maiden stole
one of the men from the city.

In time came poor Oedipus here to Thebes,
sent by the Pythian god;* and pleased
they were to see him then, though later
he brought them woe, for a victor
in the riddle the poor man wed his mother
in an abomination of a marriage,
and brought pollution to the city.
Piling bloodshed on bloodshed
he strikes his children down with curses,
compelling loathsome conflict, the wretch.
We rejoice, we rejoice for him who goes
to death for his country's sake,
for though he may leave Creon in tears,
yet he will confer glorious victory

on the city of the seven towered gates.
May we be mothers thus, may we be blessed
with noble sons, we pray to Pallas,*
who caused the dragon's death by stoning,
by inspiring Cadmus to his task,
whence destruction fell on this land
thanks to the depredations of the gods.

Enter MESSENGER, who goes over to the palace doors.

MESSENGER (*loudly*). Hello! Is there anyone at the palace doors? Open up, and fetch Jocasta outside. Hello again! You're taking your time, but you must come out.

Enter JOCASTA from the palace.

JOCASTA. My dear friend, what news? You were Eteocles' constant companion in the ranks and protected him from enemy missiles, so I'm sure you haven't come with bad news, to tell me that he's dead. Is my son dead or alive? Tell me.

MESSENGER. No, he's alive, don't worry. You have no cause for alarm on that score.

JOCASTA. What about the fortifications, the seven towers? Are they all right?

MESSENGER. They stand unbreached, and the city has not fallen.

JOCASTA. But they were in danger from the Argive army?

MESSENGER. Yes, the situation was extremely hazardous, but the Mycenaean troops were no match for Theban Ares.*

JOCASTA. There's one thing you must tell me, please. Do you have any information about Polynices? For another thing that concerns me a great deal is whether he is still alive.

MESSENGER. Both your sons are still alive at the moment.

JOCASTA. Bless you for that. So how did you repel the Argive forces from the gates after they had blockaded the city? Tell me, because I'd like to go and cheer up the blind old man indoors, now that Thebes has been saved.

MESSENGER. Creon's son stood on the top of the fortifications and thrust his dark sword into his throat, to bring salvation to this land. After this patriotic death, your son assigned seven companies and captains to the seven gates of the city, to mount a defence against the Argive forces, and organized cavalry reserves for the cavalry, and foot soldiers for the foot soldiers, so that any weak part of the walls could rapidly be reinforced. From the high towers we saw the Argive army with their white shields leave Teumessus* and approach the trench. Simultaneously, from their side and from us on the walls, war-cries and trumpets rang out. We fought first with bows and javelins, with far-reaching slings and with crushing rocks. The battle was going our way, when Tydeus and your son* suddenly yelled: 'Men of Argos, why wait until you are torn to shreds by their missiles? Make a concerted assault on the gates in full force—light troops, cavalry, and charioteers!'

This cry roused everyone to immediate action. Many fell with bloodied heads, and on our side you would have seen large numbers of men hurtle to the ground in front of the walls. The dry earth became saturated with rivers of blood. Then the son of Atalanta—no Argive, but an Arcadian*—fell on one of the gates like a hurricane, calling for fire and axes to raze the city to the ground. But his furious advance was checked by Periclymenus, the son of the sea-god,* who hurled at his head a chunk of masonry big enough to be carried by a cart, a coping-stone from the battlements, which shattered his head with its fair hair, splitting open the bones of the skull and drenching his newly dark beard with blood. He'll not be returning to his mother, the maiden of Mount Maenalum with the fair bow.*

When he saw that this gate had been successfully defended, your son raced over to another, with me by his side. I could see Tydeus and large numbers of men from his squadron hurling their Aetolian spears at the very edge of the fortifications, forcing the defenders to abandon the heights of the battlements. But like a hunter your son regrouped them and repositioned them on the towers.

Over to another gate we raced, to stop the rot there. How shall I describe how mad Capaneus was? On he came, carrying a long scaling-ladder, and he even went so far as to boast that not even the sacred fire of Zeus* would prevent the city from falling to him, starting with the tops of the towers. While uttering this boast he climbed, with his body coiled right under his shield against the stones that were bombarding him, one by one up the planed rungs of the ladder. He was just about to climb over the coping-stones of the battlements when Zeus struck him with a thunderbolt. To everyone's terror the ground rumbled. Down from the ladder he spun, and fell to the ground a blazing corpse.

When Adrastus saw that Zeus had taken sides against his forces, he halted the Argive army beyond the trench. On the other hand, when our men saw this favourable portent from Zeus, they charged out of the city in their chariots, on horseback, and on foot, and engaged the Argives at close quarters. All kinds of horrors happened at once. Some leapt, some fell from their chariots, wheels flew through the air, axles crashed down on one another, corpses were piled together with corpses.

Anyway, we have prevented the razing of Thebes' towers for today, but the future success of the city is the concern of the gods.

JOCASTA. The gods and fate are favourable towards me. My sons are alive and Thebes is out of danger. Poor Creon seems to have reaped the harvest of my marriage and Oedipus' troubles, since he has lost his son, which is a personal calamity, but fortunate for the city. But please resume your story. What did my sons do next?

MESSENGER. I should ignore the rest, if I were you, since you're happy so far.*

JOCASTA. That's a worrying thing to say. No, this is not something I can ignore.

MESSENGER. What more do you want for your sons than that they are alive?

JOCASTA. I want to hear whether I shall be happy in the future too.

MESSENGER. Let me go. Your son has no one to stand next to him in the battle line.

JOCASTA. You're concealing something bad and trying to keep it from me.

MESSENGER. I certainly don't want to follow what you found to be welcome with bad news.

JOCASTA. You must, unless you can fly away from here into the sky.

MESSENGER. Oh, dear! Why didn't you let me leave once I'd finished delivering my good news? Why do you insist on my telling you bad news? Abhorrent as the undertaking might be, your two sons are poised to fight a duel, one against one, without involving the rest of the army.* Go, with whatever resources you have—physical strength or clever arguments* or magical charms—and stop your sons from this terrible contest. They are in great danger.

JOCASTA (*turning to the palace, and calling*). Antigone, my child, come out of the palace!

Enter ANTIGONE *from the palace.*

ANTIGONE. Why are you calling me outside, mother? Do you have further news to dismay your family?

JOCASTA. Daughter, your brothers' lives are lost!*

ANTIGONE. What do you mean?

JOCASTA. They've set about fighting in single combat.

ANTIGONE. Oh, no! Tell me more!

JOCASTA. There's nothing welcome to hear, but come with me.

ANTIGONE. Where? Would you have me leave the girls' quarters?*

JOCASTA. To the armies.

ANTIGONE. I would feel ashamed to appear before such a crowd.

JOCASTA. Now is not the time for modesty from you.

ANTIGONE. What would you have me do?

JOCASTA. Put an end to your brothers' dispute.

ANTIGONE. How, mother?

JOCASTA. By kneeling before them, along with me. (*To the* MESSENGER) Lead the way to the battlefield. Hurry, now! (*To* ANTIGONE) Quickly, daughter, quickly! For if I get there before my sons fight, I shall remain alive. But if they are dead, I shall lie in death beside them.

Exeunt JOCASTA, ANTIGONE, *and the* MESSENGER.

CHORUS (*sings*). Ah, woe, woe! My heart trembles,
trembles with fear! Pity pierces my flesh—
pity for a mother's unhappiness.
Which of her two sons will turn out to murder the other?
O Zeus, O Earth, alas for these trials!
In bloody conflict, which brother's neck,
which brother's life will be lost?
Oh, misery, misery! Which of them
shall I have to bewail in death, a corpse?

Oh, horror, horror! Two wild beasts,*
lusting for blood, will fall to the brandished spear,
fall presently amidst fierce bloodshed.
Why did the wretches think of single combat?
In tears I shall mourn with foreign cries
in lamentation made for the dead.
Their destiny is at hand, death is near!
The sword shall decide the future.
Horrendous is the fate that brings slaughter through the Erinyes.

Enter CREON *from the palace.*

CREON. Alas, what shall I do? Am I to weep for myself or for Thebes, which is shrouded in the kind of cloud that would propel it across the Acheron?* My son has killed himself for the city's sake—an act which, for all the pain it causes me, will make him famous for his courage. I have just fetched him from the dragon's cliff* and carried his suicide corpse in my arms—ah, the pain of it! My whole household resounds with cries of grief. I've come to find my sister Jocasta, an old man seeking an old woman, to ask her to wash and lay out my dead son.* For it is the duty of the living to attend to the dead, out of respect for the god of the underworld.

CHORUS. Your sister has left the palace, Creon, and Antigone has accompanied her mother.

CREON. Where have they gone? What has happened to make them leave? Tell me.

CHORUS. She heard that her sons were about to clash in single combat to resolve the issue of the royal palace.

CREON. What? I was too involved in lavishing affection on my son's body to realize this as well.

CHORUS. But your sister left some time ago. I imagine, Creon, that Oedipus' sons have already finished their fight to the death.

CREON. Oh, no! This looks ominous! I can see a frown on the face of a man coming with news.

Enter the SECOND MESSENGER.

MESSENGER. Alas! How shall I deliver the news and the tears I bring?

CHORUS. It is all over with us. This is not a favourable start to your message.

MESSENGER. Alas, I cry again! For the news I bring is disastrous.

CHORUS. Tell me, how did Oedipus' two sons bring about their deaths? What happened in the contest caused by their father's curses?

MESSENGER. You know of Thebes' success in defending the city, because the encircling walls are not so far away. But the two young sons of aged Oedipus arrayed their bodies in bronze armour, and went and stood in the middle of the battlefield to fight their duel. Looking in the direction of Argos, Polynices voiced the following prayer: 'Lady Hera,* I pray to you since, by reason of my marriage to Adrastus' daughter and residence in Argos, I am yours. Grant that I may kill my brother and drench my fighting arm with the blood of victory.' And Eteocles, looking towards the temple of Pallas,* the goddess with the golden shield, prayed: 'Daughter of Zeus, grant my spear glorious victory! Let it fly from my hand, propelled by this arm of mine, into my brother's chest!'

The sound of the Tyrrhenian trumpet* rose like fire into the air, signalling the start of bloody battle, and they hurled themselves at each other in a formidable charge. Like boars whetting their savage tusks they came together, their beards drenched with foam. They jabbed at each other with their spears, but they were crouched behind their shields so that the points would slide off and achieve nothing. If one of them saw the other's eye peer over the rim of the shield, he made a thrust with his spear, intent on reaching him with the point before he disappeared again behind the shield. But they kept their eyes fixed so close to the rims of their shields that spears were useless. In anguish for their friends the onlookers were sweating even more than the combatants.†

Eteocles stepped on a stone, and in brushing it aside with his foot his leg fell outside the protection of his shield. Polynices, seeing that he was being offered a chance to strike a successful blow, lunged with his spear, and the Argive weapon pierced his opponent's leg—at which the whole Argive army shouted out in triumph. Just at this point of the fight the one who had sustained the first wound saw an exposed shoulder and, to the delight of his fellow Thebans, stabbed his spear towards Polynices' chest†—only to have the head of the spear break off. With no spear to rely on now, Eteocles drew back, before picking up a marble rock* and letting fly with it. He succeeded in breaking the shaft of Polynices' spear, and so the fight was evenly balanced, since both of them had lost their spears.

Next they gripped their swords by the hilts and came to close quarters. Their shields clashed and, with their feet firmly planted on the ground, they engaged in the extreme violence of battle. It somehow occurred to Eteocles to make use of the Thessalian trick,* which he knew because of his familiarity with that land. He disengaged from the struggle they were involved in, pulled his left foot back, and, protecting his stomach in front, stepped forward on to his right foot and stabbed his sword down through Polynices' belly until it was wedged into his spine. Poor Polynices, with blood pouring from the wound, doubled up and fell. Eteocles, who was naturally certain that he had defeated his brother and won the fight, hurled his sword on to the ground and began to strip him of his armour, neglecting his own protection in favour of this task. And it was this that proved his undoing. His brother was still just breathing and had kept hold of his sword during his horrible fall, and although it was hard for him Polynices, the one who had fallen first, reached up and stabbed Eteocles in the liver. There the two of them lie, side by side, their mouths filled with dust, with the rulership of Thebes still undecided.

CHORUS. Oh, no! I grieve for you and your troubles, Oedipus! The god appears to have fulfilled your curses.

MESSENGER. But wait! There's more terrible news. With her two sons fallen and breathing their last, their poor mother burst in on the scene and, seeing their fatal wounds, sobbed out: 'I have arrived too late to help you, my sons!' Falling on each of them in turn she began to cry, and pitifully to lament all the effort of feeding them at her breasts, and their sister, her companion, joined in as well: 'O you who were to look after your mother in her old age . . . !'; 'O my darling brothers, traitors to my marriage . . . !'* With his chest heaving as he gasped out his dying breaths,† lord Eteocles heard his mother's voice and placed a damp hand on her. He spoke not a word, but the tears in his eyes spoke for him, to show his love. Polynices was still breathing and, looking towards his sister and his aged mother, he said, 'My life is over, mother. I feel sorry for you, for my sister here, and for my dead brother, a kinsman who became my enemy, but remained my own dear brother. Mother, sister, calm the anger of my fellow citizens and bury me in my native soil, so that even if I have lost my inheritance I may gain this much, at any rate, of my native land. Mother, close my eyes with your own hand'—and he himself put her hand on his eyes—'and let me bid you farewell. For darkness is beginning to overwhelm me.'

Both breathed out their unhappy lives together. When their mother saw what had happened, in extreme agony of mind she snatched up the sword from her dead sons and did an appalling thing. She thrust the sword right through her throat, collapsed to the ground, and between her beloved sons she now lies dead, her arms embracing both.

The soldiers jumped to their feet and fell to arguing, with us claiming that my master had won and then that the other brother had. The officers weren't immune to the dispute either. The men rushed to seize their arms and armour, but the Theban army, well guided perhaps by foresight, had sat down with their equipment near at hand. Since the Argive army did not yet have their weaponry to protect them, we suddenly fell on them before they could fall on us. None of them made a stand; they filled the plain as they fled, and rivers of blood flowed from the men killed by our spears. After our victory, some set up an image of Zeus as a trophy, while others of us stripped the Argive corpses of their armour and had them taken into the town as booty. Some joined Antigone and are bringing the bodies here for those who loved them to mourn over. Of the conflicts which have affected this city, some have had very fortunate outcomes, but others have been complete disasters.

Exit the SECOND MESSENGER.

Enter ANTIGONE, *with attendants carrying the corpses of* POLYNICES, ETEOCLES, *and* JOCASTA.*

CHORUS. The disaster that has befallen the royal household is no longer just something we have been told about. For now we can see the three corpses. Here they are, by the palace, joined by common death in their lot of a lifetime of darkness.

ANTIGONE (*sings*). Not hiding the delicacy of my cheek with its clustering curls,
nor in maidenly modesty the blush under my eyes, the flush on my face,
I come in frenzy for the dead, with the veil cast from my hair,
and my rich saffron gown loosened, escorting the dead in lamentation.*
Ah, woe! Alas! Alas! O Polynices, how aptly you were named, it seems!*
I cry alas, Thebes! Brother, the consummation of your quarrel
—no quarrel but successive slaughter—has destroyed
the house of Oedipus in awful bloodshed, foul bloodshed.
O house, O royal house, how shall I raise amidst tears, so many tears,
cries of grief worth anything as music or melody?
For the three bodies I bring are all members of my family,
my mother and her sons, for the delight of the deadly demon
which destroyed the house of Oedipus long before
he solved the melody of the savage Sphinx's song
and killed the creature. How clever he was, faced
with her evil cleverness! Oh, alas, alas!
Is there any woman from Greece or abroad,
or any noble past, who has borne such pain for all to see,
the pain of so much wrong, of so many mortal lives
lost in so much bloodshed?† What bird, deprived of her brood,
in the highest branches of oak or fir matches in her mourning
the expressions of grief I cry out in my wretchedness?*
With tears and lamentation I mourn these people here,
I who will spend all my remaining years in floods of tears,
I who will spend the rest of my life alone. On to which of them
first shall I cast the offering of hair torn from my head?*
Will it lie by the two dry, milkless breasts of my mother,
or by the foully mutilated bodies of my brothers?

Ah, leave your palace and bring your blinded eye out here,
old father of mine! Reveal your life of misery, Oedipus,

you who still, after casting murky darkness on your eyes,
prolong your days indoors. As you pace the courtyard with aged foot
or rest in misery on your bed, can you hear me call to you?

Enter OEDIPUS *from the palace.* OEDIPUS *and* ANTIGONE *chant or sing until 1581.*

OEDIPUS. Why, daughter, with most pitiful tears did you call me forth,
to emerge, though bed-ridden, with staff for my blind feet
from the dark of my chamber into the light of day—
a pale ghost shining with the brightness of the upper sky,
or a corpse from down below, or a winged dream?

ANTIGONE. There's grim news for you to hear, father: your sons are dead,
and so is your wife, who was always found beside your staff
in patient attendance on your blinded feet. I'm so sorry, father!

OEDIPUS. Oh, the pain, the pain! I must cry out my grief like this!
How did these three lives end? What happened? Tell me, child.

ANTIGONE. I speak not in reproach, nor in perverse delight, but in anguish.
The demon you released, heavy laden with swords and fire
and wretched conflict, fell on your sons. I'm so sorry, father!

OEDIPUS. Oh, woe!

ANTIGONE. Why this pitiful cry?

OEDIPUS. My sons . . .

ANTIGONE. Your distress is great.
But what if you still could see the Sun's four-horsed chariot
and with your own eyes had gazed upon these bodies here?

OEDIPUS. The evil that befell my sons is plain to all; but tell me, child,
what happened to my wife? How did she come to die?

ANTIGONE. Weeping bitter tears for all to see, she bore . . . she bore her breast
to her sons, a suppliant eagerly offering suppliant breast.*
Seizing a bronze sword from the bodies, in her own flesh
she dyed it red and fell in grief for her sons between their bodies.

Father, on this one day there have been gathered for our house
all kinds of grief by the god who brought this to fulfilment.†

CREON (*abruptly*). Enough mourning: now it is time to turn our minds to burial. Hear what I have to say, Oedipus. Your son Eteocles has passed on to me the rulership of this land, and has given the dowry and marriage-bed of your daughter Antigone to Haemon. I refuse, then, to let you live any longer in this land—Tiresias made it plain that as long as you are living here the city would never prosper.* So be on your way! It is not arrogance or personal hostility that makes me say this; I'm only worried that the land might suffer as a result of the vengeful demons that attend you.

OEDIPUS. O Fate, you bore me for misery right from the outset.† Even before I entered the world from my mother's womb, Apollo foretold to Laius that I, a baby still unborn, would murder my father. Oh, the suffering I have had to bear! No sooner was I born than my father in his turn tried to kill me on the grounds that I was his enemy, since he was to die at my hands. So he had me taken away, pining for my mother's breast, to make a sorry meal for wild beasts.† And then, a wretched victim of fate, I killed my own father, took my poor mother in marriage, and fathered children on her—brothers, whom I then destroyed, by passing on to them the curse of Laius which I had received. For I am not so stupid as to think that I did what I have done to my eyes and to the lives of my children without the assistance of one of the gods.

But anyway, what shall I do now, wretched victim of fate that I am? What guide for my blind feet will be my companion? She would, I'm sure, if she were alive—but she's dead. What about my fine pair of sons? No, they are gone. Do I still have the energy to find sustenance by myself? Impossible! Creon, why are you doing such a thorough job of killing me? For kill me you will if you banish me from this land. But I'm not going to play the coward and wrap my arms around your knees in supplication:* even in my misfortune I refuse to betray the nobility that once was mine.

CREON. You're right to speak of not clasping my knees, but still I cannot allow you to live here. (*He addresses the attendants*)

Now, as for these bodies, this one is to be taken inside the palace, but the other, the corpse of Polynices, who came with an army to destroy his native city, you are to cast unburied beyond the borders of the land. And the town-crier will announce to all Thebans that death will be the punishment for anyone caught adorning the corpse with a ritual garland or burying it.†* (*He turns to* ANTIGONE) Antigone, you are to stop mourning the three dead now and go indoors.†

ANTIGONE. We are to be pitied, father, for the evils that beset us. I weep for you more than I do for the dead, because there's not one of your troubles that is endurable. You are wretched in all respects, father. (*To Creon*) But I have questions for you, the new ruler of this land: why do you treat my father here in such a high-handed fashion? Why banish him? And why do you introduce regulations about a wretched corpse?

CREON. They are Eteocles' edicts, not mine.*

ANTIGONE. They are stupid, and you're an idiot for going along with them.

CREON. Why? It's right to carry out instructions.

ANTIGONE. Not if they're bad and malicious.

CREON. What do you mean? Won't it be right to let the dogs have this corpse?

ANTIGONE. No, because the punishment you're imposing on him is unlawful.

CREON. It's perfectly justified in the case of someone who made himself an enemy of the state, when he wasn't before.

ANTIGONE. Hasn't he already been punished by his destiny?†

CREON. Well, he can be punished now by the manner of his burial too.

ANTIGONE. What was his crime? He was only after his share of the land.

CREON. You can be sure that this man will receive no burial.

ANTIGONE. *I* shall bury him, even if the city forbids it.

CREON. Then you'll be burying yourself along with this corpse.

ANTIGONE. There's no disgrace in two people who are dear to each other lying in close proximity.

CREON (*to attendants*). Seize this woman and take her into the palace.

ANTIGONE (*taking* POLYNICES' *body in her arms*). You can't, because I shall not let go of this corpse.

CREON. Your wishes, young woman, go against the gods' decrees.

ANTIGONE. There's another such decree—that one is not to abuse the bodies of the dead.

CREON. No libation shall moisten the dust covering this one.

ANTIGONE. Creon, I beg you in the name of my mother, Jocasta here.

CREON. Your efforts are wasted; they'll get you nowhere.

ANTIGONE. At least let me bathe his body.

CREON. This will be one of the actions that no citizen is allowed to perform.

ANTIGONE. But won't you let me bandage his savage wounds?

CREON. No, there's no way that you will pay this corpse any mark of respect.

ANTIGONE. My darling, at least I shall kiss your lips. (*She does so before* CREON *can interfere*)

CREON. You are not to let tears blight your marriage.

ANTIGONE. Do you really think I shall ever marry your son? Not while I live!

CREON. You have little choice. After all, where will you go to escape the marriage?

ANTIGONE. The night of my marriage will be the night I become one of the Danaids.*

CREON (*to* OEDIPUS). The audacity of the girl! Did you hear her? What an insult!

ANTIGONE (*laying her hands on* POLYNICES' *sword*). I swear it by the iron of this sword.

CREON. Why do you want to avoid this marriage so much?

ANTIGONE. I shall go into exile along with my poor father here.*

CREON. There's a noble streak in you, but it's combined with stupidity.

ANTIGONE. You should know further that I shall die with him too.

CREON. Go. You will not murder my son. Leave the country.

CREON steps back among the attendants.

OEDIPUS. Daughter, I admire your determination, but . . .

ANTIGONE. What if I were to be married and you were to go alone into exile, father?

OEDIPUS. Stay and be happy. I shall submit to my trials and tribulations.

ANTIGONE. And who will look after you in your blindness, father?

OEDIPUS. I shall lie on the ground wherever my fate has me fall.

ANTIGONE. Where now is the Oedipus who solved the famous riddle?*

OEDIPUS. He is gone. A single day—the same day—brought me success and death.

ANTIGONE. And shouldn't I share your trials too?

OEDIPUS. Exile with a blind father is shameful for a daughter.

ANTIGONE. No, not if she knows her duty, father. It's a noble thing to do.

OEDIPUS. All right, then. Take me up to your mother. I want to touch her.

ANTIGONE. There. Lay your hand on her beloved cheek.†

OEDIPUS. Mother . . . wife . . . wretched woman.

ANTIGONE. Here she lies, a sorry sight, burdened with all her woes at once.

OEDIPUS. Where are the bodies of Eteocles and Polynices?

ANTIGONE. Here they are for you, stretched out side by side.

OEDIPUS. Please bring my blind hand to their poor faces.

ANTIGONE. There. Caress your dead sons with your hand.

OEDIPUS. Dear corpses, wretched sons of a wretched father.

ANTIGONE. Polynices, my darling . . . †

OEDIPUS. Now the oracle of Loxias is coming true, my child.

ANTIGONE. What oracle? Do you have a tale of further woes to tell?

OEDIPUS. It was foretold that I should die a vagabond in Athens.

ANTIGONE. Where? What fortress in Athens will take you in?

OEDIPUS. Sacred Colonus,* the home of the god of horses. But come, take care of your blind father, since you are determined to share his exile.

OEDIPUS and ANTIGONE sing or chant to the end.

ANTIGONE. Go, then, into miserable exile. Aged father,
reach out your dear hand. I shall be
your escort, as a breeze escorts a ship.

OEDIPUS. Here. I'm on my way, child.

Poor you, to be my guide.
ANTIGONE. Wretched I am indeed. No maiden
of Thebes has more to endure.
OEDIPUS. Where do I put my aged foot?
Where do I wield my staff, child?
ANTIGONE. Here! Come this way with me!
Here! Put your foot down here!
For you are as weak as a dream.
OEDIPUS. Oh, that in my old age I should wander
in wretched exile from my homeland!
Oh, what a dreadful, dreadful fate I have suffered!
ANTIGONE. Why have you suffered? Why have you suffered?
There's no Justice to watch over the bad or repay wrong.
OEDIPUS. I am he who attained the victory song, gained glory
as high as heaven, when I solved the puzzle
riddled in evil cleverness by the half-female maiden.
ANTIGONE. Why mention the Sphinx, a matter for reproach?
Give up this talk of past successes.
Sorrow and suffering were in store for you—
banishment from your country, father,
and death in some unknown place.*†

Exit ANTIGONE leading OEDIPUS; exit CREON.

SUPPLIANT WOMEN

Characters

THESEUS, *king of Athens*
AETHRA, *Theseus' mother*
ADRASTUS, *king of Argos*
HERALD, *from Thebes*
MESSENGER, *an Argive slave*
EVADNE, *widow of Capaneus*
IPHIS, *Evadne's father*
ATHENA, *goddess of Athens*

CHORUS *of Argive mothers and their slaves*
SONS *of the seven dead war-leaders, constituting a secondary chorus*

*Scene: In front of the temple of Demeter at Eleusis near Athens. The altar is adorned with suppliant branches.** AETHRA *is sitting on the temple steps, with* ADRASTUS *near by.* ADRASTUS' *head is covered by his cloak, in an attitude of grief. The* CHORUS *of suppliant Argive mothers surrounds* AETHRA*; their attendants are near by, and also the secondary chorus of* SONS *of the seven dead war-leaders.*

AETHRA. I call on you, Demeter,* protectress of this Eleusinian land, and on you servants of the goddess, who manage her sanctuary. Grant happiness to me, to my son Theseus, to the city of Athens, and to Pittheus' land,* where my father raised me, Aethra, amid prosperity in his palace until at Loxias'* command he married me to Aegeus the son of Pandion. This prayer of mine is prompted by the sight of these women here, who for all their advanced years have left their homes in Argos to kneel with suppliant branches and clasp my knees. They have been overtaken by terrible calamity. At the gates of Cadmus' city their seven noble sons have died, leaving them childless. Not long ago lord Adrastus led their sons to war, in his desire to gain for exiled Polynices, his daughter's husband, a portion of Oedipus' estate.* Their mothers wanted to give the war-slain dead their funeral rites, but the Theban rulers forbade them from doing so, and refused them permission to collect the bodies. This is an insult to the gods and their customs.* And here is Adrastus, who shares with these women the burden of their need of me. Here he lies, tears pouring from his eyes in remorse for the war and the ill-starred campaign he led from his home. He is urging me to plead with my son until he takes on the task of recovering the bodies, whether that requires argument or force of arms, and plays his part in seeing them buried. He wants to see this task undertaken in common by my son and the city of Athens. It so happened that, in order to sacrifice for the fertility of the land, I had left my house and come to this precinct, where the fruitful corn first appeared bristling above this soil.* And here, bound by these branches that are not bonds,* I remain by the sacred altars of the two goddesses, the Maiden* and Demeter, out of pity for these grey-haired mothers bereft of their sons and reverence for their holy wreaths. At my command a messenger has gone to the city to summon Theseus here, and the upshot will be that he will either banish from the land the distress caused by these women or discharge his obligation to help these suppliants by doing the gods some sacred service. It is reasonable for women who are wise to get men to act for them in everything.

CHORUS (*sings*). As elder to an elder, I fall in supplication at your knees,
voicing my prayer. Put an end to the lawlessness†
of those who leave in limb-dissolving death the limbs of the dead
for the beasts which dwell in the mountains to feast on,*
moved by the sight of the pitiful tears in my eyes,
and of the gashes torn by my hands in my aged flesh.*
What else could I do? I have not laid out my dead son
before my home, nor do I see any mound heaped up for his burial.

My lady, you too have shown your husband your worth as a wife
by giving birth to a son, so you can sympathize now with my plight.
I beseech your sympathy for all the grief in my dejection I feel
for my dead son. Persuade your son, I implore you,

to go to the Ismenus,* to place in my arms the body
of my still-youthful son, who has been denied burial.

It is not the sacred rites, but necessity that brings me here*
to fall before their fiery altars and implore the goddesses.
Justice is on my side, and thanks to your fine son you have the power
to remove my misery. In my sorrowful plight I beseech
your son to place in my wretched arms the body of my son,
so that I may embrace my son's sombre limbs.

The attendants of the CHORUS *make various sounds and gestures of mourning.*

Here arises a response, tears rivalling our tears,
the hands of our slaves resound the theme.
Come, you who echo our sorrows,
you who echo our grief, come
to the dance which Hades* celebrates!
Rake your cheeks with your nails
and redden with blood your pale skin! Ah, yes!
It is fine for the living to care for the dead.

As from a sheer cliff drops of water flow,
so the insatiable, agonizing pleasure
of tears induces me to shed
further tears, tears without end.
For the suffering caused by the death of sons
is a form of pain that is bound
to reduce women to tears. Ah, yes!
Would that I could die and forget this pain!

Enter THESEUS.

THESEUS. Echoing from this temple here I heard the sound of tears, of breasts being beaten and lamentation for the dead. Who is grieving here? I am restless with fear that my mother may have met with an accident, and I have come in search of her because she has been gone so long from home. Oh, no! What's this? A strange sight greets me, hard to put into words. I see my aged mother seated at the altar, along with foreign women in various attitudes of grief. Tears of sorrow pour from aged eyes to the earth, hair has been shorn, their clothing is unsuited to celebration here. What's going on, mother? You have to tell me; I'll have to listen. I expect some bad news.

AETHRA. Theseus, these women here are the mothers of the seven generals, their sons, who fell at the gates of Cadmus' city. As you can see, my son, they have hemmed me in with a circle of suppliant branches.

THESEUS. And who is this who lies here in the gateway moaning?

AETHRA. I am told that he is Adrastus, the Argive king.

THESEUS. What about the boys around him? Who are they? Are they these women's sons?

AETHRA. No, their fathers are the dead warriors.

THESEUS. Why have they come as suppliants to us?

AETHRA. I know why, but the next part of the story must come from them, my son.

AETHRA resumes her attitude of grief, with a fold of her clothes covering her head.

THESEUS (*to Adrastus*). I address my questions to you, the one shrouded in his cloak. Uncover your head, leave off your tears, and talk to me. For speech is the only way to get things done.

ADRASTUS. Theseus, glorious in victory, king of Athens, I have come in supplication to you and to your city.*

THESEUS. For what reason? What is it that you need?

ADRASTUS. You know the fatal campaign I led?

THESEUS. Yes, you made no secret of it as you marched through Greece.

ADRASTUS. The flower of Argive manhood died there thanks to me.

THESEUS. War is harsh; there are bound to be fatalities.

ADRASTUS. I went to Thebes to ask for the bodies back.

THESEUS. Because you wanted to see to their funerals? And did you make use of heralds, sacred to Hermes?*

ADRASTUS. Yes, and then their slayers refused me permission.

THESEUS. But your request was perfectly proper. What did they say?

ADRASTUS. What indeed? Their success did not teach them how to endure success.

THESEUS. So have you come to ask my advice? Or what do you want?

ADRASTUS. Theseus, I want *you* to recover the dead sons of Argos.

THESEUS. Where is that Argos we hear so much about? Is it no more than empty boasts?

ADRASTUS. After our defeat it's all over with us. That's why we have come here to you.

THESEUS. Was this your own personal decision or a decree ratified by the whole city?*

ADRASTUS. All the Argives beg you to bury the bodies.

THESEUS. Why did you lead your seven squadrons against Thebes?

ADRASTUS. As a favour to my two sons-in-law.*

THESEUS. What are their names, these Argive men to whom you gave your daughters?

ADRASTUS. My sons-in-law are not from Argos.

THESEUS. Really? You gave your daughters, Argive girls, to foreigners?*

ADRASTUS. Yes, to Tydeus and to Theban-born Polynices.

THESEUS. What made you want them as your sons-in-law?

ADRASTUS. An obscure riddle told by Phoebus insinuated itself into my mind.

THESEUS. What did Apollo say to ordain their marriage to your daughters?

ADRASTUS. That I was to give my two daughters to a boar and a lion.

THESEUS. And how did you unravel this oracular utterance of the god's?

ADRASTUS. Two exiles came under cover of darkness to my door.

THESEUS. Tell me their individual names. At the moment you're speaking of them both at once.

ADRASTUS. Tydeus and Polynices, and they fell to fighting there.*

THESEUS. So these are the men—or beasts, rather—to whom you gave your daughters?

ADRASTUS. Yes, because they fought like two wild animals.

THESEUS. What were they doing there? Why did they leave their native countries?

ADRASTUS. Tydeus was banished for killing a member of his own family.*

THESEUS. And how did Oedipus' son come to leave Thebes?

ADRASTUS. It was thanks to his father's curse. He was worried that he might kill his brother.

THESEUS. Well, that's certainly a sensible reason for choosing exile.

ADRASTUS. Yes, but the people he left behind set about wronging him in his absence.

THESEUS. Did his brother really steal his property?

ADRASTUS. It was to avenge this wrong† that I undertook the campaign which has proved my undoing.

THESEUS. Did you consult diviners? Did you inspect the flames of burnt offerings?*

ADRASTUS. Ah, you've found my weakest point.

THESEUS. So it seems that you didn't have the gods' blessing for your expedition.

ADRASTUS. It's worse than that: I went despite Amphiaraus'* warning.

THESEUS. Did you so lightly ignore the gods?

ADRASTUS. Yes, because the young men's clamour confused me.

THESEUS. You were guided by confidence rather than consideration.

ADRASTUS. Yes, and this has proved the undoing of many a military commander.† But let me appeal to you, the king of Athens and the bravest man in Greece. It embarrasses me to kneel and clasp your knees,* because I am old and was once a prosperous ruler; but I must submit to my misfortune. (*He kneels and clasps* THESEUS' *knees as a suppliant*) Please rescue the bodies. Have pity on me in my time of trouble and on these women here, the mothers of the dead warriors, now childless in their grey old age. (*He slowly gets to his feet*) They endured the journey here, the hardship of stirring their elderly bodies and placing their feet on foreign ground, and they came not as a delegation for the mysteries of Demeter,* but to bury their sons, who should by rights have been the ones to bury them in due course and see to their funerals. It is wise for a rich man to consider poverty, and for a poor man to look in admiration on the rich, to make him desire to be wealthy himself. And it is wise for those who are not cursed with misfortune to see pitiful sights ⟨. . .⟩† and a poet should find delight in giving birth to his own original compositions. If he had no such feeling of delight, if he was overwhelmed by personal disaster, he would not be able to cause delight in others—he would have no right to please them. Now, you might wonder why I ignored Pelops' land* and am trying to assign this task to Athens. This question deserves an answer from me. Sparta is hard and fickle in her ways,* and the rest of the cities are small and weak. Yours is the only city with the ability to shoulder this burden, for she has seen pitiful sights, and she has in you a vigorous, outstanding leader. Lack of this—that is, lack of such a commander—has proved the undoing of many a city.

CHORUS. I echo this appeal to you, Theseus, and ask you to have pity on us and to take on the burden of our misfortunes.

THESEUS. In the past I have debated at length with others the question whether, as some say, there is more bad than good in human life. My view is the opposite, that there is more good than bad. If this wasn't the case, we wouldn't remain alive. I praise whichever god it was who removed human life from its chaotic and bestial state and gave it order, first by imbuing us with intelligence, and then by giving us tongues to communicate our words, so that we may understand speech. He gave us the growth of crops, and to aid their growth he gave us rain that falls from the sky, not only to nurture the produce of the soil, but also to refresh our bellies with drink. Moreover, he provided us with protection from the storms of winter and the means to defend ourselves against the heat of the sun, and taught us how to sail the sea, so that by trade we might make up for any shortfall in our local crops. As for matters that are unclear and hard to assess, we have the prophecies of diviners, based on their inspection of flames, of the patterns on entrails, and of the flights of birds. Is it not self-indulgent to be unsatisfied when the god has provided for us so well? But in our arrogance we seek power greater than his, and our self-importance is such that we imagine ourselves cleverer than the gods. You seem to be one of this company, in that under the influence of Phoebus' oracle you stupidly married your daughters to foreigners—as if it were the gods who give girls in marriage—and muddied the clear waters of your house, inflicting a terrible wound on it. Anyone with any sense should not couple sound with unsound bodies, but should make his kin those who will bring prosperity into his house. For from the god's point of view there's no difference between our circumstances: he uses a sick person's ailment to destroy someone who was perfectly healthy and morally unblemished too. When you led the Argives out to war at full strength, you paid no heed to the prophetic utterances spoken by diviners; in deliberately disregarding the gods you brought ruin down on your city. You were led astray by young men who enjoy being in the public eye and multiply wars with no regard for justice or for the citizens' deaths they cause. They do this for a number of reasons, one because he wants to lead an army, another in order to acquire power and abuse it, another for financial gain, without any concern whether the general populace is harmed by his treatment of them. Citizens fall into three categories, you see. There are the rich, who are useless, always greedy for more. There are the poor, who live below subsistence level: they are dangerous, because they are guided for the most part by envy and,† deceived by the tongues of unscrupulous demagogues, shoot deadly missiles at those who are well off. Of the three classes in society it is the one that falls between these two which keeps cities safe, and preserves the officially ordained constitution, whatever it may be.

And so shall I enter into an alliance with you? What good reason could I give my fellow citizens for doing so? No, I bid you farewell. Since you have failed to exercise sound judgement, you must overcome your fortune by yourself, and leave us out of it.†

CHORUS. He made a mistake, which is inevitable in the young, and should be forgiven.

ADRASTUS. My lord, I didn't ask you to judge my faults, nor to punish me or censure me for any mistake I am found to have made. I came to ask for your help. If you're not prepared to give it, I must be content with this decision of yours. What else can I do? (*To the* CHORUS) Come, then, old women, let's go. Leave your leafy olive branches here, ribbons and all, calling on the gods, the earth, Demeter with her torch,* and the light of the sun, to witness that our prayers to the gods have proven ineffective.

CHORUS. ⟨Theseus, you are descended from Pittheus⟩† who was Pelops' son, and since we come from Pelops' land we are of the same lineage as you. What are you doing? Are you really going to betray our kinship and expel old women from the land before they've gained anything of what is owed them? Don't do it. When caught in a storm a city can cower behind the protection of another city, just as a wild animal can take refuge in a cave and a slave at the altars of the gods.* For in human life there is no such thing as permanent prosperity.

The CHORUS divides into two Semichoruses.

SEMICHORUS A.† Arise, you poor things, arise from the floor of Persephone's temple; embrace his knees and implore him to collect the corpses of our dead sons—oh, the pain we suffer!—the sons we lost at the walls of Cadmus' city.

SEMICHORUS B (*kneeling in supplication around THESEUS*). Kinsman of mine, most glorious of the Greeks, in our misery we embrace your knees and clasp your hands, and we beg you, by your beard,* to have pity on us as we come to you as suppliants, singing dirges, pitiful dirges for our sons.

SEMICHORUS A. Theseus, we implore you, don't leave our sons, your peers, as a feast for the beasts in Cadmus' land.

SEMICHORUS B. See the tears in our eyes, hear our plea at your knees to win burial for our sons.

The CHORUS reunites.

THESEUS. Mother, why these tears? Why have you shrouded your eyes with the fine cloth of your gown? Is it because of the bitter tears of these wretches here? They touched me too. Lift up your aged head and dry your eyes, since you are seated at Deo's sacred altar.*

AETHRA. Ah, woe!

THESEUS. Their grief should not be yours.

AETHRA. I feel such sorrow for them!

THESEUS. You are not their child.

AETHRA. There's something I want to say which is valid both for you and for the city. May I speak?

THESEUS. Of course. Even women often make intelligent points.

AETHRA. But I hesitate to utter aloud the words I have inside me.

THESEUS. How could you even think of keeping valuable advice from those you love? That's a shocking idea.

AETHRA. I shall not keep quiet now and then later blame myself for having lacked the courage to speak out, nor shall I leave the valid point I have to make unsaid because of worrying about the saying that fine speeches from women are useless. My child, above all I suggest you take care to avoid coming to grief as a result of having dishonoured the gods. Moreover, if it did not take courage to help victims of injustice, I would certainly have kept quiet. But as things are you should appreciate, my son, how much honour it will gain you to do what I feel no qualms about advising—to use force of arms to compel men who are committing the outrage of denying bodies burial and funeral rites to stop undermining the established practices followed by all Greeks. For you can be sure that it is the due maintenance of law and custom that holds human societies together. Now, someone will attribute to cowardice your nervous failure to take action, when you had the chance to win a crown of fame for Athens. They will say that you undertook the unimpressive challenge of hunting a wild boar,* but turned out to be a coward when, faced with the might of helmet and spear, you had a job to complete. My son, my own flesh and blood, don't do this! Do you see how your country, when taunted for lack of sound judgement, looks with fearsome eye on her taunters? She flourishes through her labours, while states which pursue their shady business with a policy of inactivity are so cautious that their looks are shaded too. Will you not help the dead warriors and their wretched mothers in their hour of need, my son? The prospect doesn't fill me with alarm, because you'll set out on a just mission, and although I can see that the Thebans are currently enjoying success, I trust that the dice may yet fall otherwise and bring them down. For everything suffers reversal at the hands of the god.

CHORUS. How it warms my heart to hear you! Your words are good for him and for me too, and so give pleasure in both respects.

THESEUS. Mother, what I told Adrastus here was the truth. I

showed him which policies, in my opinion, caused his downfall. Nevertheless, I too can see the validity of your advice, that it would hardly be in keeping with my character to shrink from danger. By the number and quality of my achievements I have already shown the Greeks that it is my practice to prove myself a punisher of wrongdoing. So I cannot now refuse this task. What would my enemies say, seeing that my mother, the one who has especial concern for my safety, is the first to suggest that I undertake this task? All right, I'll do it. I shall go and rescue the bodies. I shall prevail upon the Thebans by argument, if I can, and if that fails I shall turn forthwith to force of arms, and the gods will not begrudge me their assent. But I would also like all the citizens to agree to this plan of action. The people of Athens will agree if I want it, but they'll be more amenable if I give them a share in the discussion. For when I freed the city and distributed the right to vote equally among the citizens,* I gave them sovereign power. I shall take Adrastus with me as proof of my words, and I shall address the assembled body of citizens. Once I've gained their assent, I shall muster an élite force of young Athenians and return here. Once armed, I shall send a message to Creon* demanding the return of the bodies.

(*To the* CHORUS) Old women, would you now free my mother from the holy wreaths that restrain her? I would like to take her by her dear hand and lead her to Aegeus' palace. For it's a sad child who fails to repay his parents' services with services of his own. And, wonderfully, this repayment is itself a loan, because what he gives to his parents he receives back again in kind from his own children.

Exeunt THESEUS, AETHRA, *and* ADRASTUS.

CHORUS (*sings*). O horse-farming Argos,* land of our fathers,
did you hear that? Did you hear
the holy, god-fearing words of the king?
An important speech for Pelasgia,* for Argos.

I pray that he may put an end and more to my plight,
that he may stop us mothers raking our flesh,
raising blood, and may win the friendship
of the land of Inachus for the help he brings.

A city is graced by a sacred task and wins
undying gratitude. What will Athens resolve?
Will she ally herself with my cause?
Are we to gain burial for our sons?

Come, city of Pallas,* come to a mother's aid!
Keep our human customs free from taint!
Justice you revere, injustice you despise,
and ever prove the salvation of the wretched.

Enter ADRASTUS, *and* THESEUS *in conversation with an Athenian herald and accompanied by attendants.*

THESEUS. This is your job, to serve the city and me as occasion demands by delivering messages. I want you to cross the Asopus* and Ismenus' waters and say this to the haughty king of Thebes: 'Theseus requests that you be so good as to allow the dead their funerals. He thinks it right, since his land borders yours, that you grant this request and keep on good terms with the people of Athens, the descendants of Erechtheus.'* If they accede, thank them and hurry back home; if they refuse, here is my second message: 'Prepare for the arrival of my band of revellers, carrying shields. My army has passed muster and is here waiting in readiness around the sacred Callichorus.* When they saw that I was in favour, the citizens gave the undertaking their willing and wholehearted approval.'

But here I must break off. I see someone approaching. Who can it be? He looks to me, though I can't be certain, like a Theban herald.* You had better wait. He might have come to forestall my designs, which would relieve you of your task.

Enter HERALD.

HERALD. Who is the sole ruler of this land? To whom should I deliver the message given me by Creon? For Creon now rules Cadmus' land, following Eteocles' death by the seven gates of the city at the hands of his brother Polynices.

THESEUS. You went wrong there right at the beginning of your speech, stranger, when you asked for the sole ruler here. The city is free, not under the dominion of just one man. The people rule, with government following government in yearly succession.* We don't privilege a man because of his wealth; the poor have equal power.

HERALD. This point of yours gives me the advantage, as one might in a game of draughts. For the city from which I've come is ruled by one man, not a rabble. It's impossible for anyone to make our city over-confident and turn it this way and that for his private gain. In the short term, such a man finds favour by his gross flattery, and even later, when he does the city harm, he conceals his earlier mistakes behind fresh slanders and escapes punishment. Besides, how could the common people correctly govern a city when they can't even correctly assess a speech? Time is a better teacher than haste. Even if a poor smallholder is not disqualified by stupidity, the work he does makes it impossible for him to turn his attention to politics. It is indeed a threat to the better members of society when a bad man gains respect and dominates the common people with his eloquence, when formerly he was a nobody.

THESEUS. What a marvellous herald this man is! So smart with uncalled-for words! All right: since it was you who initiated this contest, listen to what I have to say. After all, it was you who proposed the debate. There's nothing more pernicious for a city than a sole ruler, above all because in such a situation there are no public laws, and one man has usurped the law and taken rulership for himself. That spells the end of equality. A written code of law guarantees both weak and wealthy an equal share of justice, so that it is possible for a weaker member of society, when accused by someone who is well off, to respond in the same terms, and for an insignificant man to defeat an important man, if his case is just. Here is where freedom lies: 'Which of you has good advice for the city and is prepared to open it up to public debate?' All it takes to gain distinction is the willingness to do this; anyone who chooses not to keeps quiet. How could any political system deliver more equality than that?

Moreover, when the common people hold the reins of government, they value the younger members of society, seeing them as a resource. A king, however, regards the existence of vigorous young men as a threat; he puts to death the bravest of them and those he regards as intelligent, since he is in constant fear for his tyranny. How could a city ever be strong, when its youth is mown down and harvested like the new growth of a meadow in spring?* What point is there for a man to gain wealth and a comfortable life for his sons when all his efforts serve only to improve a tyrant's life? Why should he raise his daughters at home in the proper maidenly virtues, when the ruler wants the kinds of pleasure tyrants delight in and the parents are only paving the way for their daughters' tears? I would rather die than see my daughters bedded against their will.

This is what I have to say in response to the points you made against me. But now tell me for what reason you have come here. Indeed, if you were not on an official mission for your city, your gratuitous words would make you regret your visit. A messenger should deliver the message he has been told to deliver and then swiftly make his way home again. In future, let Creon send to my city a less talkative herald than you.

CHORUS. Amazing! When fortune favours evil men, in their insolence they assume their prosperity will last for ever.

HERALD. Now I shall speak. We can agree to differ on the issues we have just been debating. The message I have for you—and I speak for all the Thebans—is this: do not admit Adrastus into your land. If he is here already, then before the sun sets you should override the sacred mystery of suppliant wreaths and banish him across your borders. Nor are you to seek to recover the corpses by force, since you have no real connection with Argos. If you comply with these demands, the waters through which you steer your city will be calm. If you refuse, great waves of war will break over Athens and Thebes, and all your allies too.

These words of mine may arouse your anger, since you claim that your city is free, but beware of giving a response which is based on an inflated idea of your meagre resources. Hope is unreliable, and has often brought states to war by stirring up excessive anger. For when the people are to vote for or against war, no one takes into consideration the possibility that he himself may die, but diverts this misfortune on to someone else. If death were visible as votes were cast, Greece would never be destroyed by the madness of war. And yet, when faced with two arguments, we can all tell which is the better; we can all recognize what is good and what is bad, and how much better peace is for us than war. In the first place, there is nothing more precious to the Muses than Peace, and nothing more inimical to the goddesses of feud. Also, children flourish under the delighted gaze of Peace, and prosperity is her pleasure.* Yet in our iniquity we reject all this, involve ourselves in wars, and suppress the weak, with one man making another his slave, one state another state.

And do you now seek to help our enemies, who died in battle? Do you want to recover and bury men who were destroyed by their own insolence? Do you then think it wrong that the body of Capaneus, the man who set his ladders upright against the gates of Thebes and swore that he would sack the city whether or not the gods approved, is still smoking from the thunderbolt? Or that the notorious seer* was swallowed up, chariot and all, by a chasm? Or that the other war-leaders lie by the gates, their skulls shattered by stones? You have a choice: either vainly to rank your intelligence above that of Zeus, or to admit that it is right for the gods to destroy evil men. Anyone with any sense should love first his children, and then his parents and his country. He should strengthen rather than wreck his country, but an impulsive leader is just as dangerous for it as an impulsive seaman is for a ship. A wise man is one who chooses the right moment for inaction; foresight too is courage.

CHORUS. Zeus' punishment was sufficient; this arrogant insolence in you is unnecessary.

ADRASTUS. You complete and utter villain . . .

THESEUS. Quiet, Adrastus. Curb your tongue and wait till I have had my say. I am the object of this herald's mission, not you, and so it is for me to reply.

I shall respond first to the first point you made. As far as I am aware, Creon is not my master, nor are his resources greater than mine. I don't see, then, how he can compel Athens to do what he wants. The world will be turned upside down if we let ourselves be ordered about by him like this. This war is not being made by me; I didn't even march with the Argives to Cadmus' land. I think I'm perfectly justified in seeking, in conformity with pan-Hellenic law, to bury the bodies, since I did no harm to your city and initiated no death-dealing contest of arms with you. Is there anything wrong in this? Granted that you may have suffered at the hands of the Argives, but they have died for it. Your resistance to your enemies brought credit to yourselves and disgrace to them, and justice has been done. So you should now let the bodies be buried, and each part return to the place from where it first arose into the light of day—the soul to the bright sky, the body to the earth. For we are no more than tenants of the bodies we possess as our own, and finally the earth which nourished them must receive them back.

Do you think you are harming Argos in refusing the bodies burial? Far from it. When someone keeps the dead unburied and deprives them of their due rites, the whole of Greece is involved, because if this law is instituted, brave men will become cowards.* Although you came issuing terrible threats against me, does the prospect of the corpses being buried make you afraid? What do you think might happen? Are you afraid that after they are buried they may raze your city to the ground? Or that in the recesses of the earth they may father sons to come and take their revenge on you? But it's a foolish waste of breath for me to tell you that these fears are base and empty.

No, don't be so stupid. You should appreciate that we humans are beset with troubles, and that life is a struggle. Some men prosper now, some later, some in the past. Only the gods live a life of ease, in that they receive worship and honour from the unfortunate who hope to prosper, and are glorified by the fortunate who fear death. Anyone who appreciates this should put up with being wronged with relative equanimity, not with anger, and should commit only wrongs which will have no repercussions.

Well, then, how is it to be? Will you give us the dead bodies and let us bury them? After all, this is a sacred duty we are willing to take on. Otherwise, the consequences should by now be obvious to you: I shall come and I shall bury them by force of arms. I will not have it noised abroad in Greece that the ancient law of the gods came to me and the city of Pandion* only to be confounded.

CHORUS. Keep up your courage. As long as you maintain the light of justice you put yourself beyond the reach of all criticism.

HERALD. Shall I respond to what you say? It won't take long.*

THESEUS. By all means. (*Sarcastically*) It would be unlike you to keep silent.

HERALD. You'll never recover those men of Argos from our land.

THESEUS. Now it's my turn, if you don't mind, to respond to you.

HERALD. Go ahead. I can't refuse you your turn.

THESEUS. I shall remove the bodies from Thebes and bury them.

HERALD. But not before you've gambled on the outcome of war.

THESEUS. You won't be the first against whom I have undertaken such labours.

HERALD. So were you born a match for all?

THESEUS. Yes, for all who choose insolence, at any rate. I never make an example of decent men.

HERALD. You and your city have a habit of interfering in other people's business.

THESEUS. It's precisely because we take on a lot that we prosper a lot.

HERALD. Come, then. Our force of Sown Men is waiting to hurl you in the dust.

THESEUS. How could any warlike dash come from a serpent?*

HERALD. Experience will give you your answer. At the moment you're still a callow youth.

THESEUS. Your taunts aren't going to provoke me to anger. Now leave this land, and take with you the empty words you brought—empty, because we have got nowhere.

Exit the Theban HERALD.

I call on every man, foot-soldier or charioteer, to set out, and for horses to race to Cadmus' land, mouthpieces dripping with foam. For I shall march in person to the seven gates of Cadmus' city, my sharp sword in my hand; I shall be my own herald. I charge you, Adrastus, to stay here, so that your fortune remains separate from mine. For I have fresh cause for undertaking this expedition, with the help of my guardian deity, and I bring fresh war to Thebes. All I need is for those deities who respect justice to be on my side, since their support brings victory. Human courage is no good unless it has the backing of the gods.

Exeunt THESEUS, *Athenian herald, and attendants.*

The CHORUS *divides, and chants or sings until 633.*

SEMICHORUS A. You mothers, sorrowing for the sorry dead,
my innards are disturbed by pale fear . . .
SEMICHORUS B. What's this? What new thought are you trying to convey?
SEMICHORUS A. . . . for which way things will go for the army of Pallas.
SEMICHORUS B. Through fighting, you think, or negotiation?
SEMICHORUS A. The latter would be welcome. But what if the result
is bloody death in battle? What if Athens' streets
resound with the beating of breasts in grief?
Ah, me! What charges then will be brought against me?

SEMICHORUS B. But however exalted a man is by success, still the time will come
when fate will destroy him. This is what gives me good cheer.
SEMICHORUS A. The gods in your view, then, are just.
SEMICHORUS B. Yes, for in whose hands but theirs lie all our fates?
SEMICHORUS A. But I see how often the gods' designs differ from those of men.
SEMICHORUS B. That's because you're laid low by your former fear.
But justice summons justice, blood calls on blood,
and the gods give mortal men relief from pain,
since they control the limits of all things.

SEMICHORUS A. Why can't I leave the sacred waters of Callichorus
and go to the plains where fair towers rise?
SEMICHORUS B. If some god gave you wings
and to the twin-rivered city* you went,
you would know—ah, yes!—you'd know
the fortune of our loved ones.
SEMICHORUS A. What fate, what destiny awaits
the mighty lord of this land?

SEMICHORUS B. We call once more on the gods we have called on before, but this is the first refuge of faith in time of fear.

SEMICHORUS A. I call on Zeus, who sired a son on Inachus' daughter,
the heifer-girl, the foremother of our race,*
to look kindly on our city
and support her in her fight.

SEMICHORUS B. Bring back for the pyre from dishonour
the pride, the foundation of your city!

Enter MESSENGER.

MESSENGER. Women, I am here with plenty of good news. Not only have I myself been rescued (I should say that I was taken prisoner during the battle fought by the seven dead war-leaders by the river Dirce), but I bring news of Theseus' victory. To cut a long story short, I was a slave of Capaneus,* whom Zeus burnt to ashes with his fiery thunderbolt.

CHORUS. My very dear friend, it's good to hear of your return and the news about Theseus. If the Athenian army is safe too, all your news is welcome.

MESSENGER. The army is safe and has achieved what Adrastus intended to achieve with the Argive force he dispatched from the Inachus* and launched against Thebes.

CHORUS. What happened? How did Aegeus' son and his fellow warriors come to erect the victory trophy, sacred to Zeus? Tell us, please. A firsthand account is just what we need, since we weren't there.

MESSENGER. The sun's rays illuminated the earth and made everything clear to see as I stood on the tower by Electra's gate,* which afforded me a good view. I saw the Athenian army, which was divided into three sections. The foot-soldiers stretched up towards the Ismenian hill, as I heard it called, and the right wing was occupied by the king himself, the glorious son of Aegeus, and the troops stationed with him, natives of the ancient land of Cecrops.* Then there was Paralus,* wielding a spear, right by the spring of Ares.* The massed cavalry was arrayed on the outside edges of the army, and there were just as many of them as the infantry. And below the sacred tomb of Amphion* were the chariots. The Theban troops took up a position in front of the walls, with the corpses for which they were fighting located behind them. Armed horsemen faced horsemen, chariots faced war-chariots.

Theseus' herald spoke for all to hear as follows: 'Quiet, men! You Theban troops, quiet there, and listen! We have come for the bodies. Our intention is to bury them, in conformity with pan-Hellenic custom, but we have no desire for further bloodshed.' Creon made no reply through his herald to these words, but remained where he was, fully armed, silent. Then the shepherds of the war-chariots initiated the battle. They drove their chariots across to the opposing lines and dropped off their men-at-arms, who formed up and began to battle it out with their weapons, while the charioteers wheeled their horses round towards the fighting, back to the men-at-arms. Phorbas,* the commander of the Athenian horsemen, saw the mêlée in which the chariots were engaged, and so did the officers in charge of the Theban cavalry; they added their might to the battle, and now one side, now the other had the upper hand. I saw the action firsthand; I didn't have to be told about it, because the struggle in which the chariots and the men-at-arms were involved was taking place right where I was. I don't know which of the many tragic sights I saw there I should recount first. Should I tell about the vast quantity of dust that rose up into the sky? The men dragged bouncing in their reins? The rivers of red blood flowing, as some fell and others were hurled headlong from their shattered chariots to the ground and died near the wreckage of their chariots?

When Creon noticed that our side was winning, thanks to our horsemen, he grasped his shield and advanced before his men lost heart. But Theseus' cause was not undone by any hesitation: straight away he snatched up his gleaming weapons and charged. The two main armies clashed together in the middle of the field, and set about killing and being killed. Orders were bellowed out to one another along the line: 'Strike now!' and 'Stand firm against the Athenians!' The company of those who had come to manhood from the serpent's teeth proved a formidable adversary; they were beginning to turn our left wing, while on our right the Theban troops had been defeated and were in flight. The contest hung in the balance, but this was the moment when our commander showed his admirable qualities. Not satisfied merely with victory on the right, he went over to those of his troops who were hard pressed and called out an appeal which resounded all over the land: 'Men, Pallas' city is undone if you fail to contain here the Sown Men, for all their staunch prowess!' This boosted the morale of the whole Athenian army. Theseus seized his fearsome weapon, his mace from Epidaurus,* and set to on all sides; his whirling club snapped necks like stalks and harvested the helmets on their heads.

The enemy only just managed to turn and flee. As for me, I shouted for joy, danced a jig, and clapped my hands. The Thebans were making for the city gates. The streets were filled with the shouts and wailing of young and old, and they flocked to the temples in their fear. But although he could have entered, Theseus stopped at the walls, declaring that he had not come to sack the city, but to demand the return of the dead. I tell you, he is the very model of the generals we should choose: he is brave in the face of danger, and he loathes insolence in a people who, when they are faring well, strive to climb to the topmost rung of the ladder of success,* and so destroy the prosperity they could have enjoyed.

CHORUS. I never thought the day would come! Now I believe that the gods exist, and I feel some relief from my misfortunes, since the Argives have met with the punishment they deserved.

ADRASTUS. Zeus, why do people attribute intelligence to us poor human beings, when we depend on you and our actions are just what you happen to want us to do? There was a time when we regarded Argos as invincible, thanks to the size of our population and the might of our fighting men. And so, when Eteocles was ready to be reconciled with us,* to enter into a treaty, we spurned his offer—and this caused our ruin. But then the Theban people, like a poor man who has suddenly come into possession of wealth, let success go to their heads, and in their mindless arrogance they in their turn have now been ruined. Oh, the stupidity of humans, who aim too high and, despite the frequency and harshness of the penalties for this, refuse to listen to their friends' advice, but learn only from events! And how stupid cities can be, when they could negotiate their way out of trouble, but choose slaughter rather than dialogue as their means of achieving their goals. But why do I bother with these reflections? I'd like to hear how you came to be saved. Afterwards, I'll have further questions for you.

MESSENGER. When the city was disturbed by the chaos of war I left through the gate by which the army was entering.

ADRASTUS. And have you brought back the corpses for which the battle was fought?*

MESSENGER. Yes, at any rate those who were in command of the seven glorious companies.

ADRASTUS. What do you mean? Where are the rest of the dead, the mass of common soldiers?

MESSENGER. They've been buried in the glens of Cithaeron.

ADRASTUS. On this side of the mountain or on the far side? And who buried them?

MESSENGER. Theseus, by the shady hill of Eleutherae.*

ADRASTUS. Where did you leave the bodies he didn't bury?

MESSENGER. Not far away. All that effort is close to its fruition.

ADRASTUS. I suppose the slaves hated bringing them from the field of death?

MESSENGER. The job wasn't given to any slaves.

ADRASTUS. ⟨So did Theseus himself show them this signal honour?⟩†

MESSENGER. You'd say so if you'd been there when he cared for the bodies.

ADRASTUS. Did he himself wash clean the poor men's wounds?

MESSENGER. Yes, and he made up their biers and dressed their bodies.

ADRASTUS. What an awful and demeaning task!

MESSENGER. How could there be anything demeaning for a person in other people's misfortunes?

ADRASTUS (*overcome by distress*). Oh, how much better it would be for me to have died alongside them!

MESSENGER. There's no point in crying, and you're making these women here weep too.

ADRASTUS. You may think so, but in fact it is they who are my teachers. But I'm off to greet the dead with a salute and sing songs of lamentation in which I may express my affection for those whose loss has brought on the desolation I mourn in my sorrow. For human life is the only thing which, once lost, may never be retrieved; there are always ways to make money.

Exit ADRASTUS *and* MESSENGER.

CHORUS (*sings*). Some things have gone well, some badly.
True, both Athens and her generals
have gained the honour of glorious victory,
but for me to see my son's body is very hard.
And yet I never thought the day would come,
and to see him will be wonderful—
and that is the fiercest pain of all.

Would that Time, ancient father of days,
had left me unwed to this day.
What use to me were sons?
Once I'd have dreaded the terrible pain
of never finding a husband,
but now I see that the most certain evil
is losing beloved sons.

But look! Here are the bodies of our dead sons! The pain of it!
I wish I could die with them and go down to Hades by their side.

Enter ADRASTUS, *with attendants carrying the seven bodies.* ADRASTUS *and the* CHORUS *chant or sing until 836.*

ADRASTUS. Sing out, sing out your lamentation, mothers,
for those who have died and gone to Hades,
in response to the lamentation you hear me sing!
CHORUS. O children—ah, how hard it is for loving mothers
to address you thus!—I call on you in your death!
ADRASTUS. Oh! Oh!
CHORUS. Yes, I cry out in my woe!
ADRASTUS. Alas!
CHORUS. ⟨. . .⟩†
ADRASTUS. Oh, the pain we feel!
CHORUS. The most savage of all possible pains!
ADRASTUS. O city of Argos, do you not see what has become of me?
CHORUS. They see me too, bereft of my child.

ADRASTUS. Bring forth, bring forth the bloody bodies of the wretched dead

who died an unworthy death at the hands of unworthy men,
among whom the contest was fought out to its appointed end.

CHORUS. Let me take my son in my arms!
Let me cradle him close to my breast!

ADRASTUS. Here! Here!

CHORUS. Yes, my woes are weight enough!

ADRASTUS. Alas!

CHORUS. Is your dirge not for us, their mothers?

ADRASTUS. You can hear it is.

CHORUS. Your tears are for the plight of mothers and sons alike.

ADRASTUS. I wish the Theban ranks had destroyed me in the dust!

CHORUS. And that I had never been taken to share my husband's bed!

ADRASTUS. Look upon an ocean of pain,
you poor mothers of these men!

CHORUS. We have raked our cheeks with our nails,
poured ashes on our heads.*

ADRASTUS. Ah, alas! Alas! May the earth engulf me!
May the storm-winds rend me!
May the flame of Zeus' fire descend upon me!*

CHORUS. Bitter was the wedding you saw,
Bitter the oracle you heard from Phoebus.
The grim curse has left the house of Oedipus*
and torments us instead!

Enter THESEUS, with freed Argive prisoners.

THESEUS. I was going to ask you this before, Adrastus, but I didn't want to interrupt you while you were pouring out your woes for the dead warriors; but I'll ask you now, if I may: how did these men come by their signal reputation for courage? Your knowledge of them makes you better equipped than anyone to answer this question, so do please tell these young men from our city.† But there's one question I won't ask you, which is who each of them grappled with in the course of the battle—that is, which of the enemy inflicted the wounds each of them received. That is a ridiculous question to ask; the answer is no more than idle chatter, of no help at all to either listener or speaker. For in a battle situation, with missiles flying thick and fast before one's eyes, who can say with certainty who is brave? I couldn't ask such a question, nor could I believe anyone who went so far as to answer it. When faced with the enemy one is scarcely able to see to immediate emergencies.

ADRASTUS. All right, I'll tell you. I'm delighted that you give me the opportunity to say what I'd like to say—which will be nothing but the truth and their due—in praise of my friends.* For I saw the acts of courage, too extraordinary to describe, with which they hoped to capture Thebes.† Do you see the one who lies shattered by the violence of the bolt that struck him? That is Capaneus. He was a man of substance, but was the last person to let his wealth make him haughty. His humility was that of a poor man, and he avoided people who despised mere sufficiency and took excessive pride in the feasts they could lay on, because it was his opinion that virtue lay not in filling one's stomach, but in being content with a moderate amount. He was a true friend to his friends—and they were few—whether they were with him or not. He had an honest disposition, he was politely spoken, and he never acted abusively towards his slaves or fellow citizens.

In the second place, I turn to Eteoclus,* an excellent young man, but in a different way from Capaneus. He was not well off, but there was no one who was held in higher esteem in Argos. His friends would often offer him money, but he always refused to accept it in case he should become slavishly attached to riches. He hated transgressors, but not their cities, on the grounds that although a bad leader may give a city a bad reputation, it is not actually to blame.

Third there's Hippomedon, and this is what he was like. Even at an early age he was tough enough to resist the pleasures offered by the Muses and the easy life. He lived in the countryside and enjoyed devoting himself to hard activities which would develop courage. So, for instance, he used to go out hunting, he loved riding, and he used to practise archery, because he wanted to be physically useful to his city.

Next comes Parthenopaeus, the son of the huntress Atalanta, an outstandingly good-looking man. Although he was Arcadian, he came to the river Inachus and was brought up in Argos. During his formative years there, his chief characteristic was the one foreign residents of a place should have—that is, he never made a nuisance of himself, was never offensive to the city, and wasn't stubbornly contentious in an argument, which is the worst fault anyone can have, whether citizen or foreigner. He took his place in the ranks and fought in defence of Argos as if he had been born there; he was glad when the city did well, and upset by her failures.†

As for Tydeus, it will not take long to sing his praises. He was not an outstanding orator, but he was a skilled and highly innovative sophist of war.† What I have said should be enough to dispel any surprise you may harbour, Theseus, that these men had the courage to die before the battlements of Thebes, because a sense of honour is the outcome of a good upbringing. Any man who has been trained in virtue is ashamed of cowardice. Courage is teachable,* for after all a child can be taught to speak and to take in things he doesn't yet understand. And the things one learns as a child are invariably preserved all the way up to old age. Therefore, train your children well.

CHORUS (*sings*). Ah, my son! I bore you in my womb, endured the pain
of childbirth, and reared you—all for you to suffer misfortune.
And now, alas!, Hades holds the fruit of my toils,
and I have no one to look after me in my old age,
for all that I bore a son. Ah, poor me!

THESEUS. What's more, the gods seized Oecles' noble son* alive and took him down to the innermost recesses of the earth, along with his war-chariot—a clear sign of the honour in which they hold him. And as for Polynices, Oedipus' son, I can truthfully tell his praises, because he stayed with me during his period of self-imposed exile from Thebes, before he made his way to Argos. But do you know what I want you to do for these bodies?

ADRASTUS. No, I don't—but you can be sure that I shall do as you suggest.*

THESEUS. As for Capaneus, struck by Zeus' thunderbolt . . .

ADRASTUS. Do you want to bury him separately, on the grounds that his body is sacred?*

THESEUS. Yes. But you can burn all the others on a single pyre.

ADRASTUS. Where will you put the tomb of Capaneus here, once he has been dealt with separately?

THESEUS. I'll erect it here, by the temple.

ADRASTUS. Well, this is a job my slaves can take care of straight away.

THESEUS. And I'll take care of the rest of them. Let's take up the bodies and go.

ADRASTUS (*to the CHORUS*). Women, sorrowful mothers of these men, approach the corpses.

THESEUS. No, Adrastus, that's an inappropriate idea.

ADRASTUS. Why? What's wrong with mothers laying hands on their children?

THESEUS. It would devastate them to see how disfigured these men are.

ADRASTUS. Yes, the corpses' bloody wounds would be a distressing sight.

THESEUS. So why do you want to upset them?

ADRASTUS. I take your point. (*To the CHORUS*) You must be patient. Theseus is right. After they've been consigned to the fire, you can collect the bones.

O miserable mortals! Why do you take up spears and make bloody war on one another? Stop this behaviour! Put an end to these trials of strength, and instead take care of your cities as men of peace alongside men of peace. Life is short, and we should make it as easy as possible to get through it without trouble.

Exeunt ADRASTUS, THESEUS, and the sons to attend to the cremations.

CHORUS (*sings*). No longer blessed with offspring, robbed
of my son,
the happiness of Argive women with sons is not for me.
The midwife Artemis* has no words of cheer for the childless.
Life is a burden to me now. I am driven here and there,
like a cloud by grim winter storms.

We seven mothers bore, to our misery, the seven
most illustrious young men Argos had ever seen.
And now childless, robbed of my son, I grow old
in utter misery, numbered neither among the living
nor among the dead, my fate set apart from both.

Tears are all that remain to me. My home contains sad reminders of my son—
strands of hair cut in mourning, ungarlanded locks, libations to the dead,
songs that will never find favour with golden-haired Apollo.*
Every morning I shall be awoken by my tears, and my weeping
will for ever soak the clothes that drape my breast.

EVADNE appears on high above the backdrop, dressed as a bride.

Look! There's Capaneus' resting-place, his sacred tomb,
and outside the temple Theseus is giving the dead their funerals.
And there, near by, is glorious Evadne, daughter of lord Iphis,
wife of this man the thunderbolt blasted. Where is she going?
Why is she standing there, on the high cliff that soars above this temple?

EVADNE (*sings*). What light, what radiant light the sun and moon
drove that day across the sky, ⟨ . . . ⟩†
when at my far-famed wedding the city of Argos†
raised my heart as high as a tower in happiness,
and the heart of my groom, bronze-armoured Capaneus.
In frenzied haste I have run here from my house,
for I desire to share his funeral pyre and his tomb,
in order to end in death the wearisome burden of living.
For no death is more sweet than dying with the dead you hold dear,
and I pray that fate may grant me such an ending!

CHORUS. Look, there's the pyre! You can see it close to where you're standing. It's a treasury, sacred to Zeus,* and on it lies your husband, who was struck down by the bright thunderbolt.

EVADNE (*sings*). Here where I stand I see my death! May fortune assist my fall!
Fair fame I shall win with a sudden leap from this rock
into the flames. In the blazing fire I shall join my body
with that of my precious husband. With skin close to skin

I shall reach my marriage chamber in Persephone's halls.
Never shall I betray him in his death by staying alive on this earth!
Bring on the wedding-torch, bring on my marriage.
I pray that the virtue of my marriage may be seen by Argos' young,
and that my husband may be fused with the guileless spirit of a noble wife.

CHORUS. Look! Your aged father Iphis is approaching. He cannot anticipate the unwelcome news you have for him; when he hears it, he will be devastated.

Enter IPHIS, attended by slaves.

IPHIS. In my old age I find myself sharing your misery, women. Two painful family concerns have brought me here. First, I've come to take on board my ship* the body of my son Eteoclus, who died at Thebes, and carry him back to his homeland. Second, I'm looking for my daughter, Capaneus' wife, who dashed out of sight away from home and longs to join her husband in death. She had been confined indoors before, but under pressure from the troubles that are currently besetting us I relieved those who were watching her of their duties and she immediately left. I think it most likely that she has come here: can you tell me if you've seen her?

EVADNE. Why are you asking these women? Here I am, father, perched like a bird on the cliff, hovering in my misery over Capaneus' pyre.

IPHIS. Daughter, what spirit, what mission brought you here? Why did you steal away from home and come to this land?

EVADNE. If I told you what I was planning, you'd be angry, father. I don't want to tell you.

IPHIS. What do you mean? I'm your father. Don't I have a right to know what's going on in your life?*

EVADNE. You lack the insight to judge what I have in mind.

IPHIS. Why are you dressed in these clothes?

EVADNE. These robes of mine have a glorious significance, father.

IPHIS. You certainly don't look like a wife in mourning for her husband.

EVADNE. That's because I've dressed for another purpose.

IPHIS. Then why have you come here, right by the funeral pyre?

EVADNE. I have come here a glorious victor.

IPHIS. What victory are you talking about? Tell me, please.

EVADNE. Victory over every woman who has ever lived.

IPHIS. For your skill at Athena's crafts,* or for the soundness of your judgement?

EVADNE. Thanks to my virtue. For I shall lie in death with my husband.

IPHIS. What are you saying? What does this pernicious riddle mean?

EVADNE. I'm going to dash myself on to this pyre, where Capaneus' body lies.

IPHIS. Daughter, don't say this in front of all these people!

EVADNE. My intention is precisely that all Argos shall know what I do.

IPHIS. No! I won't let you do it!

EVADNE. It makes no difference: you can't reach up and grab hold of me. And so I let my body fall. For all your disapproval, it is just what I and the husband with whom I shall burn want.

EVADNE throws herself on to Capaneus' funeral pyre, as it were behind the backdrop.

CHORUS. Oh, Evadne! This is an appalling thing you have done!

IPHIS. Too much pain, women of Argos! This is the end of me.

CHORUS. After all your terrible suffering, can you bear to see this cruel deed?

IPHIS. There is no one in the world more wretched than I.

CHORUS. I feel for you, old man. Oedipus' curse has descended on to you and my poor city.

IPHIS. Oh, why is it impossible for people to have a second youth and then grow old again? If something is not right in our domestic affairs, we can rethink the situation and set things right, but we cannot change the course of our lives. If we could repeat our youth and old age, in our second lifetime we could correct any mistakes we made. In my case, for instance, the sight of others with children made me want children of my own, until I began to be sick with longing for them. But if I had found myself in the position of experiencing what it's like for a father to lose his children, I would never have found myself in the wretched state I am now in.

Anyway, what should I do now in my misery? Shall I go home—only to gaze upon empty rooms and the prospect of a helpless life? Perhaps I ought to go to Capaneus' house instead. There was certainly a time, when my daughter here was alive, when there was nothing I liked more, but now she is dead. I remember how she used to take my head in her hands and pull on my beard for a kiss. There is nothing a father enjoys more in his old age than a daughter. Males have too much self-esteem and lack the sweetness of disposition to give and take caresses. (*To his slaves*) Take me home, then, quickly now! Give me to the darkness, where I can starve my aged body to death! What good will it do me to collect my daughter's bones?

Old age is such a struggle! I hate it! And I hate everyone who seeks to lengthen his life with food and drink and magic charms, and tries to avoid death by diverting water into his dried-up channel. Such people are a burden on the earth; they should die and make way for the next generation.

Exit IPHIS.

Enter the second Chorus of SONS,* *carrying urns containing their fathers' ashes and bones. The Choruses of Argive mothers and sons chant or sing to 1164.*

CHORUS. Ah, now the bones of our dead sons are being brought here.
Hold me up, slaves! I am weak and old,
exhausted by grief for my son. Long years have I lived,
and many cares have worn me down. What greater pain
could there be for mortals than having to see their children dead?

SONS. From the funeral pyre, sorrowful mother, I bring them—
I bring my father's remains, a burden made heavy by grief,
for this one small urn holds all that is dear to me.
CHORUS. Oh, my son, you bring tears for the mother of the dead

and little enough ash to replace bodies once famed in Mycenae.*

SONS. You are childless, childless, and in my misery, a fatherless orphan,
I inherit an empty house, given not by the hands of him who fathered me.

CHORUS. Oh, where now is the pain endured for my son? Where is the joy of his birth?
Where is the mother's milk and the nights spent without sleep,
caring for him? Where are the loving kisses given and received?

SONS. Gone, they are lost and gone. Alas for my father!

CHORUS. The bright sky holds them now, their bodies reduced to ashes
by the fire. They have winged their way to Hades.

SONS. Father, do you hear your son lamenting? Will I ever take up my shield
and repay your murder? Would that this may come to pass for your son!†
If the gods will it, justice may yet come for my father.

CHORUS. This wrong is not yet asleep. Alas for my misfortune!
Do I not already have enough cause for tears, for grief?

SONS. Asopus' gleaming waters will receive me some day at the head
of an army of bronze-armed Argives to avenge my father's death.
I still seem to see you, father, before my very eyes . . .

CHORUS. . . . placing a kiss on your precious cheek . . .

SONS. . . . but gone are your words of encouragement, borne away on the wind.

CHORUS. Sorrow he has bequeathed to both of us—to me, his mother,
and the pain of your father's loss will never leave you.

SONS. The weight of this pain is enough to kill me.

CHORUS. Bring me the urn, that I may clasp the ashes to my breast.

SONS. Oh, how the horror of your words affects me and brings tears to my eyes!

CHORUS. Gone, you are gone, my son! Never again will I see you, the precious pride and joy of your mother!

Enter THESEUS and ADRASTUS.

THESEUS. Adrastus! Women of Argos! You can see these young men here bearing in their hands the remains of their noble fathers, whose bodies I recovered. To them we—the city of Athens and I—present these remains. But I charge you to preserve the memory of what has happened in gratitude for all the good I have done you and to remind these young men likewise to respect this city of Athens and to pass down from generation to generation the record of all the benefits you have received. And may Zeus and the gods in heaven witness the kinds of favours we granted you on your visit.

ADRASTUS. Theseus, we recognize all the kindness you have shown Argos and the favours you have performed for her in her hour of need, and our gratitude will never fade. You have behaved nobly towards us and we owe you the same in return.

THESEUS. Is there anything else you would like me to do for you before you go?

ADRASTUS. No, I bid you farewell—for faring well is what you and your city deserve.

THESEUS. It shall be so. And may you do just as well yourself.

ATHENA appears above the backdrop.

ATHENA. Theseus, I am Athena! Listen to my instructions and learn how you can improve your situation† by carrying them out. You are not simply to relinquish these bones to these young men here and let them take them back to Argos. In repayment for all your efforts and those of Athens, you should first extract a solemn promise. As their king, Adrastus here has the authority to take an oath on behalf of all the Argives, and he is to swear as follows: that Argos will never undertake an armed invasion of this land, and will take up arms against anyone else who attempts to do so.* If they break their word and march on the city, pray that terrible ruin is visited upon the Argive land. Now listen to my instructions regarding the vessel over which the victims' throats are to be cut. At home you have a bronze-footed tripod—the one which, after razing Troy to the ground and before setting out on another task, Heracles once told you to set up at the Pythian altar.* After you have cut the throats of three sheep and caught the blood in this vessel, engrave the oath on the inside of the hollow part of the tripod and then give the tripod for safe keeping to the god whose domain is Delphi, to commemorate the oath and to make all Greece bear witness to it. And you are to bury the sharp-bladed knife you use to cut the victims and inflict the fatal wound on them deep within the earth by the funeral pyres of the seven heroes. If the Argives ever march on Athens, the sight of this place will fill them with fear and give them an evil journey home. Once you have done all this you can escort the bodies away from Athens. And you are to leave the place by the Isthmian crossroads,* where the bodies were purified by fire, just as it is, a precinct sacred to the god.

So much for what I have to say to you. Here are my words to the sons of the fallen Argives. When you reach maturity you shall avenge your fathers' deaths with the sack of the Ismenian city. Aegialeus,* in the vigour of your youth you shall take your father's place as military commander, and the son of Tydeus, whom his father named Diomedes, will come from Aetolia to help you. As soon as beards start to darken your chins, you are to raise an army of bronze-rich Argives and march against the fortifications of Thebes, city of seven gates. They will rue the day you come, lion-cubs, now fully grown, and sack their city. This is how it shall be. Future generations in Greece will name you the Successors and make you the subject of songs. What an expedition you will make, with the help of the god!

THESEUS. Athena, my lady, I shall do as you say, for it is you who guide me and keep me from error. I shall bind Adrastus here with oaths. But I pray that you may keep me from error, since as long as you look kindly on the city we shall manage the future in safety.

CHORUS. Let us go, Adrastus. Let's make our pledge to Theseus here and to his city. They deserve our respect for all their efforts on our behalf.

Exeunt both Choruses, ADRASTUS, THESEUS, *and* ATHENA.

EXPLANATORY NOTES

ION

1 *s.d.*: Hermes, who gives details of his ancestry in 1–4, probably appears on the stage, not on top of the stage building where Athena will appear at 1549. He doubtless wears his usual attributes, winged shoes, a staff with two snakes represented as a figure of 8 at the top, and a large-brimmed hat. In Homer's *Odyssey*, as here, he is the messenger of Zeus. More generally, he communicates between gods and men (4).

1–2 *Atlas, whose adamantine back wears out the sky*: Atlas was one of the Giants who fought against Zeus, the king of the gods. As his punishment, he was turned into a mountain (Mount Atlas in North Africa) and condemned to carry the vault of the sky on his shoulders.

2–3 *fathered Maia by one of the goddesses*: the goddess was Pleione.

5 *Delphi*: here Phoebus Apollo (he can be called by either name or by both), god of prophecy, had his greatest cult-centre. His sanctuary, set on a dizzying cliff on the slopes of Mount Parnassus in central Greece, was considered to be at the centre of the world. A round navel-stone (5, 222), a copy of which survives in the Museum at Delphi, marked the spot where two eagles, sent by Zeus from opposite edges of the earth, met and thus established its central location.

Apollo did not in fact chant his oracles and prophecies himself (6–7). He worked through his priestess, the Pythia. Crowned with laurel, she sat on a tripod (a three-legged stand), became possessed by the god, and prophesied under divine inspiration.

8 *a rather famous city in Greece*: this is Athens, the main city of Attica, which was named after its patron goddess, Pallas Athena. Pallas' hill (12) is the Acropolis, on which her great temple, the Parthenon, stands. On this hill was a colossal bronze statue of Athena the Champion made by Pheidias. Her spear had a gilded point (9) which was visible from a considerable distance. The cave where Apollo raped Creusa is below the Long Rocks (13), the cliffs on the northern side of the Acropolis. The theatre of Dionysus, where *Ion* was first performed, is on the south-eastern slopes of this hill.

9 *Erechtheus*: the father of this Attic hero was Erichthonius (21),

the son of Gaia (Earth) after her impregnation by Hephaestus' semen which fell on her after his failed rape of Athena (Eratosthenes, *Catasterismi* 13).

17–18 *in which she and the god had lain together*: 'the place was chosen to remind Apollo of his obligations which he duly met' (*Ion*, ed. K. H. Lee (Warminster, 1997), n. at 17).

19 *the rounded hollow of a crib*: the standard Greek–English dictionary suggests, somewhat bizarrely, that this is a pram! In fact, it is a round wickerwork basket with a hinged lid. It is described at 37ff. and 1337ff.

23 *Aglaurus' daughters*: Aglaurus married Cecrops, king of Athens. Their three daughters were Aglaurus, Herse, and Pandrosus. The names all suggest dew, meaning 'the sparkling one', 'dew', and 'the all-bedewed one' respectively.

25 *golden snake-ornaments*: snake-ornaments of this kind are common in Etruscan and Pompeian jewellery. They prove of importance twice later in the play, at 1427ff. and 1575ff.

29 *whose roots lie in the land where they live*: the reference is to the Athenians' ancestor Erichthonius (father of Erechtheus—see n. at 9) who was born from the soil of Attica. (His identity later fused with that of Erechtheus.) Athenians were also proud of the fact that they had occupied Attica from time immemorial.

35–6 *I'll take care of him after that*: 'Apollo's speech ends with an emphatic statement of his paternity and his interest in what is to happen. This will be important to the audience in the face of his apparent neglect in the course of the play' (Lee, n. at 35–6).

36 *Loxias*: a name for Apollo which occurs twenty-three times in this play. It may mean 'slanting', which would be appropriate both to his 'slanting' journey through the sky as the sun-god and to his enigmatic oracles as the god of prophecy.

53 *when he reached manhood*: how old is Ion? This is an important question in a play which deals with his journey to adulthood. Though physically mature, he is extremely inexperienced in the ways of the world. Lee comments (n. at 53) that 'his youthfulness is stressed repeatedly (cf. 57, 780, 794, 1034, 1218, 1132), and, despite the important duties he has, we should imagine him as no older than 20 and in a period of transition'.

58 *Xuthus*: this figure, whose non-Athenian ancestry is stressed (63–4)—it is to prove a highly significant motif—had been banished by his brothers and become a soldier of fortune.

60 *Euboea*: a long thin island to the east of Attica and Boeotia.

62 *his reward was marriage with Creusa*: the marriage has been imposed on Creusa because of Xuthus' services to Athens in war.

71–2 *once inside his mother's house and recognized by Creusa*: in fact, mother and son will recognize each other at Delphi before the end of the play. Apollo's programme does not go according to plan.

74 *Ion, the founding father of Asia*: i.e. the eponymous founder of *Ion*ia, the collective name for the Greek towns and islands on the central part of the west coast of Asia. At the time *Ion* was written, the Athenians controlled this area and they shared with its inhabitants a common Ionian culture.

76–7 *Well, I had better . . . to the boy*: Hermes, who is to play no further part in the drama, hides in order to see what will happen. Does he suspect that the programme he has himself laid out in his prologue will not go altogether to plan (see n. at 71–2)?

80 *laurel branches*: the laurel is commonly associated with Apollo.

80–1 *Here Ion comes . . . the name that awaits him*: 'it is appropriate that Hermes in role of herald proclaims the boy's name' (Lee, n. at 80–1). The name means 'the one who comes'.

82 *Here is the gleaming four-horse chariot!*: here, as frequently in classical literature (cf. 41), the Sun-god is portrayed as driving a chariot of fire drawn by four horses.

89 *desert incense*: incense either from Arabia, a region of deserts, or dry as distinct from oily.

95 *the Castalian spring*: all who came to Delphi with a religious objective purified themselves by washing all or part of themselves in this spring, which is reached before the entrance to the sanctuary.

103–6 *with boughs of laurel . . . dampen the ground with sprinkled water*: Ion is probably using a broom of laurel shoots bound together by the garlands. One can still see people sweeping wetted pavements in exactly the same way as Ion.

109 *when I had no mother or father to look after me*: a wonderful ironical touch, the first of many in the play.

122 *the sun's swift wing*: cf n. at 82.

125 *Paean*: this is an address to Apollo in his role as healer.

127 *son of Leto*: Leto gave birth to Apollo (and his sister Artemis) on the island of Delos, supporting herself on the branches of a palm tree (Theognis 1.5). The birth was accompanied by the singing of swans (Euripides, *Iphigenia among the Taurians* 1104–5,

Callimachus, *Hymn to Delos* 249–52) on a circular lake (which has been drained by French archaeologists).

128–30 *Phoebus, out of reverence . . . count the toil fair*: compare, from George Herbert's *The Elixir*:

> A servant with this clause
> Makes drudgery divine;
> Who sweeps a room as for Thy laws
> Makes that and th' action fine.

153–4 *Aha! Here they come now!*: 'it is early morning; so the birds are beginning to come' (*Ion*, ed. A. S. Owen (Oxford, 1939), n. at 154). Then as now, bird droppings were a problem for buildings and sculptures. The Chorus-leader in Aristophanes' *Birds* refers to 'crescents', metal umbrellas fixed over the heads of statues to protect them from birds (1114).

158–9 *Herald of Zeus*: i.e. an eagle (Homer, *Iliad* 24.293).

167 *the lake of Delos*: see n. at 127.

171 *Another bird of some kind*: 'the bird is not named, but is most likely the swallow, which arrives in Greece in March, the month of [the dramatic festival of] the Great Dionysia, when the play was probably performed' (Owen, n. at 171).

174–6 *by the swirling Alpheus / or in the sacred grove on the Isthmus*: i.e. near Zeus' temple at Olympia on the river Alpheus or the temple of Poseidon on the Isthmus of Corinth at Isthmia, beside which there stood a pine grove. Owen notes, sourly but truthfully (n. at 174–5), that the 'ministrant of Apollo does not seem to mind if the shrines of other gods are defiled by the birds, nor even what happens in Apollo's own shrine in Delos (167)'.

183 *s.d.*: the Chorus consists of fifteen of Creusa's slave-women. It looks as if Euripides' own imagination played a considerable part in their description of the representations on the temple. Recent scholarship has observed that 'both the scenes with the monsters and the gigantomachy [the revolt of the Giants against the gods] impress on the audience the struggle between Olympian, civilizing powers and monstrous earth-born figures which represent violence and uncultivated brutality'. In the play as a whole, Euripides deals with 'the struggle within humans, especially those whose outlook and behaviour are conditioned by blood and heritage, to find an equilibrium between violent, darker tendencies and acceptance of a higher order' (Lee, n. at 184–236).

Vivid visual representations are a major feature of the play. See, most notably, the tapestries described at 1141 ff.

188–9 *twin faces gleam with fair-eyed light*: i.e. (probably) the two pediments of the temple reflect the early morning light.

191–2 *The son of Zeus is slaying the Lernaean Hydra*: the Hydra, which lived at Lerna near Argos, had between five and a hundred heads. These Heracles cut off 'with a golden sword' (perhaps represented in gilded bronze fitted into the stone-work) while his nephew Iolaus cauterized the wounds (194–200), thereby preventing the heads from growing back again as they otherwise would have done.

196–7 *while at work on my loom*: were such stories told as they work, or were they—as the Greek could also mean—woven into the fabric?

204 *a three-bodied fire-breathing monster*: Bellerophon, riding on the winged horse Pegasus, killed the monstrous Chimaera, the fire-breathing compound of a snake, a lion, and a goat.

209–10 *against Enceladus her shield with its Gorgon heads*: Enceladus was one of the Giants (cf. n. at 183); the Gorgons were the snake-haired women whose gaze turned men to stone. Perseus decapitated the most famous of them, Medusa.

212–13 *the mighty thunderbolt, flaming at both ends*: the thunderbolt was Zeus' weapon. It was commonly represented this way, especially in sculpture.

215 *Minas*: one of the Giants.

216–18 *unwarlike though it is*: Bromius (= the Roarer) is the god of wine, Dionysus or Bacchus; the Bacchants are his followers; the Earth's children are the Giants; the ivy-entwined wand is the thyrsus, a rod of fennel in which ivy is held fast by a pine cone. In Euripides' *Bacchae*, it proves to be a violent missile.

226 *a honey-cake*: a batter-like mixture of barley, honey, and milk.

252–4 *Oh, how wretched . . . ruin us?*: 'Creusa's agitation is expressed in the accumulation of clipped ejaculations and perplexed questions' (Lee, n. at 252–4)

264–368 *In fact, that . . . suffers in her misfortune*: this section is in *stichomythia*, the dramatic convention by which characters address each other in single lines. It is a device particularly well suited to violent argument, but here, in what is in fact the longest stichomythia extant, it proves finely sensitive in its suggestion of the uncomprehended closeness between mother and son. Contrastingly, it is used in 517–62 to convey the polarized feelings and language of the two speakers and in 934–1028 it proves an expressive vehicle for interrogation and gradual revelation.

269 *And was it Athena who raised him up out of the ground?*: Earth handed over the baby Erichthonius to Athena, who had rejected Hephaestus' advances, to bring up. See n. at 9.

271 *Are the traditional paintings correct?*: there is 'a small terra-cotta group of the early fifth century in Berlin . . . in which the Earth goddess gives the babe to Athena, who is reaching out her arms to it, while Cecrops with serpent-tail is nearby' (Owen, n. at 271).

278 *Yes, he hardened . . . country*: Erechtheus sacrificed his daughters to guarantee success in the war against Eleusis. Euripides wrote a play on this subject, his *Erechtheus*, a substantial amount of which survives.

281 *And is it true that the earth opened up and swallowed your father?*: though Erechtheus defeated the Eleusinians, Poseidon, his father, in an earthquake, struck the acropolis with his trident and Erechtheus was swallowed up—as befitted his autochthonous birth—in the earth.

285 *the Pythian lightning*: 'the numinous character of the place and its continued link with Apollo is noted by Ion' (Lee, n. at 285). This is in fact a puzzling line. Owen (n. at 285) observes that it 'was customary on three days and three nights each month to watch for lightnings, which appeared at Harma on Mt Parnes, and, when they appeared, an embassy was sent to Delphi. Strabo (9.2.404) tells us that the place of outlook was . . . nowhere near the Long [Rocks].' No doubt poetic licence overrules geography here.

298 *gaining my dowry as a reward for his help in the war*: by marrying Creusa, Xuthus gained rule over Athens. 'Are we meant to see in Creusa's fulsome description of herself resentment at her status as a gift to a helpful foreigner?' (Lee, n. at 298).

300 *Trophonius*: Trophonius was a Boeotian seer whose oracle was 15 miles from Delphi. 'By allowing Xuthus to consult Trophonius, Euripides neatly achieves two ends: Creusa and Ion are able to meet alone, and Xuthus gives Creusa the advance information that they will not return childless from Delphi, thus deepening the reversal of expectation when the Chorus tell her that she will never have a child' (Lee, n. at 300).

318–19 *And which woman . . . brought me up*: 'Creusa's question shows her deep anxiety about never having reared her child (cf. 963, 1492f.), and her interruption to Ion's answer shows her eagerness to discover what she failed to do for her own child' (Lee, n. at 319–20).

338 *One of my friends*: 'the device of the fictitious friend standing for oneself goes back to the false tales of the *Odyssey* (cf. 18.300 ff.)' (Lee, n. at 338).

359 *Alas! Her misfortune and my pain are so similar!*: i.e. she has no child and he has no mother.

366 *the tripod on which he sits is open to all Greeks*: the oracle at Delphi, which may have dated from the eighth century BCE, was of international importance. At the time *Ion* was written, the oracle was thought to be pro-Spartan and therefore anti-Athenian. It was believed that it had prophesied that the Spartans would win the Peloponnesian war (431–404 BCE—waged between Sparta and her allies and Athens and hers) if they fought according to their ability, and that Apollo would help them, when invited and when not (see A. Powell, *Athens and Sparta* (London, 1988), 395, who cites Thucydides 1.118.3, 1.123f. and 2.54.4f.). For the Athenian audience, this belief may have added to the doubts about Apollo expressed in the play.

369 *No one will act as the god's spokesman for you on this matter*: normally, the Delphians would act as spokesmen, taking questions to the oracle and returning with the answer. See also 413–16.

406 *How may the child-seed from the two of us be blended together?*: the Greeks had two theories about the woman's role in conception. Either she was simply a receptacle for the male seed, or—as here—she also produced seed and the child was formed from the mingling of male and female seed.

407–9 *He chose not . . . the oracular shrine*: as opposed to the evasive Apollo, Trophonius gets it right: as Lee remarks (n. at 407–8), both Xuthus and Creusa 'will find Ion in a different way'.

410 *divine lady, mother of Phoebus*: Leto—see n. at 127. 'Creusa turns in prayer to Leto partly because her earlier attempt to approach Apollo had been futile and partly because she hopes for the sympathy which a mother might feel for her case' (Lee, n. at 410).

419–20 *the victim offered in front of the temple for all visitors*: if the omens derived from this victim were auspicious, the oracle could be consulted.

422–3 *take branches around the laurel-laden altars*: suppliants would lay their laurel branches, the token of their supplication, on the altars.

445–6 *Poseidon and Zeus . . . for all the rapes you've committed*: Poseidon and Zeus were both notorious rapists, the former with Melanippe, Alope, and Tyro, the latter with Leda, Danae, Semele, and Alcmene (among others).

452–7 *Athena . . . blessed Victory*: Eleithuia, goddess of childbirth, played no part in the birth of Athena, who sprang fully armed from the head of Zeus after it had been hacked open, traditionally by Hephaestus, here by Prometheus, the son of one of the Titans (the six sons of Uranos and Gaia). Athena is identified here with Victory. The cult of Athena-Nike (Victory) was a popular one after the Persians wars, and a temple to this goddess had recently been built by the entrance to the Acropolis. (It can still be seen.)

458 *the Pythian god*: Apollo, who had killed the Python who lived at Delphi before his arrival and taken on its powers as well as its name.

459 *Olympus*: the mountain in north-east Greece where the gods lived.

465–6 *you and Leto's daughter—both goddesses, both virgins*: the two virgin goddesses are Athena and Artemis, both daughters of Zeus and therefore Apollo's sisters. (See n. at 127 for the birth of Artemis.)

492–6 *O abode of Pan . . . daughters of Aglaurus dance*: Pan, a god of shepherds and flocks, was half-man, half-goat. He played the reed pipe. His association with Apollo is thus through music (of which Apollo was the god); in addition, his cave beneath the Acropolis was just to the west of Apollo's.

For the daughters of Aglaurus, see n. at 23. It may be that they are visualized as returning to dance after their deaths. One of the editors (M. A. Bayfield (London, 1924), n. at 492 ff.) comments lyrically: 'This picture of the daughters of Aglaurus returning after death and dancing through the summer night on the top of the Acropolis, while Pan pipes to them from his cave below, is an exquisite invention . . . It is a scene of idyllic loveliness unsurpassed even in the lyrics of Euripides, and one that will for the imaginative reader lend some of the colour of its romance even to the severer associations of the spot.'

517–62 *My son . . . made me happy*: this lively episode begins in stichomythia (see n. at 264–368) and gathers further momentum when (from 530) the lines are divided.

542 *Children aren't born from the ground*: since the Athenians *did* originally spring from the ground (see n. at 29), Xuthus here shows himself the foreigner we know him to be.

550 *the torchlit ceremony in honour of Bacchus*: Bacchus was celebrated in torchlit mysteries on Mount Parnassus. 'Religious

festivals and ceremonies, because they allowed women relative freedom, are regularly associated with sexual liaisons and clandestine births' (Lee, n. at 550).

653 *the birthday sacrifices*: sacrifices were offered on the fifth or seventh day after a child's birth when the baby would be carried round the hearth. It would be named on the tenth day.

660–3 *And I name you 'Ion' . . . shrine*: the Greek word Ion means 'the one who comes' (see n. at 80–1).

671–2 *I pray that my mother . . . freedom of speech*: 'Ion means that if his mother is an alien he will feel inhibited from speaking his mind, a particular quality of Athenian life . . . The importance of one's mother's blood was underlined by Pericles' law of 451 BCE, which restricted citizenship to those with both parents citizens' (Lee, n. at 672).

707 *cake*: this is the same as the honey-cake in 226 (see n. there).

725–6 *You once were tutor to my father Erechtheus*: this slave must be very old indeed. It is not surprising that he finds the steep climb difficult (738–9).

760 *I shall speak, then, even at the risk of doubling the threat of death*: the Chorus have in mind Xuthus' threatening injunction that they should *not* tell their mistress (666–7).

796–9 *May I fly . . . I suffer!*: 'Creusa shares the desire of the Psalmist (Psalms 55:6) to escape from intolerable affliction' (Owen, n. 796). The sentence from Psalms reads: 'And I said, Oh that I had wings like a dove, for then would I flee away and be at rest!' It is in fact a common tragic prayer—cf. 1238–9 and e.g. Euripides, *Hippolytus* 732.

813ff. *For he came to Athens a foreigner . . .* : the Old Man 'is inventing without any correction from the Chorus, who had heard what Xuthus said (546). Nor is he even convincing, for had Ion been born after Creusa's marriage, he would be younger than his actual age' (Owen, n. at 813ff.). Owen sums up the Old Man's character as follows (p. xxx): 'He is utterly unscrupulous and without pity; he invents lies on the spur of the moment without any evidence for them (815 ff.); he proposes that Creusa should burn Apollo's temple or kill her husband (974–6). He is a minister of evil like the Nurse of Phaedra [in *Hippolytus*] . . . His passionate loyalty to the queen is his best quality, and it makes him ready to face the prospect of death (850–3) if he can serve her; but apparently he had not contemplated the prospect of torture, which makes him give evidence against her (1215).'

842 *the house of Aeolus*: i.e. his own people (63).

863 *The contest now is not one of virtue*: she means that, now that she believes Xuthus to be false, she has no need to consider her own reputation.

871–3 *the goddess . . . Triton's deep-watered lake*: Athena, who was born at the Tritonian lake in North Africa, or came there after being born from Zeus' head.

881–4 *You whose song . . . . of the Muses*: Apollo was the god of music, and was frequently represented holding a lyre. The curved side pieces are here described as being made from the horns of dead animals.

887–90 *You came to me . . . for a flower festival*: with this idyllic setting for the rape, compare Milton's Sicilian meadow in which Pluto (Dis) seized Proserpina (*Paradise Lost* 4. 268–71):

> . . . that fair field
> Of Enna, where Proserpin gathering flowers
> Herself a fairer flower by gloomy Dis
> Was gathered.

896 *Cypris*: a name for Aphrodite, the goddess of love, who was born from the foam of the sea and came to land at Paphos in Cyprus.

906 *paeans*: songs associated with Apollo. See n. at 125. Creusa's bitterness is extreme here. 'You just go on making music!'

909 *the golden seat*: i.e. the oracular seat, golden either because of Apollo's association with gold (cf. 887) or because of the vast quantity of treasure amassed at historical Delphi.

919 *Delos*: see n. at 127.

938–1028 *Yes, close to where Pan . . . trying to keep from you*: stichomythia.

953 *Hades' halls*: Hades was the god of the underworld.

967 *Why have you covered your head, old man?*: 'covering the head was a traditional gesture of mourning, symbolising withdrawal from the inescapable cause of grief or shame' (Lee, n. at 967).

988 *Phlegra*: Pallene, the western promontory of Chalcidice, is named elsewhere too (Euripides, *Heracles* 1194) as the site of the battle in which the earth-born giants tried unsuccessfully to overthrow the gods. To help her sons, Earth created a monster, the Gorgon, which Pallas Athena killed. (The usual story—see n. to 209–10—makes Perseus the killer.) Athena then used the Gorgon's snaky skin as a kind of breast-plate, the so-called aegis.

997 *A name it acquired when she rushed to join the ranks of the gods*: in a characteristically Euripidean display of etymology, the poet

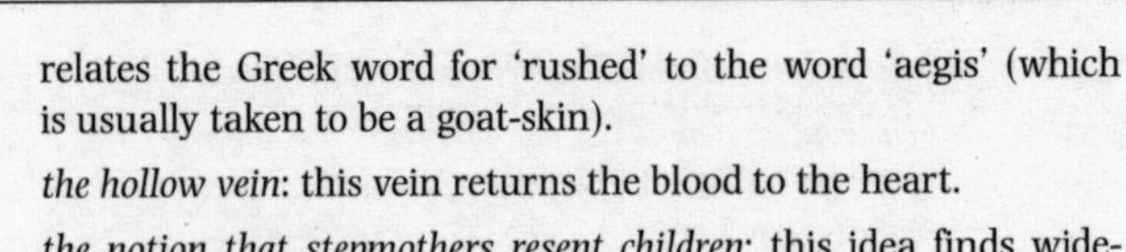

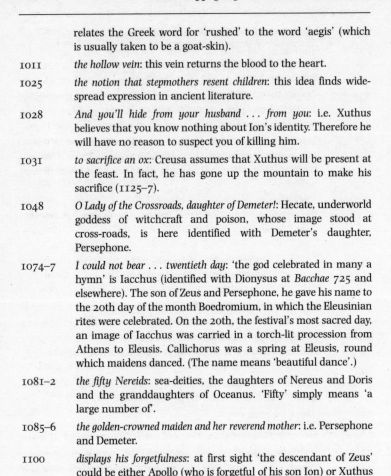

relates the Greek word for 'rushed' to the word 'aegis' (which is usually taken to be a goat-skin).

1011 *the hollow vein*: this vein returns the blood to the heart.

1025 *the notion that stepmothers resent children*: this idea finds widespread expression in ancient literature.

1028 *And you'll hide from your husband . . . from you*: i.e. Xuthus believes that you know nothing about Ion's identity. Therefore he will have no reason to suspect you of killing him.

1031 *to sacrifice an ox*: Creusa assumes that Xuthus will be present at the feast. In fact, he has gone up the mountain to make his sacrifice (1125–7).

1048 *O Lady of the Crossroads, daughter of Demeter!*: Hecate, underworld goddess of witchcraft and poison, whose image stood at cross-roads, is here identified with Demeter's daughter, Persephone.

1074–7 *I could not bear . . . twentieth day*: 'the god celebrated in many a hymn' is Iacchus (identified with Dionysus at *Bacchae* 725 and elsewhere). The son of Zeus and Persephone, he gave his name to the 20th day of the month Boedromium, in which the Eleusinian rites were celebrated. On the 20th, the festival's most sacred day, an image of Iacchus was carried in a torch-lit procession from Athens to Eleusis. Callichorus was a spring at Eleusis, round which maidens danced. (The name means 'beautiful dance'.)

1081–2 *the fifty Nereids*: sea-deities, the daughters of Nereus and Doris and the granddaughters of Oceanus. 'Fifty' simply means 'a large number of'.

1085–6 *the golden-crowned maiden and her reverend mother*: i.e. Persephone and Demeter.

1100 *displays his forgetfulness*: at first sight 'the descendant of Zeus' could be either Apollo (who is forgetful of his son Ion) or Xuthus (who is forgetful of his obligations). The following lines resolve the ambiguity in favour of Xuthus.

1126–7 *the two cliffs*: the double peak of Parnassus was famous.

1137 *a plethron*: a hundred feet. As a square measure, this comes to 10,000 square feet.

1141 *the treasuries*: many Greek cities built small treasuries in Delphi in which they stored precious objects. Ion has access to these (54–5).

1145 *the spoils he took from the Amazons*: in one of his labours Heracles fought the Amazons, fierce women who lived beyond the Black

Sea. One of the spoils, the girdle of their queen Hippolyte, was preserved in a temple at Mycenae.

1149 *Hesperus*: the evening star.

1150–1 *Meanwhile, dark-cloaked Night . . . traceless chariot*: Night is a lesser divinity than the Sun and so has only two horses as opposed to the Sun's four. Night has no trace-horses. See n. at 82.

1152–4 *Pleiades*: a seven-star group in the constellation Taurus; *Orion*, the giant huntsman, son of Euryale and Poseidon (or Hyrieus), is here seen with a sword and not his traditional club—the Pleiades are in constant flight from his dogs; the *Bear* is the constellation of Ursa Major, also known as the Plough—his tail was a noted feature.

1156 *the Hyades*: three (or five) stars making up the head of Taurus. Their 'morning setting marked the onset of the stormy season in November and the closure of the seas' (Lee, n. at 1156).

1160 *ships well equipped with oars drawn up opposite Greek vessels*: no doubt evoking for the Athenian audience such great naval victories of the Greeks over the Persians as those at Lade (496 BCE), Salamis (480), and Eurymedon (*c*.466).

1161 *hybrid semi-human creatures*: such as centaurs, which were half-man, half-horse.

1163–4 *Cecrops with intertwining coils and daughters near by*: Cecrops' 'snakey tail recalls the autochthonous origins of Ion's future city' (Lee, n. at 1163–5). Athena had placed the infant Erichthonius in a chest with two serpents to protect it. She then gave the chest to Cecrops' daughters, forbidding them to open it. However, they did so, were driven mad by the sight of the serpents, and hurled themselves over the cliffs of the Acropolis (see 273–4).

1169–80 *they put wreaths . . . state of happiness*: 'the order of proceedings here seems to reflect those at an Attic symposium: the meal (at which no wine was drunk) was followed by hand-washing and perfuming of the room (1174 f.). Undiluted wine was then drunk (for this the small cups mentioned in 1175 and 1179 were used) before the singing of the paean to the accompaniment of flutes (1177). This ceremony ushered in the symposium proper which was preceded by libations of wine that had been mixed with water in a common bowl.' (Lee, n. at 1169 ff.) The old man plays the role of the master of ceremonies, the 'symposiarch' (1171 ff.).

1195 *wine from Biblos*: the grape from which this was produced came from Thrace, which was noted for the strength and bouquet of its wines.

1198 *a flock of doves, which dwell fearlessly in Loxias' temple*: Owen (n. at 1198) observes that they 'must have been privileged birds, as Ion had been scaring off others. Travellers to Venice will be reminded of the pigeons in St Mark's Square, which for centuries were maintained by a special provision of the republic.' But surely there is a characteristic Euripidean irony in the fact that the very birds which Ion has been scaring away reveal the murder plot against him.

1210 *Who has designs upon my life?*: Ion has learnt authority with impressive speed.

1219 *Pythia*: i.e. Delphi. See n. at 458.

1222–3 *The lords of Delphi unanimously decreed death by stoning for my mistress*: stoning is a punishment which a community administers collectively. Thus it is inevitably a response to a heinous offence which has damaged the community as a whole.

1232–3 *Dionysus' clusters*: i.e. wine (from the grapes of the wine-god).

1256 *Killing a suppliant is forbidden by divine law*: provided suppliants maintained contact with the altar, it was an unthinkable violation to kill them.

1261 *Cephisus, bull-headed Cephisus*: Cephisus was the chief river of Athens and Creusa's great-grandfather. River-gods were frequently visualized with bull-like features. The bull was suggestive of their roaring waters.

1263 *one of those snakes whose fiery eyes shoot out deadly flames*: snakes which could, like the basilisk, kill with a glance.

1284–1311 *What do you and Phoebus . . . made me unhappy*: stichomythia. The answer to Ion's question, 'What do you and Phoebus have in common?' is of course Ion himself.

1289 *And now I am his, while you no longer are*: the play of irony here illuminates the abyss of incomprehension into which Ion and Creusa have fallen.

1293 *you set fire to the house of Erechtheus*: Creusa speaks metaphorically. Nevertheless, the remark stands as a devastating exposure of the absurdity of the threats which the Old Man has led her to believe that Ion poses to her house.

1299 *Yes, but a mercenary has no true rights to the land*: 'she speaks contemptuously of her husband as a foreign *condottiere* who could not hold landed property in Attica' (Owen, n. at 1299). Cf. n. at 58.

1321 *this wall here*: the low wall marking off the innermost sanctuary.

1324–56 *Welcome, mother . . . limits of Europe*: stichomythia.

1354 *What a day! These revelations make it a really happy one for me!*: most Greek tragedies take place within a day. Ion's growth to maturity is fast, but he has experienced much.

1380–1 *But now I'll take this crib and dedicate it to the god*: 'even as he speaks of his mother's loss of joy in him, Ion proposes to make that loss permanent, as Creusa herself had nearly done twice, by returning the crib to Apollo ... Even at the last moment Euripides endangers the recognition; this is not a metatheatrical ploy to amuse the audience, but a further instance of human emotion coming near to derailing divine arrangements' (Lee, n. at 1380ff.).

1406–26 *Oh, this is awful . . . just this piece?*: stichomythia.

1421–3 *There's a Gorgon . . . like an aegis*: 'Athena's victory over the monster was raised in connection with Creusa's apparent protection of her house from an intruder (989ff.). Here it recurs pictorially at the moment the rightful heir is to be discovered' (Lee, n. at 1421–3).

1433–4 *the original olive tree that grew on Athena's rock*: an olive tree, putatively the descendant of the one that Athena gave the Athenians originally, still grows in front of the west porch of the Erechtheion on the Acropolis. This wreath, the final recognition token, is an appropriate symbol for an Athens which will never fade thanks to its re-founder Ion (1465).

1441–2 *in Persephone's realm*: Persephone was the goddess of the underworld and the wife of its king, Hades. (She in fact divided her time between the underworld and the world above.)

1454 *Ah, woman*: Creusa addresses the absent Priestess.

1482 *the rock of the nightingales*: Athens was famous for its nightingales (Sophocles, *Oedipus at Colonus* 16). Owen (n. at 1482) says that he heard them in the National Garden there. Lee (n. at 1482) comments that nightingales are introduced because the horrific story of Procne, who was transformed into a nightingale, involves rape and the death of a son.

1486 *in the cycle of the tenth month*: this does not in fact mean that it was a long pregnancy, since the Greeks counted these in lunar months.

1523–7 *Are you sure, mother . . . really no god is?*: Ion's scepticism calls for the objective pronouncement of the *deus ex machina* (Athena, who appears above the stage building to end the play).

1534–6 *he just gave you to him . . . guardian of his house*: the fifth-century practice of adoption in fact demanded that the name of the real father had to be given.

1558 *in case his past deeds should provoke you to open criticism*: 'we cannot be surprised that Apollo should prefer sending an emissary to appearing in person. He has had a discreditable incident in his past made known; Delphi has been proved to have given a false oracle; his plans have gone wrong, and he has been shown to have limits to his divine powers. Athena makes the best of a bad job ...' (Owen, n. at 1557–8). Another way of regarding the situation is to follow H. Strohm (*Euripides: Interpretationen zur dramatischen Form* (Munich, 1957), 162, n. 3) in feeling that Apollo 'distances himself from a dispute conducted in terms of mortals' limited perspective'.

1570 *I harnessed my chariot*: Athena may have actually appeared aloft on a chariot. Cf. *Medea* 1317 ff.

1575–8 *For his sons . . . inhabitants of my cliff*: before Cleisthenes' reforms of 508, the people of Attica were divided into four tribes.

1579–81 *Geleon . . . Aegicores*: Geleon gave his name to the Geleontes tribe; Hopletes, Argades, and Aegicores are usually explained as 'warriors', 'workers', and 'goatherds', but Euripides relates the last to Athena's aegis (see nn. at 988 and 997).

1583 *the Cyclades*: usually assumed to be not just the islands around Delos but generally all the states in the Athenian empire in or on the Aegean.

1591 *the Dorian city*: Sparta.

1592 *Rhium*: a port on the south side of the entrance to the Gulf of Corinth.

1602 *so that Xuthus can remain in blissful ignorance*: does Xuthus' continuing ignorance cast a shadow on the general optimism with which the play ends?

ORESTES

4–7 *that happy man . . . looming over his head*: Tantalus was happy once, not only because he was extremely rich but also because he was said to be the son of Zeus, but his 'unbridled tongue' (10) led him to disaster when he either rashly asked to have all that the gods have (a request which Zeus granted but stopped him from enjoying the experience by suspending the rock over him), or gave away the secrets of the gods to men. The punishment of the looming rock is not as familiar to us as his 'tantalization' by fruit and water, but was well established in ancient literature. Euripides, however, appears to have invented the idea of a flying Tantalus (see also ll. 982 ff.).

As Electra explains, Tantalus stands at the head of the calamitous family tree, of which she and Orestes are pitiful survivors.

12–13 *and Atreus . . . against his brother Thyestes*: a golden lamb was discovered in Atreus' flocks. Whichever of Tantalus' grandsons, Atreus and Thyestes, possessed the lamb was entitled to be king of Argos. Atreus had it first since Pan brought it to him. However, Thyestes seduced Atreus' wife, Aerope, and with her assistance carried off the lamb and laid claim to the kingdom. In response to this impious behaviour Zeus reversed the course of the sun and stars. Atreus kept his throne and took the grisly revenge that Electra now describes.

16 *I pass in silence over what happened next*: this may be the story told in Sophocles' lost play, *Thyestes in Sicyon*, involving Thyestes' incest with his daughter Pelopia and the resulting birth of Aegisthus.

18 *Aerope of Crete*: Aerope had an adulterous union with Thyestes (see n. at 12–13). Cretan women were especially vulnerable to the power of love.

19–20 *Helen, who was loathed by the gods*: the end of the play shows that the gods hate her no longer (1629–43).

25 *she trapped her husband in the coils of an endless cloth*: when Agamemnon, king of Argos, returned from his victory at Troy, Clytemnestra took him to his bath. While he was in it, she flung over him the cloth referred to here—a vase of 470 BCE shows it as having a filmy, see-through texture—and it prevented him from defending himself.

26–7 *Her motives it would be improper for a young woman like myself to mention*: she refers obliquely to Clytemnestra's adulterous liaison with Aegisthus, which she sees as the incentive to the murder. In fact, Clytemnestra had other motives: Agamemnon had sacrificed their daughter Iphigenia so that his armada could sail to Troy, and he had brought back from that city the prophetess Cassandra as his mistress.

28–9 *Next, Phoebus . . . persuaded Orestes to murder his mother, the woman who bore him*: the oracle of Phoebus Apollo (he can be called by either name) at Delphi had urged Orestes to kill his mother Clytemnestra in requital for her murder of his father Agamemnon. Electra's criticism of Apollo for sponsoring this act of matricide finds an echo in *Electra* (1244–6), when Castor tells Orestes that Clytemnestra 'has justice—though you have not acted justly. But Phoebus, Phoebus—yet he is my lord and so I say nothing.'

34–8 *The upshot is . . . the divine Eumenides*: Orestes' act of matricide has called up the Eumenides, spirits of vengeance, especially for crimes within the family, and embodiments of a guilty conscience. The name Eumenides means 'the kindly ones' and is 'apotropaic', i.e. it seeks to 'turn away' the ominous foreboding of their real nature. At 409, Menelaus prefers not to name them at all. It is an interesting feature of *Orestes* that these goddesses are repeatedly referred to in it as the Eumenides: elsewhere in Euripides they are called Erinyes (Furies).

39–42 *This is now the sixth day . . . bathed his body*: Orestes clearly presents a terrible appearance. Cf. 219–20, 223–6, and 385–91.

48–50 *And this is the decisive day . . . stoned to death*: whatever an audience may feel about the proceedings described by the Messenger in 866ff., the fact remains that the decision is arrived at by democratic means. In addition, stoning is a democratic punishment since the whole community is involved in its performance. See *Ion*, n. at 1222–3.

54 *Nauplia*: the port of Argos, about seven miles away from the city.

56–7 *the mass-murderer Helen*: the Greek Helen had run off with the Trojan Paris, thus causing the Trojan war in which so many died. Electra's loathing of Helen comes across vividly here and in 19–20.

72 *still unwed after all these years*: there is a play on words here, since the name 'Electra' suggests 'alektros', Greek for 'unwed'. The words are highly charged in view of the fact that Helen has been married three times.

75 *I incur no pollution in addressing you*: In his edition of the play (Warminster, 1987), Martin West remarks laconically (n. at 75): 'If everyone shared the Argives' horror of speaking to the matricides (47), it would be hard to write a play.'

88–109 *How long . . . looking after her*: stichomythia; see *Ion*, n. to 264–368. It is well suited to this edgy scene in which Electra can scarcely keep her taunts in check.

96 *these hair-trimmings of mine*: the gift of a lock of hair was a customary tribute at the tomb of a hero. Since the head and the hair signified strength and life, the cutting of the latter symbolized submissive grief.

116 *stand on top of the mound*: Neoptolemus is said to have mounted Achilles' tomb to sacrifice Polyxena (Euripides, *Hecuba* 524).

128 *Did you see*: Electra addresses the audience. This is a very rare occurrence in Greek tragedy.

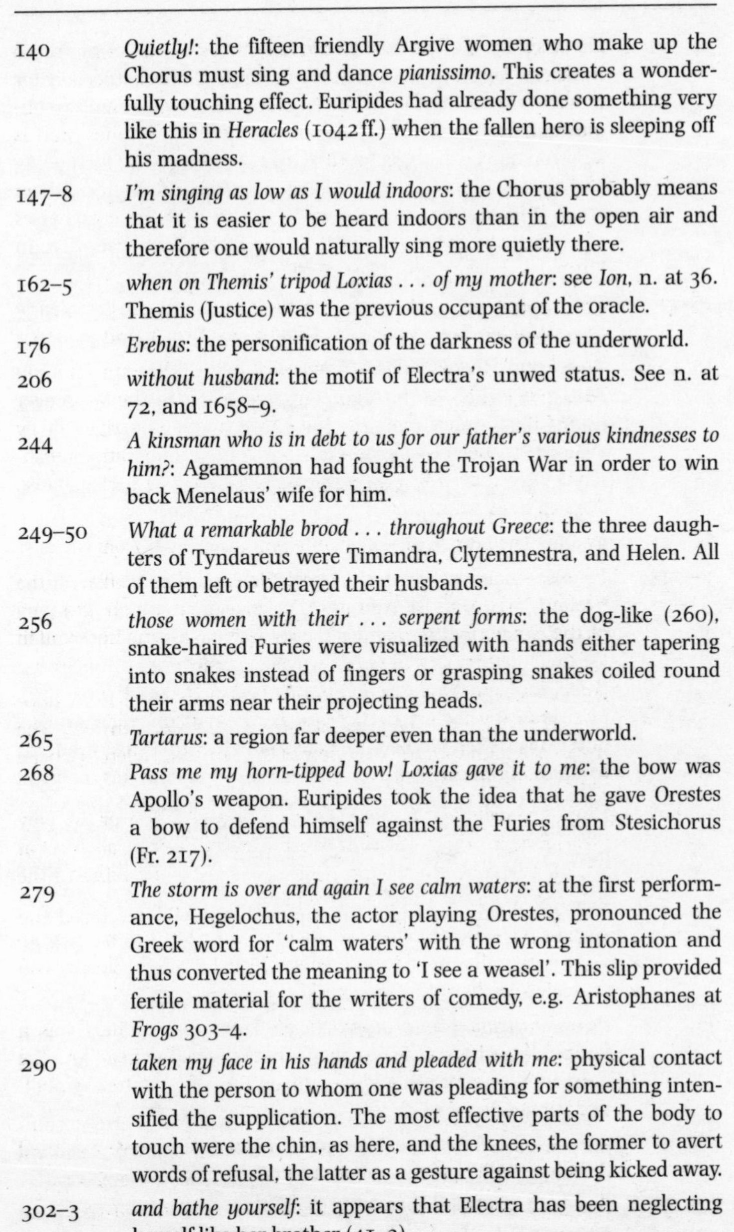

140 *Quietly!*: the fifteen friendly Argive women who make up the Chorus must sing and dance *pianissimo*. This creates a wonderfully touching effect. Euripides had already done something very like this in *Heracles* (1042 ff.) when the fallen hero is sleeping off his madness.

147–8 *I'm singing as low as I would indoors*: the Chorus probably means that it is easier to be heard indoors than in the open air and therefore one would naturally sing more quietly there.

162–5 *when on Themis' tripod Loxias . . . of my mother*: see *Ion*, n. at 36. Themis (Justice) was the previous occupant of the oracle.

176 *Erebus*: the personification of the darkness of the underworld.

206 *without husband*: the motif of Electra's unwed status. See n. at 72, and 1658–9.

244 *A kinsman who is in debt to us for our father's various kindnesses to him?*: Agamemnon had fought the Trojan War in order to win back Menelaus' wife for him.

249–50 *What a remarkable brood . . . throughout Greece*: the three daughters of Tyndareus were Timandra, Clytemnestra, and Helen. All of them left or betrayed their husbands.

256 *those women with their . . . serpent forms*: the dog-like (260), snake-haired Furies were visualized with hands either tapering into snakes instead of fingers or grasping snakes coiled round their arms near their projecting heads.

265 *Tartarus*: a region far deeper even than the underworld.

268 *Pass me my horn-tipped bow! Loxias gave it to me*: the bow was Apollo's weapon. Euripides took the idea that he gave Orestes a bow to defend himself against the Furies from Stesichorus (Fr. 217).

279 *The storm is over and again I see calm waters*: at the first performance, Hegelochus, the actor playing Orestes, pronounced the Greek word for 'calm waters' with the wrong intonation and thus converted the meaning to 'I see a weasel'. This slip provided fertile material for the writers of comedy, e.g. Aristophanes at *Frogs* 303–4.

290 *taken my face in his hands and pleaded with me*: physical contact with the person to whom one was pleading for something intensified the supplication. The most effective parts of the body to touch were the chin, as here, and the knees, the former to avert words of refusal, the latter as a gesture against being kicked away.

302–3 *and bathe yourself*: it appears that Electra has been neglecting herself like her brother (41–2).

329–31 *the oracle spoken by Phoebus from the tripod . . . the navel of the world*: see *Ion*, n. at 5. Cf. n. at 28–9. A round navel-stone, a copy of the original, is the first thing one sees as one enters the museum at Delphi.

346 *that first union from the gods*: Tantalus was said to be the son of Zeus (5) and Pluto, the daughter of Cronus or of Atlas. He married Dione, a daughter of Atlas.

352–3 *the thousand-shipped invasion of Asia*: a thousand was the 'canonic' number of the Greek ships which sailed to Troy. (See Christopher Marlowe, *Doctor Faustus*: 'Was this the face that launched a thousand ships . . . ?') In Homer's *Iliad* the number is 1,186, and Thucydides (1.10) rounds it up to 1,200.

362 *Malea*: this cape at the south-east tip of the Peloponnese was traditionally the first sight of Greece for soldiers returning from Troy (Homer, *Odyssey* 3.287).

383 *lack a suppliant's leafy boughs*: for the process of supplication, see n. at 290. A fully equipped suppliant would, unlike Orestes, carry a leafy olive branch adorned with strands of wool.

385–447 *Ye gods . . . as bad as it could get*: stichomythia. In his edition (Oxford, 1986), C. W. Willink (n. at 385–447) writes, 'The goal of this stichomythia, among the most "intellectual" and intellectually demanding in Greek tragedy, is the *pitying* conclusion [I feel for you. Your situation is as bad as it could get—447]. Menelaus is shocked by Orestes' deed (376) and appearance, but properly concerned to determine the full extent of his troubles, in terms both of his "disease" and of his political peril . . . Only perhaps in retrospect are we aware of the subtly "negative" touches (423, 425) in line with Menelaus' later conduct.' West (n. at 395–411) observes that 'Menelaus interrogates Orestes in the manner of a doctor, the sort described in Plato, *Laws* 720d, who asks how the ailment began and developed and who learns from the patient as well as advising him as best he can.'

404 *I was outside, waiting for the bones to be collected for burial*: Clytemnestra's body was cremated on a funeral pyre (403) and the bones which the pyre had failed to burn were then collected to be buried in a funeral mound (402).

406 *Pylades*: Pylades was not only Orestes' loyal friend and accomplice but also his first cousin. He was the son of Strophius, king of Phocis, by Anaxibia. It was to Strophius' court that Orestes had been smuggled away after the murder of Agamemnon.

424 *he is true to his own*: i.e. he will help Orestes in the end.

429 *haven't you even purified the blood on your hands in the customary way?*: the 'customary way' was for the polluted person to sit at someone else's hearth. His host then sacrificed a sucking pig and let its blood run down the killer's hands. Pure blood washes away impure.

432–3 *Oeax . . . Palamedes*: Oeax was the brother of Palamedes, who was 'framed' by Odysseus at Troy on a false charge of treason to his fellow Greeks and stoned to death.

464–5 *Leda . . . Castor and Polydeuces*: Leda was the wife of Tyndareus, the mother of Clytemnestra, Helen, Castor, and Polydeuces. Zeus changed himself into a swan in order to make love to her and was the father of Helen, Castor, and Polydeuces.

471–2 *While I was pouring libations at Clytemnestra's tomb*: this is the explanation for the fact that the old king of Sparta is in Argos.

476 *whose wife was also loved by Zeus*: see n. at 464–5. Tyndareus is supposedly honoured by the fact that the king of the gods loved his wife.

511 *how long will these horrors go on?*: Tyndareus makes a good point in his condemnation of an endless chain of vendetta killings.

621 *until she set the palace ablaze—though not with fire*: Willink notes (n. at 621) that 'Electra's "incendiary" behaviour is thematically connected both with the present "kindling" of Tyndareus' fury (609) and with the "palace-burning" climax of the plot (1618, etc.); for the 'fire' theme, cf. also 697, 820, 1150.'

623 *our kinship*: Tyndareus was, of course, Menelaus' father-in-law.

658 *As for the sacrifice of my sister at Aulis*: the Greek fleet had assembled at Aulis to sail to Troy but was held there by adverse weather. Agamemnon sacrificed his daughter Iphigenia to the goddess Artemis to obtain the winds which would allow the ships to go on their way. Agamemnon thus killed his daughter in order to get Menelaus' wife back for him. Is there a hint in the next line that Menelaus' own daughter Hermione would have been the appropriate victim?

692 *the Pelasgian Argives*: one tradition made Pelasgus the first king of Argos.

713 *. . . that are besetting you*: reactions to what Menelaus says vary widely. P. Vellacott and H. D. F. Kitto believe he is completely justified, Kitto opining that he makes 'the only possible reply'. R. P. Winnington-Ingram and A. P. Burnett view him as a villain, the former dubbing him 'a cold calculating sophistical politician who would like the throne for himself'. Both responses

are surely too extreme. The present writer feels that Menelaus' speech is a brilliant exposition of evasiveness as the speaker hides behind a smoke-screen of verbiage. In the event, he says nothing at the assembly, despite 704–5, and may not even have gone there.

725–6 *But I can see my closest friend Pylades . . . from Phocis*: see n. at 406. Orestes and Pylades are the model of committed friendship. Pylades tries to persuade Orestes to let him die together with him in Euripides' *Iphigenia among the Taurians* (674–686).

734–98 *To explain . . . my mother's tomb*: stichomythia. The excitement of the dialogue (conducted in trochees, not iambics, starting from 729 and continuing to 806) increases when the lines are divided between the speakers from 774 on.

772 *But the masses can be terrifying when they gain unscrupulous leaders*: it is tempting to see a reference to contemporary Athenian politics here, when the so-called demagogues such as Cleophon could manipulate popular opinion.

788 *And wouldn't that be a significant omen?*: i.e. Electra's tears would prove inauspicious.

809 *beside Simois' streams*: Simois is one of the rivers of Troy.

812–13 *the dispute over the golden lamb*: see n. at 12–13.

818 *the twofold house of Atreus*: i.e. the families of Agamemnon and Menelaus.

871–3 *the hill where they say Danaus . . . a legal hearing*: the fifty daughters of Danaus, king of Argos, killed their husbands, the fifty sons of Danaus' brother, Aegyptus. However, one of them, Hypermestra, spared Lynceus because he had allowed her to remain a virgin, and it was Lynceus who secured a peaceful arbitration before an Argive assembly. It was held on the hill known as the Haliaia (Halia) (= Assembly(-place)) referred to here.

888 *Talthybius*: in *Hecuba* and *Trojan Women* Talthybius is a highly sympathetic go-between for the Greek vistors and their Trojan captives. Here he is far from favourably presented. Euripides may be developing Cassandra's devastating critique of him in *Trojan Women* 424–6.

898 *Diomedes*: this lustrous Homeric figure is sympathetically viewed here. In Homer, he is the 'lord of Argos', but that has been conveniently forgotten.

932 *Inachus*: the founder of Argos.

955–6 *his Pythian tripod*: see *Ion*, n. at 5.

960 *Pelasgia*: i.e. Argos. See n. at 692.

963–4 *the fair maiden goddess / Persephone, queen of the dead below the ground*: disfiguring the cheeks and beating the head are customary actions in mourning those travelling to Persephone's realm.

965–6 *the Cyclopian land*: the stones which constitute the walls of Mycenae and Tiryns in the Argolid are so huge that it was considered that only the one-eyed giants, the Cyclopes, could have built them. Euripides uses the names of the cities Mycenae and Argos without differentiation. Thus the latter city is granted Cyclopean walls too.

969–70 *those about to die, / who once led Greece to war*: the identity of the children of Agamemnon is subsumed under that of their father.

974–5 *the bloody vote, / cast in hatred by the citizens of this place*: the decision was taken democratically, even though it was swayed by the promptings of a man the Messenger saw as a mob-orator (902–16). The Messenger—witness his words at 868–70—and the Chorus are certainly not free from bias. They are well disposed towards Orestes and Electra, and there is no need to assume that the dramatist shared their point of view.

984 *Olympus*: the home of the gods. It is the highest mountain in Greece (rising to 9,573 feet or 2,918 metres), on the borders of Macedonia and Thessaly.

989–95 *First there were winged colts . . . the swell of the waves*: in order to win Hippodamia as his bride, Pelops, like all her other suitors, had to vanquish her father Oenomaus in a chariot race. This was a race that Oenomaus would inevitably win since his horses were unbeatable; and when he overtook the suitor, he would kill him. For the race with Pelops, however, Oenomaus' charioteer Myrtilus sabotaged his chariot, replacing its axle-pins with wax pegs and thus causing an accident fatal to Oenomaus. Pelops, however, refused Myrtilus his bribe of the first night with Hippodamia and flung him out of his flying chariot into the sea near Geraestus in southern Euboea. Myrtilus then cursed (996) Pelops and his line. This story, with its amalgam of lust, treachery, cheating, and murder, is characteristic of the disastrous house of Tantalus.

1001–6 *Then Strife . . . the Pleiades with their seven tracks*: Thyestes' shocking behaviour in his conflict (hence Strife) with Atreus over the golden lamb caused Zeus, in horrified disgust, to reverse the course of the sun and stars (see n. at 12–13). The Pleiades are a group of seven stars, but here they stand for the stars generally.

1007 *that death*: the death of Myrtilus.

1008 *the banquet that bears the name of Thyestes*: Electra has told us about this in her prologue (15).

1009 *Aerope*: Atreus' treacherous wife. See n. at 12–13.

1058 *He wasn't even anywhere to be seen*: see n. at 682–713.

1060 *Let's make sure we die in a noble fashion*: for a Roman, suicide was ennobling when it led to the preservation of personal integrity; for a Greek, the situation was more problematic. In *Heracles*, Theseus talks the hero out of suicide, and, when Ajax kills himself in Sophocles' play, his action has dire consequences. Orestes' wish to die 'in a noble fashion' is not as straightforward as that of Cleopatra (in Shakespeare's *Antony and Cleopatra*) to die in 'the high Roman fashion'. He strikes a faintly ludicrous pose.

1094 *Delphi, the citadel of the Phocians*: when Euripides wrote this play, Delphi was territorially independent of Phocis, but, as Willink remarks (n. at 1094), tragedy had its own mythical topography.

1100–30 *My dearest friend . . . your implication*: stichomythia. Seth Schein (*WS* 88 (1975), 62) refers to this as 'a mad stichomythia . . . in which Orestes and Pylades distort the meaning of their words . . .'

1105 *Let's kill Helen*: a shattering moment, comparable with Beatrice's sudden demand that Benedick should 'Kill Claudio!' in Shakespeare's *Much Ado about Nothing*.

1108 *In fact she's putting her seal on all my property*: she is behaving as if she and Menelaus already owned the place. This gives some colour to Orestes' comment (1058–9) that Menelaus has his hopes set on the throne.

1109 *Hades*: the king of the underworld.

1111 *Phrygian*: i.e. Trojan. Quite possibly, Euripides here lays the ground for the entry of the Phrygian slave at 1369. It is a commonplace of classical literature to contrast robust Europeans with effeminate easterners.

1150 *we'll set fire to this palace here*: for the palace-burning theme, see n. at 621.

1158 *not only did you devise the mischief we made against Aegisthus*: Pylades is far more of an *agent provocateur* in this play than in his other appearances in Greek drama.

1167–8 *Agamemnon, who became the leader of Greece on his merits*: in Euripides' Athens, generals were elected by vote while all other state officials were chosen by lot. This election process enhanced the prestige of the generalship. Agamemnon too had been actually chosen to lead the Greeks (though by the kings, not the ordinary people).

1181–90 *Listen, then . . . for us three companions?*: a short burst of stichomythia.

1213 *whelp*: Euripides frequently uses animal words to refer to young people. Here the word 'whelp' seems to be used pejoratively. It is certainly appropriate to the victim of a hunt (cf. 1315–16, 1346).

1233–4 *Agamemnon, close kin of my father*: in Euripides' *Iphigenia among the Taurians* (918), it is in fact Strophius' *wife*, Anaxibia, who is the close kin of Agamemnon, being his sister.

1246 *Mycenae*: this name for the city is used interchangeably with Argos. Cf. n. at 965–6. The two places are in fact 6 miles apart.

1310 *Scamander*: one of the rivers at Troy. It was called Scamander by mortals but Xanthus by the gods.

1326–36 *Well, you'd expect . . . for an outcry?*: stichomythia. The convention comes under strain when Hermione is forced to speak a virtually meaningless line (Who? Tell me. I don't want to remain in ignorance. (1333)), and West (n. at 1333) believes that this line was the model for A. E. Housman's parody in his *Fragment of a Greek Tragedy*:

> —A shepherd's questioned mouth informed me that—
> —What? For I know not yet what you will say.
> —Nor will you ever, if you interrupt.

1364–5 *that pernicious, baneful man from Ida, / Paris*: Paris, the second son of Priam, king of Troy, had been an oxherd on Mount Ida, the mountain range behind Troy where he had been left out to die. Here it was that he had judged the beauty competition between the three goddesses Hera, Athena, and Aphrodite. He awarded the prize to Aphrodite, who had bribed him with the offer of the most beautiful woman in the world. This was Helen, and when Paris subsequently abducted her from her husband Menelaus' palace in Sparta, he precipitated the catastrophic Trojan war.

1369 *s.d.* PHRYGIAN: this oriental figure *sings* his great aria. He is entertainingly ludicrous in his abject cowardice.

1372 *Doric triglyphs*: triglyphs were grooved tablets above the columns of a temple. Doric describes an architectural 'order'.

1377–8 *bull-headed Oceanus*: the river-god whose waters embraced the disk-shaped Earth. River-gods were often visualized with bull's horns. See *Ion*, n. at 1261.

1385–7 *that bird-born, / swan-feathered whelp of Leda*: see n. at 464–5. Because of the circumstances of her conception, Helen was born from an egg, but it would probably be wrong to take it that she literally had the feathers of a swan.

1391 *O Dardanus' wretched land!*: i.e. Troy, the city which Dardanus built.

1392 *Ganymede*: Zeus fell in love with this beautiful Trojan boy and took him up to Mount Olympus to be his cup-bearer as well as his catamite. This is the only reference to him as a horseman.

1404 *Odysseus*: the hero of Homer's *Odyssey*, a poem in which his inventiveness is a highly appealing attribute, is usually seen in a far from flattering light in Greek tragedy. (The portrayal of him in Sophocles' *Ajax* is the exception that proves the rule.)

1409–10 *the archer Paris*: in Homer's *Iliad*, the bow is seen as a coward's weapon since the archer avoids hand-to-hand fighting. Paris is certainly an archer in that poem—and as such will prove to be the dastardly killer of great Achilles—but he also engages in more heroic conflict, though with decidedly ignominious results.

1427–9 *with rapid movement . . . I was wafting a breeze*: the Phrygian slave is a punkah-wallah. Egyptian, Assyrian, and Persian kings were fanned by such slaves. The 'firm, feathered fan' is an exotically Eastern touch.

1431–3 *her hands wound . . . to the floor*: 'the fingers of the spinner's right hand twirl strands from the distaff into a single thread attached to the top of the pendent rotating spindle; when the latter reaches the ground, the yarn is wound on to it, and the process begins again' (Willink, n. at 1430–3).

1453–4 *O great mother, mighty Idaean mother, / mighty goddess Antaea!*: the Asiatic Earth-mother was worshipped under many names. Antaea means either 'confronting in battle' or 'invoked in prayer'. Ida is the mountain range behind Troy.

1481 *as Phrygian Hector, / or as Ajax*: Hector was the Trojans' greatest fighter; after Achilles, Ajax was the mightiest Greek warrior.

1493 *Bacchants*: frenzied devotees of Bacchus, the god of wine and the liberated spirit.

1506–26 *Where's the man . . . good news*: stichomythia.

1528 *although you're not a woman, you're no man either*: this probably is simply a scathing reference to the Phrygian's cowardice, but it could well be literally true since Helen's attendants were likely to have been eunuchs.

1532 *flaunting his yellow hair on his shoulders*: Menelaus has blond hair in Homer's poems. The poet Archilochus disapproves of the dandyish type of general suggested here (114).

1541–4 *But look . . . Tantalus' house*: the 'palace-burning' theme nears its culmination. Cf. notes at 621 and 1150.

1548 *because of the fall of Myrtilus from the chariot*: see n. at 989–95.

1576–1617 *Are there questions . . . put you there*: stichomythia.

1592 *His silence is agreement*: in fact Pylades must remain silent. His part is now being perfomed by a mute so that the actor who had played him can assume the role of Apollo. (There were only three speaking actors in a Greek tragedy at this time.)

1618–20 *Hey, Electra . . . to the torch!*: the 'palace-burning' theme reaches its climax.

1625 *s.d.* 'There is now a spectacular tableau on four levels, unique in ancient drama: the chorus in the orchestra; Menelaus and his followers in battle array before the house; the conspirators with their swords and torches on the roof, probably symmetrically stationed on either side of their captive; and the two beautiful deities above them all. Perhaps about forty persons in total' (West, n. at 1625).

1636–7 *she will sit enthroned . . . a saviour to sailors*: Castor and Polydeuces did constitute a constellation, Gemini, but there is no other reference to a marine cult of Helen.

1646 *named after the fact that you passed your exile there*: Parrhasia is in southern Arcadia, where there was a town called Orestheion or Oresthasion.

1653–4 *As for Hermione . . . she is destined to be your wife*: how comic is this intended to be?

1654–7 *Neoptolemus . . . of his father Achilles*: the story of the death of Neoptolemus, son of Achilles, to whom Menelaus had promised Hermione at Troy, is told (rather differently) in Euripides' *Andromache*.

1661 *As for Argos, let Orestes rule it*: compare 'Go out and govern New South Wales!'—Hilaire Belloc, 'Lord Lundy'.

1685–6 *Hera and Hebe, Heracles' wife*: Hera was the queen of the gods, the wife of Zeus; Hebe, their daughter, was the personification of Youth. Heracles was the son of Zeus by Alcmene; the great strong man of the ancient world, he was famous for his twelve labours.

PHOENICIAN WOMEN

1 *s.d. Thebes*: *Phoenician Women* is one of Euripides' extant Theban plays. (The others are the equally alarming *Heracles* and *Bacchae*; and note the savage Theban element in *Suppliant Women.*) In an important essay ('Thebes: Theatre of Self and Society in Athenian Drama', in J. J. Winkler and F. I. Zeitlin (eds.), *Nothing to do with Dionysus?* (Princeton, 1990), 130–67), Froma Zeitlin writes helpfully of the way in which the Attic damatists made use of the Theban myths. She suggests that 'through the specific myths associated with Thebes on the Athenian stage, certain clusters of ideas, themes, and problems recur which can be identified as proper to Thebes—or rather Athenian tragedy's representation of Thebes as a mise-en-scène . . . The Athenian theatre . . . portrays a city onstage that is meant to be dramatically "other" than itself. Thebes . . . provides the negative model to Athens' manifest image of itself with regard to its notions of the proper management of city, society, and self. As the site of displacement, therefore, Thebes consistently supplies the radical tragic terrain where there can be no escape from the tragic in the resolution of conflict or in the institutional provision of a civic future beyond the world of the play . . . .Thebes is the place . . . that makes problematic every inclusion and exclusion, every conjunction and disjunction, every relation between near and far, high and low, inside and outside, stranger and kin. . . . Thebes functions in the theatre as an anti-Athens, an other place . . . Thebes, we might say, is the quintessential "other scene" . . . There Athens acts out questions crucial to the *polis*, the self, the family, and society, but these are displaced upon a city that is imagined as the mirror opposite of Athens. . . . Thebes is . . . the obverse side of Athens, the shadow self, we might say, of the idealized city on whose other terrain the tragic action may be pushed to its furthest limits of contradiction and impasse' (pp. 131, 134, and 144).

1–2 *O Sun . . . swift steeds*: here, as frequently in classical literature, the Sun-god is portrayed as driving a chariot of fire drawn by four horses.

5–6 *when Cadmus reached this land from his coastal home of Phoenicia*: Cadmus left the Phoenician port of Tyre where Agenor, his father, was king in order to search for his sister Europa after her abduction by Zeus.

7 *Harmonia, the daughter of Cypris*: Cypris is Aphrodite, goddess of love. She is so called because it was on the island of Cyprus that she eventually came to land after she had been born from the

foam of the sea. Jocasta makes no mention of the less than harmonious fact that Harmonia's father was Ares, god of war.

15 *Phoebus*: the god of prophecy, Phoebus Apollo, had his most famous sanctuary at Delphi. Such consultation was entirely normal; cf., in this volume, Xuthus' consultation of Apollo in *Ion*.

24 *Hera's meadow by the cliffs of Cithaeron*: Hera was the queen of the gods, the wife of Zeus. Cithaeron is a mountain range near Thebes, and a resonant name in the tragic tradition, above all in Sophocles' *Oedipus the King*.

27 *Oedipus*: the name means 'swell-foot'.

28 *Polybus* was the king of Corinth. His wife (29) was Merope.

42 *the tendons of his feet*: see n. at 27. It is no wonder that this remained a vulnerable area.

45–6 *With the Sphinx preying savagely on the city*: the Sphinx was a monster with a woman's face, a lion's chest and feet, and the wings of a bird of prey. Her riddle was: 'What creature has four legs in the morning, two at midday, and three in the evening?' Oedipus gave the correct answer—man, since he crawls on all fours as a baby, stands upright on two legs in the prime of his life, and supports himself with a stick in his old age. When Oedipus had solved the riddle, the Sphinx self-destructed by throwing herself from the top of a rock.

77 *Adrastus*: the king of Argos. Polynices' bride was called Argeia.

79 *the walls with their seven gates*: Thebes was celebrated for its seven gates, a traditional element in this story. Cf. Aeschylus, *Seven against Thebes*.

87 *the same person*: i.e. herself.

87 *s.d.*: the evidence that this scene takes place 'above the backdrop' is in 90 where we discover that Jocasta has allowed Antigone to come to the edge of the upper part of the palace, and in 100 where the Slave tells Antigone to 'climb up to the top of the old cedar-wood ladder'. The model for the scene is the *teichoscopia* (view from the wall) in *Iliad* 3.121–244 in which Helen identifies for Priam the Greek heroes below them on the plain.

89–90 *your mother has given you permission*: Antigone's dependence on her mother is stressed. She will grow to maturity in the course of this terrible day.

93–6 *one of your fellow citizens . . . for what we're doing*: in Euripides' Athens it was considered inappropriate for a woman to leave the women's quarters and venture into the public view. The dramatist applies this convention to this woman from the heroic age.

101–2 *the rivers Ismenus and Dirce*: these rivers provide local colour in *Bacchae* too.

107 *Pelasgian*: one tradition made Pelasgus the first king of Argos.

109–10 *O lady Hecate, daughter of Leto*: Hecate is an underworld manifestation of Artemis. It is the latter, the goddess of virginity, who is referred to here. She is the daugher of Leto by Zeus.

115–16 *the wall, built by Amphion*: Amphion, son of Zeus and Antiope, had charmed the stones of the walls of Thebes into place with the music of the lyre which had been given to him by Hermes.

126 *Lerna*: a Greek site south of Argos. The supposed ruin of Hippomedon's house could be visited here in the day of the travelogue writer Pausanias (2.36.8), who lived in the second century CE.

135–7 *Old man, is he the one . . . Polynices' new wife?*: there had been a double marriage of Adrastus' daughters, Argeia to Polynices (see n. at 77) and Deipyle to Tydeus (cf. 417–28).

145 *Zethus' tomb*: this tomb, where Zethus was buried with his twin brother Amphion (see n. at 115–16), was a landmark at Thebes (Pausanias 9.17.4).

150 *Parthenopaeus*: the name of this sexy young man means either 'girl-face' or 'girl-boy'.

159–60 *the tomb of Niobe's seven daughters*: Niobe, wife of Amphion (see n. at at 115–16), had boasted that she had a larger family than Leto, the mother (the father was Zeus) of Apollo and Artemis. Leto's children killed all of Niobe's.

173 *Amphiaraus*: see *Suppliant Women*, n. at 158.

175–6 *O Moon . . . goddess of golden, circling light!*: the description of the moon refers to the source of the moonlight, the sun, and the implication is that the moon is at the full, a time of magic and mystery.

180–1 *There he is, working out . . . from top to bottom*: Capaneus is calculating the length of the scaling ladder he needs to bring (1173–86).

182 *O Zeus' loud-rumbling thunder*: Zeus was the weather-god, the wielder of the thunderbolt, and the punisher of sin.

185–9 *Here is the man . . . Amymone*: Mycenae is a name used interchangeably with Argos. (The cities are 6 miles apart.) The spring at Lerna (cf. n. at 126) was usually called Amymone. It was also called Trident (= Poseidon, named after his staff with three prongs at the head) because here it was that Amymone had pulled Poseidon's trident from the rock after he had rescued her from a satyr.

201 *s.d.*: the chorus are 'in plainly non-Greek costume' because they have been chosen, on the basis of their beauty, in the Asian city of Tyre to be sacred slaves at Delphi. The action of the play catches them at Thebes on the way to that sanctuary.

203 *Loxias*: see *Ion*, n. at 36.

206–7 *in the place where . . . under Parnassus' snow-girt ridges*: i.e. at Delphi. See *Ion*, n. at 6.

208 *the Ionian Sea*: the Adriatic. The women seem to have taken a circuitous route from Tyre.

211 *Zephyrus*: the west wind.

217 *of Agenor's descendants*: see n. at 5–6.

222 *the Castalian waters*: see *Ion*, n. at 95.

227–8 *the twin peaks of Dionysus*: the twin peaks are no doubt the Phaedriades (= the shining rocks) on the slopes of Mount Parnassus, which tower over Delphi. Here Dionysus, god of wine and of the liberated spirit, was second in importance only to Apollo. The 'Bacchic fire' (226) came from the torches of the ecstatic worshippers of Dionysus.

232 *the serpent's lair*: i.e. the Corycian cave on Parnassus where the Python had lived and been slain by Apollo. The first possessor of the Delphic oracle had been Earth and next had come her daughter Themis. The Python, another child of Earth, defended the shrine for his mother and sister. Apollo then slew the Python and took possession of the oracle, banishing Themis.

241 *Ares*: god of war.

248 *horned Io*: Io was seduced by Zeus, and when Zeus' wife Hera discovered this, she turned her into a white cow. As for the ancestral tradition, Io is usually associated with Argos rather than Thebes.

255 *the Erinyes*: the Furies activated by Oedipus against his sons.

258–60 *For the son . . . has justice on his side*: is the audience being tempted to give a sympathetic hearing to Polynices?

346 *Ismenus*: the Theban river (see n. at 101–2) here stands for the ritual bath which was an important part of the celebration of a marriage.

368 *the training-schools*: the centres for physical exercise and social intercourse for the young men not only of the heroic world but of Euripides' Athens too.

388–426 *What is it . . . to come here with you?*: stichomythia; see *Ion*, n. to 264–368.

391 *freedom of speech*: the Athenians prided themselves on this.

411 *a boar and a lion*: i.e. Polynices who married Argeia and Tydeus who married her sister Deipyle. See n. at 135–7. It is unclear which of the two is the boar and which the lion. The point appears to be the fierce animal imagery. Tydeus had had to leave his homeland, Aetolia, after committing homicide. Through this oracle, Apollo characteristically communicates a man's fate to him and by the communication ensures that the man brings his fate on himself (413).

422 *the son of Talaus*: Adrastus.

455–6 *You're not looking at the Gorgon's decapitated head*: the gaze of the three Gorgons, monstrous females whose heads were wreathed with snakes, turned men to stone. The hero Perseus decapitated one of them, Medusa, and used her head for this purpose.

574 *the river Inachus*: Inachus is the river of Argos.

596–624 *He is close by . . . go to hell*: stichomythia. From 603 the lines are split between the speakers. The effect is of tense, excited antagonism.

606 *the white-horsed gods* . . . : Amphion and Zethus. See nn. at 115–16 and 145.

624 *the demons brought down by your father's curse?*: cf. n. at 255.

631 *Phoebus Agyieus*: an image representing Apollo standing before the house in the street (the meaning of Agyieus). Such an image may actually be present on the stage.

636 *Polynices*: the name means 'man of much strife'. The Greek tragic dramatists, unlike their comic counterparts, could not invent appropriate names for their dramatis personae, but when a character's name had an independent meaning, they were not slow to exploit the opportunity offered them by this. Thus, for example, Sophocles makes use of the fact that the name Oedipus means 'swell-foot' (and see n. at 27 here), and Euripides in *Bacchae* of the fact that the play's victim Pentheus has a name that means 'man of sorrow'.

638–41 *Here to this land . . . the untamed heifer*: the Delphic oracle instructed Cadmus to found a city and to choose its site by following a heifer until it collapsed from exhaustion. This he did, and on the site he killed a dragon, the offspring of Ares and the god's ancient guardian of the place, with a marble rock (657ff.). Athena gave him half of its teeth to sow, and, when he did this, 'Sown Men' sprang from the ground. They then slaughtered each other. Only five survived, and together with Cadmus they built the citadel of Thebes.

649–50 *after union with Zeus his mother gave birth to Bromius*: the myth tells how Hera, jealous at Zeus' affair with the Theban princess Semele, who was now pregnant by him, persuaded her to ask him to come to her in his divine form. Zeus, who had sworn to grant any of her requests, appeared to her as the god of thunder and lightning. Thus Semele was incinerated, but the river Dirce received the baby in its waters. On Bromius, see *Ion*, n. at 216–18.

666 *the motherless goddess*: Pallas Athena was born directly from her father, Zeus.

676–8 *And you, Epaphus . . . child of Zeus*: Io was transformed by Hera into a cow as a punishment for her affair with Zeus (see n. to 248). Driven by a gadfly, she came to the Nile and regained her human form. Here she gave birth to Epaphus, who was the father of Agenor, the father of Cadmus (cf. n. at 248).

684–8 *Persephone and her loving mother Demeter . . . fire-bearing goddesses*: Demeter, goddess of fertility, is here assimilated with Earth. She and her daughter are associated with torches. When Persephone was taken off to the underworld by Hades, Demeter carried torches in her search for her; and in their cult, torches signified the insight of the initiate.

707–47 *What? I don't know . . . the other is lacking*: stichomythia.

726–8 *Night brings equality . . . while they are eating?*: the Athenians had had recent experience of both a night battle (Thucydides 7.44) and a meal interrupted by an attack (Thucydides 7.40) in their disastrous expedition to Sicily (415–413 BCE). In *Iliad* 10, Odysseus and Diomedes conduct a devastating night attack on the Trojan camp, an episode which is dramatized in [Euripides'] *Rhesus*.

746–7 *Should I choose . . . if the other is lacking*: in Homer's *Iliad*, the heroes tend to be valued through a polarity between martial prowess and sound judgement. None of them possesses these in an ideal equipoise.

751 *It would take too long to mention each of their names*: in her edition of the play (Warminster, 1988), E. Craik remarks (n. at 751), 'Eteocles' comment is surely intended by Euripides to be a reference to the long central passage in Aeschylus' *Seven against Thebes*, where the warriors are individually named and

described, whether in ironic criticism, respectful deference or literary display.'

784 *Ares*: the god of war. See n. at 638–41.

785 *Bromius*: see *Ion*, n. at 216–18. Dionysus was the god not only of wine but also of the liberated spirit.

792 *the thyrsus-goading god . . . the fawnskins*: the thyrsus (see *Ion*, n. at 216–18) was carried and the fawnskin worn by Dionysus' ecstatic worshippers.

795 *the Sown Men*: see n. at 638–41.

801–2 *O Cithaeron . . . Artemis*: for Cithaeron, see n. at 24. Artemis was the goddess of hunting; she was associated with Mount Cithaeron, and indeed with any mountain.

806–7 *the winged maiden Sphinx*: see n. at 45–6.

810 *Hades*: god of the underworld. By saying that Hades sent the Sphinx against Thebes, the Chorus simply mean that her victims were killed and went down to the realm of Hades.

822–3 *the children of heaven came to Harmonia's wedding*: the gods paid the same honour to Peleus and Thetis when they attended their wedding, another instance of a god marrying a mortal.

823–4 *the walls of Thebes . . . Amphion's lyre*: see n. at 115–16.

826–7 *in front of Ismenus . . . Dirce*: the two rivers run roughly parallel to each other and meet in the plain north of Thebes.

828–9 *our horned foremother Io bore the line of Theban kings*: see n. at 676–8. Euripides here places Epaphus' birth at Thebes, not Egypt.

832 *s.d.*: Tiresias is blind; the daughter who leads him was called Manto, a name clearly linked with *mantis*, the Greek for 'seer'.

838 *the lots*: evidently notes which the seer makes after observing the flight of birds.

841 *And young Menoeceus, Creon's son*: Menoeceus does not answer, but his presence is pointedly established so that the audience can be fully aware who it is that overhears the exchange between Tiresias and Creon.

852–4 *I got back . . . Eumolpus and his army*: Eumolpus, king of Thrace, had assisted the Eleusinians who were revolting against Erechtheus, king of Athens. Erechtheus won, but had to sacrifice one of his daughters for the city, presumably on Tiresias' advice. (Euripides dealt with this subject in a now fragmentary play, *Erechtheus*.) The events at Athens clearly find an echo in the Menoeceus subplot of *Phoenician Women*.

896–929 *Wait there, old man . . . to me and my son?*: mainly stichomythia. The divided lines at the start, a remarkable feature, express intense agitation.

919 *The city can look after itself*: we are reminded of Eteocles' shocking disavowal of his house at 624.

923 *I implore you by your knees and your venerable white hair*: see *Orestes*, n. at 290.

943 *a pure descendant on both your mother's and your father's side*: Creon was descended from Echion, one of the sown men. We do not know who his mother was. The importance of one's mother's blood was underlined for the Athenian audience by Pericles' law of 451 BCE, which restricted citizenship to those with both parents citizens. Menoeceus, not his brother Haemon, must be the victim because by his engagement to Antigone the latter has lost his pure status and embarked on the journey to full adulthood.

947 *roam free*: as animals sacred to a deity were allowed to roam untethered.

966 *no one would give his own son to be killed*: we may think of Abraham's willingness to sacrifice his son Isaac in Genesis 22. In Euripides, the parent's agonizing is liable to be made irrelevant by the victim's readiness to die, as in the cases of Polyxena in *Hecuba*, Iphigenia in *Iphigenia at Aulis*, and Menoeceus here.

977–85 *Where shall I go . . . Thank you, father*: an agitated stichomythia, with the lines for the most part divided between the speakers.

982 *Dodona*: the sanctuary of Zeus in Epirus, reputedly the oldest Greek oracle. The oracle communicated through the rustling leaves of the sacred oak or from doves sitting in it.

1019–20 *offspring of Earth and underworld Echidna*: Echidna, an earth demon, half woman, half serpent, was the daughter of Keto, in her turn daughter of Earth and Pontus. Echidna lived in the bowels of the earth. Her offspring was the Sphinx (see n. at 45–6).

1031–2 *And bloody is the god whose work this was*: which god is referred to? Apollo, Hera, Dionysus, or Ares? In his commentary on the play (Cambridge, 1994), D. J. Mastronarde (n. at 1032) comments that 'the tragic poet often prefers the ominous uncertainty of anonymity'.

1043 *the Pythian god*: i.e. Apollo, who had assumed the Python's powers when he killed him. See n. at 232.

1062 *Pallas*: i.e. Pallas Athena. She can be referred to by either name.

As a goddess of warfare and victory, she had been instrumental in Cadmus' killing of the dragon.

1081 *Theban Ares*: metonymy is here employed. Ares, the god of war, is used to stand for the spirit of martial prowess.

1100 *Teumessus*: a low rocky hill about 5 miles north-east of Thebes.

1144 *Tydeus and your son*: for Tydeus, see n. at 411. 'Your son' is Polynices.

1153 *the son of Atalanta—no Argive, but an Arcadian*: Parthenopaeus. See n. at 150.

1156–7 *Periclymenus, the son of the sea-god*: Periclymenus was the son of Neleus by a Theban woman, and therefore the grandson of Poseidon, the sea-god.

1162 *the maiden of Mount Maenalum with the fair bow*: the boyishly beautiful Parthenopaeus was the son of Atalanta, who, because her father wanted only sons, was exposed on Mount Maenalum in Arcadia in southern Greece and subsequently became a huntress there.

1175 *the sacred fire of Zeus*: Zeus was the god of lightning and thunder.

1209–16 *I should ignore . . . into the sky*: stichomythia.

1219–20 *Abhorrent as the undertaking might be . . . the rest of the army*: while one would have thought that the avoidance of general bloodshed through single combat would win approval, it is notable that the Messenger, Eteocles' attendant, expresses horrified revulsion, because the duel is between brothers.

1259 *physical strength or clever arguments*: the Messenger's absurd appeal to Jocasta to use physical strength against her sons underlines the futility of any intervention from her. The reference to clever arguments reminds us that her efforts to reason with her sons (460, 530) had achieved nothing earlier.

1272–8 *Daughter, your brother's lives . . . along with me*: the lines in this stichomythia are divided. The effect is one of extreme agitation.

1275 *Would you have me leave the girls' quarters?*: this looks back to 89.

1296 *Two wild beasts*: Craik aptly observes (n. at 1296), 'The bestial character of the brothers already insinuated (263, 411–12, 420, 455–6, 699, 1169) is now openly asserted; cf. simile 1573.' Note also the 'wild boars' simile at 1380.

1312 *Acheron*: one of the rivers of the underworld. To go across Acheron was to die.

1315 *I have just fetched him from the dragon's cliff*: Menoeceus presumably committed suicide by throwing himself down from 'the highest point of the battlements' (1009) to the dragon's cave at their foot.

1317–19 *I've come to find . . . lay out my dead son*: it was the role of the female relatives to lay out a corpse for mourning and burial.

1365 *Lady Hera*: Hera is the chief goddess of Argos—as well as, relevantly here, being the patron of marriage. Mastronarde observes (n. at 1365) that 'Polynices' invocation of the foreign goddess evokes again the disenfranchisement of the exile and the new relationships on which he has been forced to depend'.

1372 *Pallas*: see n. at 1062.

1377–8 *The Tyrrhenian trumpet*: the military trumpet was considered an Etruscan invention, and Etruscan bronzework in general was celebrated. An ancient commentator tells us that before the trumpet was invented, the signal for battle was given by throwing a lighted torch into no man's land. Hence the metaphor in 'rose like fire'.

1401 *a marble rock*: it was with such a rock that Cadmus had killed the dragon. See n. at 638–41.

1407–8 *the Thessalian trick*: presumably some feint in fencing or wrestling. Thessaly is in north-east Greece.

1436–7 *traitors to my marriage . . .!*: her brothers would have normally seen to the marriage arrangements for her.

1479 *s.d.*: nowhere else in Greek tragedy are three corpses of characters who have taken part in the play carried on to the stage at the same time. It is a powerful visual emblem of the appalling destruction wrought upon the house of Oedipus.

1485–92 *Not hiding . . . in lamentation*: Antigone has strikingly abandoned any maiden modesty. See n. at 1275.

1493 *O Polynices, how aptly were you named, it seems!*: see n. at 636.

1515–18 *What bird . . . in my wretchedness?*: Antigone no doubt has the sorrowing nightingale in mind. The story of the transformation of Procne into this bird is first told at *Odyssey* 19.518–23: 'You know how Pandareus' daughter, the tawny nightingale, perched in the dense foliage of the trees, makes her sweet music when the spring is young, and with many turns and trills pours out her full-throated song in sorrow for Itylus her beloved son, King Zethus' child, whom she mistakenly killed with her own hand' (trans. E. V. Rieu).

1524–5 *the offering of hair torn from my head*: see *Orestes*, n. at 96.

1568–9 *a suppliant eagerly offering suppliant breast*: what was described at 1428 ff. is scarcely a formal supplication (see *Orestes*, n. at 290), but emotional appeals of this kind from mother to son occur elsewhere in classical literature, e.g. at Homer, *Iliad* 22.80 and Euripides, *Orestes* 527.

1591–2 *Tiresias made it plain . . . the city would never prosper*: Creon here puts words into Tiresias' mouth.

1622 *wrap my arms around your knees in supplication*: see *Orestes*, n. at 290.

1627–33 *as for these bodies . . . burying it*: here Euripides looks back to the story dramatized in Sophocles' *Antigone* (as well as a play of his own on the subject), in which the heroine disobeys Creon's edict and attempts to bury Polynices' corpse. To cast the corpse of a traitor to his native land beyond its boundaries was normal practice. To forbid any fellow countryman to bury it, on the other hand, was not.

1646–1707 *They are Eteocles' edicts . . . the home of the god of horses*: stichomythia.

1675 *The night of my marriage will be the night I become one of the Danaids*: for the killing of their husbands by the daughters of Danaus, see *Orestes*, n. at 871–3. There is a further meaning here as well, for 'Danaids' could mean 'the men of Argos'.

1679 *I shall go into exile along with my poor father here*: the shared exile of Oedipus and Antigone is movingly dramatized in the final masterpiece of Greek tragedy, Sophocles' *Oedipus at Colonus*.

1688 *Where now is the Oedipus who solved the famous riddle?*: see n. at 45–6.

1707 *Colonus*: the main deity of this village near Athens was Poseidon, the horse-god (as well as the sea-god). Here is the ground where fate will have Oedipus fall (1687).

1736 *death in some unknown place*: Antigone is simply referring indefinitely to somewhere that is not Thebes.

SUPPLIANT WOMEN

1 *s.d.*: suppliant branches are branches tied round with wool carried to add religious authority to the suppliants' plea. The definitive summation of the process of supplication is that of John Gould in *JHS* 93 (1973), 74–103.

1 *Demeter*: the Mother Goddess of the Earth, goddess of corn. Her

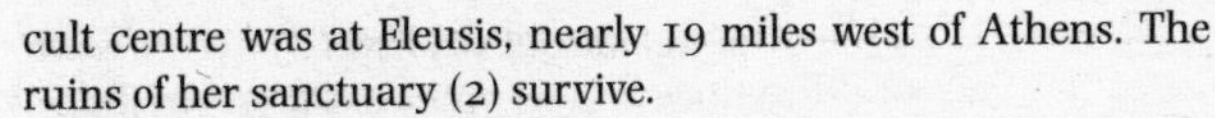

cult centre was at Eleusis, nearly 19 miles west of Athens. The ruins of her sanctuary (2) survive.

4 *Pittheus' land*: this is Troezen, located opposite Athens on the southern side of the Saronic Gulf.

5 *Loxias'*: i.e. of Apollo, god of prophecy whose greatest cult centre was at Delphi. He is also known as Phoebus. This command of his met with a successful outcome, unlike his prompting (138, 200) of the marriages of Adrastus' daughters .

11–16 *At the gates of Cadmus' city . . . Oedipus' estate*: the story is fully told in *Phoenician Women*, to which this play is a kind of sequel, though it was almost certainly written first. Oedipus ceased to be king of Thebes (Cadmus' city) when he was revealed as having killed his father and married his mother. The two sons of his incestuous union, Eteocles and Polynices, agreed to share the kingship of the city by alternating as ruler every year, but at the end of the first year, Eteocles refused to step down. In consequence, Polynices, whose name means 'man of much strife', marched on Thebes with an army led by seven Argive warriors. This army was disastrously defeated and all its leaders slain.

16–19 *Their mothers . . . their customs*: to deny corpses burial was a violation of a fundamental religious value. Homer's *Iliad* and Sophocles' *Antigone* give particularly powerful expression to this.

30–1 *this precinct, where the fruitful corn first appeared bristling above this soil*: it was at Eleusis that Demeter taught Triptolemus, a hero of the place, the skill of ploughing and handed him the first ear of corn.

32 *bound by these branches that are not bonds*: Aethra means that, while the branches certainly put pressure on the person supplicated to accede to the suppliants' plea, they do not force him or her to do so.

34 *the Maiden*: i.e. Persephone, Demeter's daughter, who shared the sanctuary at Eleusis with her.

42–6 *As elder to an elder . . . to feast on*: Chaucer's version of the story in *The Knight's Tale* describes the widows of the war-dead exclaiming thus:

> And yet now the olde Creon, weylaway!
> That lord is now of Thebes the citee,
> Fulfild of ire and of iniquitee,
> He, for despit and for his tirannye,
> To do the dede bodies vileinye
> Of alle oure lordes whiche that been yslawe,
> Hath alle the bodies on an heep ydrawe,

And wol nat suffren hem, by noon assent,
Neither to been yburied nor ybrent [burnt],
But maketh houndes ete hem in despit.

50–1 *the gashes torn by my hands in my aged flesh*: this ritualized expression of mourning indicates that the mourners, in disfiguring themselves, identify with the suffering of the dead. Solon tried to prevent the practice at Athens (Plutarch, *Solon* 21).

61 *the Ismenus*: a river of Thebes, to the east of the city.

63 *It is not the sacred rites, but necessity that brings me here*: they are dressed as mourners and, as such, could not attend the ceremonies at Eleusis. Suppliants were fined a thousand drachmas for approaching during the festival.

75 *Hades*: the god of the Greek underworld and thus of the dead.

114–62 *Theseus, glorious in victory . . . many a military commander*: stichomythia; see *Ion*, n. to 264–368. The dramatist has already made use of it in 104–9. The earlier passage shows the ready communication between mother and son, while the later one is distinctly edgy in tone. By calling Theseus 'glorious in victory', Adrastus is hinting—to Theseus and to the audience as well—at the outcome he desires. Cf. 163.

121 *heralds, sacred to Hermes*: Hermes was the god who communicated between gods and men and thus an appropriate patron for messengers.

129 *Was this your own personal decision or a decree ratified by the whole city?*: this raises the theme of the democratic monarch and is thus a precursor to 349–53.

132 *As a favour to my two sons-in-law*: compare *Phoenician Women* 408–29. For the boar and the lion (140) see *Phoenician Women*, n. at 411.

135 *You gave your daughters, Argive girls, to foreigners?*: after Pericles' racist legislation of 451 BCE, Athenian citizens were not allowed to marry foreigners. Hence, perhaps, Theseus' surprise.

142–4 *Two exiles came . . . fell to fighting there*: we discover in *Phoenician Women* (415–21) that they fought over who was going to get the bed at Adrastus' house.

148 *Tydeus was banished for killing a member of his own family*: it is uncertain which relative the Aetolian Tydeus had killed. It may have been an uncle.

155 *Did you inspect the flames of burnt offerings?*: divination could be based on the shape, strength, and smokiness of flames. See the note of C. Collard (*Supplices* (Groningen, 1975)), at 155.

158 *Amphiaraus*: famous for his integrity, Amphiaraus was both a seer and a warrior.

165 *clasp your knees*: this customary mode of supplication may have been a ritualized way of averting being kicked away with the rejection of one's plea.

173 *the mysteries of Demeter*: the annual festival of the mysteries at Eleusis attracted initiates from all over the Greek-speaking world. See n. to 63.

184 *Pelops' land*: i.e. the Peloponnese (the massive peninsula that constitutes southern Greece), named after the disreputable hero Pelops.

187 *Sparta is hard and fickle in her ways*: Collard (n. at 187) writes: 'This severe criticism of Sparta reflects perhaps not only natural feeling against Athens' enemy [in the Peloponnesian war], but also a widespread contemporary disgust with Spartan conduct (Thucydides 5.28.2).'

261–2 *Demeter with her torch*: Demeter carried a torch to search for her daughter in the underworld, whither Hades had taken her. Torches were a feature of the Eleusinian mysteries.

268 *a slave at the altars of the gods*: in ancient Athens slaves could indeed take refuge at the altars of the gods. The temple of Theseus was an especially favoured place of sanctuary for them.

277 *by your beard*: like the knees (see n. at 165), the chin was a customary part of the body for suppliants to touch, presumably a ritualized way of averting harsh *words* from the mouth of the person supplicated.

290 *Deo's sacred altar*: Deo is a poetic name for Demeter.

316–17 *the unimpressive challenge of hunting a wild boar*: like Heracles, Theseus had his labours (see 339–40), the most famous being his killing of the Minotaur. The one referred to here is his slaying of a murderous boar at Crommyon between Corinth and Megara.

352–3 *For when I freed the city and distributed the right to vote equally among the citizens*: unhistorically—but with great dramatic effectiveness—Euripides portrays Theseus as the founder of Athenian democracy. For Froma Zeitlin's view of the contrast between Athens and Thebes in Greek tragedy, see *Phoenician Women*, n. at 1 *s.d.*

358 *Creon*: the brother-in-law of Oedipus and hence the uncle of Eteocles and Polynices, Creon now rules in Thebes.

365 *horse-farming Argos*: this is Homer's description of Argos (see e.g.

Iliad 2.287). It may have become something of a poetic formula subsequently.

368 *Pelasgia*: i.e. the Peloponnese. Pelasgus was one of the traditional first kings of Peloponnesian Argos. Inachus (372) was the other.

377 *city of Pallas*: i.e. Athens, the city whose patron was the goddess Pallas Athena.

383 *Asopus*: a river in Boeotia half way between Eleusis and Thebes. For Ismenus, see n. at 61.

387 *the descendants of Erechtheus*: i.e. the Athenians, descended from the hero Erechtheus who was born from the soil of Athens. See *Ion*, n. at 9.

392 *Callichorus*: the most famous of the sacred springs of Eleusis.

396–7 *He looks to me, though I can't be certain, like a Theban herald*: presumably he can be identified as a herald from his wand of office and as a Theban from his distinctively Theban costume.

406–7 *with government following government in yearly succession*: another anachronistic reference (cf. n. at 352–3) to the operations of Athenian democracy in Euripides' day with its elective annual magistrates and council.

448–9 *when its youth is mown down and harvested like the new growth of a meadow in spring?*: is there a reference here to the story told in Herodotus (5.92) of the tyrant Thrasybulus taking Periander's messenger to a cornfield and, by continually cuttting off the taller ears, indicating to Periander how to deal with the more notable of his citizens?

490–1 *children flourish under the delighted gaze of Peace, and prosperity is her pleasure*: in the Staatliche Antikensammlungen und Glyptothek in Munich is a Roman copy of a Greek statue by Cephisodotus dating from around 375 BCE. This shows Peace holding a baby (Wealth) in her left arm. The idea behind the image is that 'Peace is the nurse of Wealth; that if nurtured by Peace, Wealth will flourish and grow—a fact of life much appreciated in basically agricultural communities' (S. Woodford, *An Introduction to Greek Art* (London, 1986), 152). The Messenger makes the point (489) that the arts will flourish too.

500 *the notorious seer*: i.e. Amphiaraus. See n. at 158.

540–1 *brave men will become cowards*: i.e. if they cannot feel confident that they will be buried if they are killed, men will be unwilling to take the risk of fighting.

562 *Pandion*: a legendary king of Athens.

566–80 *Shall I respond . . . you're still a callow youth*: confrontational stichomythia.

578–9 *Come, then . . . a serpent?*: see *Phoenician Women*, n. at 638–41.

621 *the twin-rivered city*: Thebes is situated near the two rivers Ismenus and Dirce.

628–9 *Inachus' daughter, / the heifer-girl, the foremother of our race*: Zeus had an affair with Io, a descendant of the river god Inachus (cf. n. at 645). See *Phoenician Women*, nn. to 248, 676–8.

639 *Capaneus*: one of the 'seven against Thebes'. His fate was described at 496–9.

645 *the Inachus*: the river of Argos.

651 *Electra's gate*: the south-east exit from Thebes towards Cithaeron, the great mountain near Thebes, a resonant name in Greek tragedy.

658 *natives of the ancient land of Cecrops*: Cecrops was a mythical king of Attica, the land of which Athens was the major city.

659 *Paralus*: this Athenian hero invented the warship. One of the two official Athenian triremes was called *Paralus* in his honour.

660 *Ares*: the god of war.

663 *the sacred tomb of Amphion*: see *Phoenician Women*, n. at 115–16.

680 *Phorbas*: this shadowy figure may have been Theseus' tutor and accompanied him in the battle with the Amazons.

714 *his mace from Epidaurus*: in one of his labours, Theseus killed Periphetes, the robber of Epidaurus, and took his club.

729–30 *strive to climb to the topmost rung of the ladder of success*: Collard (n. at 726–30) observes that the image 'reminds us of the Theban's sneer at Capaneus' fall from his arrogant ladder, 496–9'.

739 *when Eteocles was ready to be reconciled with us*: compare Eteocles' total unwillingness to negotiate in *Phoenician Women*, 504 ff.

754–71 *And have you brought back . . . who are my teachers*: stichomythia.

759 *Eleutherae*: a village just inside the border of Attica.

826–7 *We have raked our cheeks with our nails, / poured ashes on our heads*: for such extreme modes of lamentation, see n. at 50–1.

831 *May the flame of Zeus' fire descend upon me!*: as it had upon Capaneus. Zeus was the weather-god and he wielded the dreaded thunderbolt.

835–6 *The grim curse has left the house of Oedipus*: see n. at 11–16.

858–9 *to say what I'd like to say . . . in praise of my friends*: a funeral oration was a feature of funeral rites hallowed by long tradition. The most famous is that of Pericles, Thucydides' version of which is given in his history (2.34 ff.).

872 *Eteoclus*: Collard comments (n. at 871b–2) that Eteoclus 'is a shadowy figure'. He should not be confused with Eteocles.

913–14 *Courage is teachable*: a central theme of Plato's *Protagoras*.

925 *Oecles' noble son*: Amphiaraus: see n. at 158.

933–46 *No, I don't . . . to upset them*: stichomythia.

935 *on the grounds that his body is sacred*: 'special superstition attached to those killed by lightning, requiring their separate burial, often at the place of death, and subsequently tabooing it' (Collard, n. at 935).

958 *Artemis*: among her functions, Artemis was the goddess of childbirth.

975–6 *songs that will never find favour with golden-haired Apollo*: the god of harmonious music will take no joy in dirges.

1010 *a treasury, sacred to Zeus*: 'the pyre holds in Capaneus' body something "special" to Zeus' (Collard, n. at 1009–11), because it had been struck by his lightning.

1037 *to take on board my ship*: Iphis has come from the Peloponnese to Athens by ship, and will return by ship too.

1052–68 *What do you mean . . . I won't let you do it!*: stichomythia.

1062 *Athena's crafts*: the goddess Athena presided over spinning, weaving, and embroidery.

1114 *s.d.*: *Enter the second Chorus of SONS*: in one of the ceremonies performed in the theatre at the outset of the dramatic festival of the Dionysia, a herald would lead into the theatre the orphans whose fathers had died in war. They would be clad in full armour. The herald would then declare that these young men had been brought up to adulthood by the people, who have now clad them in armour and are sending them on their way with prayers for success. After that, they would be invited to sit in the front seats of the theatre (Aeschines, *Against Ctesiphon* 114). In a remarkable *coup de théâtre*, these orphans in the front seats now find themselves represented on stage. This is not only an arresting instance of a civic ceremony directly impinging on a play which it preceded; it also adds a powerful tragic charge, especially to the lines where the sons in the play wonder whether they will ever take up their shields to repay their father's murder (1143–4), for the orphans in the front seats are fully armed. Collard (i. 27) comments that now 'the Sons join the Chorus to complete the simulation of family mourning in all its generations'.

1131 *Mycenae*: i.e. Argos. The two cities, which are in fact about 6 miles apart, are synonymous in Greek tragedy.

1191–3 *Argos will never undertake an armed invasion of this land . . . who attempts to do so*: in Euripides' lifetime, Argos was twice in alliance with Athens (461, 420 BCE).

1197–1200 *At home you have a bronze-footed tripod . . . the Pythian altar*: a tripod was a three-footed stand on which a cauldron could be placed. It was frequently used as a dedicatory offering. For the word Pythian, see *Ion*, n. at 458.

1210 *the Isthmian crossroads*: Isthmia is by the isthmus between north and south Greece, 10 miles east of Corinth. It is beside the modern Athens–Corinth road.

1216 *Aegialeus*: the son of Adrastus.

TEXTUAL NOTES

ION

285: Reading *Φοῖβος* with Matthiae.

286: The beginning of this line is irredeemably corrupt.

303: Reading *ποίων*, as suggested by Diggle.

390: Reading *ἀλλ' οὖν ἐὰν χρὴ τοιάδ'* with Collard ap. Lee *ad loc*.

594: Reading *⟨καὐτὸς⟩ μηδὲν κοὐδένων* with Seidler.

602: Reading *αὖ λεγόντων* with Schaefer.

709: I have filled the lacuna in the text with what must be the sense without pretending to know what the original Greek might have been.

721–2: Some text is lost.

828: Reading *λαθών* with Musgrave.

844–58: Retaining these lines.

909: Reading *⟨ἐλθοῦσιν⟩ θάκους* with Page.

1035: Omitting this line, with Paley and others.

1107: Again, I have filled the lacuna with what must be the sense without pretending to know what the original Greek might have been.

1171: Reading *δαιτός* with Reiske.

1214: A line of text is missing.

1232–4: Reading *σπονδαί γ'. . . μειγνύμεναι* with Page.

1288: Reading *ἀλλ' ἐγενόμεσθα· πατρὸς ἀπουσίᾳ λέγω* with Kraus.

1360: Reading *ὅτου δέ γ'οὕνεκ'* with Badham.

1424: Reading *θαύμαθ'ὡς εὑρίσκομεν* with Collard (private communication).

1489: Reading *δὲ σᾶς ματέρος* with Paley.

1579: There is a lacuna, a line or two in extent, which would have completed the list of the four sons of Ion, and begun the list of the tribes named after them.

1614: Reading *ἀμείνονα* with Musgrave.

ORESTES

15: Retaining this line.

35: Reading *πεσών τ'* with Reiske.

424: Reading *ἔφυ θεός* with West.

491: Reading ἀσοφίας with Bothe.

545: Retaining this line.

706–7: The woolliness of these lines is perhaps not sufficient reason not to attribute them to Euripides (or to his character Menelaus).

731: Retaining this line.

813: Reading ⟨ἕνεκ'⟩ ἦλθε with Hermann.

895–7: Retaining these lines.

921: Deleting, with Di Benedetto, the comma after δέ.

964: Reading πότνα with Herwerden.

1000: Reading ⟨ποίμναις ἐν⟩ ἱπποβώτα.

1006: Deleting Ζεὺς μεταβάλλει with Biehl.

1007: Reading τῶν δ' ἔτ' with West.

1016: Reading ⟨δεῦρ'⟩ (Willink) εὐθύνων (Wecklein), and deleting Ὀρέστου with Elmsley.

1046: Reading τῇ σῇ γ' ἀδελφῇ σῶμα with West.

1106: Reading ᾔνεσ' with Willink.

1269: Reading [προσέρχεται] τίς ὅδε; τίς ὅδ' with Hermann.

1447: Reading ἄλλᾳ with West.

1467: Reading κτύπησεν κάρᾳ τε with Willink.

1484: Omitting ἐγένοντο and reading ἀλκὰν ⟨ἀλκὰν⟩ with West.

1609: Reading ψευδὴς δ' ἔφυς with West.

1610: Certain lines have been re-ordered to make better sense.

1638–42: I retain 1638 and transpose these lines to after 1663, with Willink.

PHOENICIAN WOMEN

Note: *Phoenician Women* has suffered from extensive interpolation, though scholars argue about precisely how much. I largely follow the non-conservative OCT in its deletions; this means, most drastically and apart from shorter interpolations, that I have not translated any of 1104–40 or 1221–58; however, I end the play at 1736 (omitting 1737–66) rather than 1581, although (see below) I delete some lines within this section.

26–7: Retaining these lines.

345: Deleting ὡς πρέπει with Nauck, rather than ἐν γάμοις—that is, if anything needs deleting.

361: Reading οὕτω δ' ἐτάρβησ' with MSS Rw.

504: Reading αἰθέρος with Stobaeus.

567: I retain this line.

623b, 624b, 625: I follow Mastronarde (and some of the MSS) in the distribution of these lines between Eteocles and Polynices.

646: The corrupt final word may conceal an epithet of Dirce.

697: Reading ἐμόχθησ' with Geel.

792: Reading πῶλον with some MSS.

795: Reading γένναν with some MSS.

815–17: The text is corrupt and my translation is based on elements of the text and of common sense.

868–9: I retain these two lines of the chunk bracketed in the OCT.

1388–9: I retain this couplet.

1397: Reading ἔπι instead of βίᾳ, with Paley.

1438: Reading δύσθνητον with MS M.

1514: Reading τάλαιν' οἷς ἐλελίζω with Willink, and transposing the line to after 1518.

1582–3: I omit these lines. Although I suspect the chorus would have had a couplet at this point, this cannot be it.

1596: Omitting this line with various editors.

1604–7: Omitting these lines with Hartung and others.

1634: Omitting this line, with most recent editors.

1637–8: Omitting these lines, with Dindorf and others.

1653: Reading ἔδωκε τὴν δίκην τῷ δαίμονι with Purgold.

1694: Reading παρειᾶς φιλτάτης with Schmidt.

1702: Reading ὄμμα instead of ὄνομα, with Purgold.

1734–66: I omit these lines with Mastronarde.

SUPPLIANT WOMEN

44: Reading ἀνόμους κατάπαυσαι with Campbell and Collard.

154: Reading ταῦτ' ἐκδικάζων with Hermann.

162: Retaining this line.

179: One line is missing from the text.

242: I can see no need for Kirchoff's added τ'.

249: Reading ἡμᾶς δ' ἐὰν with Nauck.

262: I have written what must be the sense of the missing line, without pretending to know quite what the Greek would have been.

271–81: I think, along with other editors, that at this point the chorus divided into two.

763: I have written what must be the sense of the missing line.

806: The Chorus's response has been lost.

844–5: Transposing these lines, with Camper, to between 859 and 860.

859: See previous note.

899–900: I delete these lines, with Dindorf and Collard.

904–8: I delete these lines rather than 902–6.

993–4: The text is too corrupt to translate.

995: Reading ⟨*εὐδοκίμων*⟩ with Diggle.

1144: Reading *τέκνοις* with Diggle.

1184: Reading *τὰ σά* with Musgrave.

A SELECTION OF OXFORD WORLD'S CLASSICS

	Classical Literary Criticism
	The First Philosophers: The Presocratics and the Sophists
	Greek Lyric Poetry
	Myths from Mesopotamia
Apollodorus	The Library of Greek Mythology
Apollonius of Rhodes	Jason and the Golden Fleece
Apuleius	The Golden Ass
Aristophanes	Birds and Other Plays
Aristotle	The Nicomachean Ethics Physics Politics
Boethius	The Consolation of Philosophy
Caesar	The Civil War The Gallic War
Catullus	The Poems of Catullus
Cicero	Defence Speeches The Nature of the Gods On Obligations Political Speeches The Republic and The Laws
Euripides	Bacchae and Other Plays Heracles and Other Plays Medea and Other Plays Orestes and Other Plays The Trojan Women and Other Plays
Herodotus	The Histories
Homer	The Iliad The Odyssey

A SELECTION OF **OXFORD WORLD'S CLASSICS**

Horace	**The Complete Odes and Epodes**
Juvenal	**The Satires**
Livy	**The Dawn of the Roman Empire** **Hannibal's War** **The Rise of Rome**
Marcus Aurelius	**The Meditations**
Ovid	**The Love Poems** **Metamorphoses**
Petronius	**The Satyricon**
Plato	**Defence of Socrates, Euthyphro, and Crito** **Gorgias** **Meno and Other Dialogues** **Phaedo** **Republic** **Selected Myths** **Symposium**
Plautus	**Four Comedies**
Plutarch	**Greek Lives** **Roman Lives** **Selected Essays and Dialogues**
Propertius	**The Poems**
Sophocles	**Antigone, Oedipus the King, and Electra**
Statius	**Thebaid**
Suetonius	**Lives of the Caesars**
Tacitus	**Agricola and Germany** **The Histories**
Virgil	**The Aeneid** **The Eclogues and Georgics**
Xenophon	**The Expedition of Cyrus**

A SELECTION OF OXFORD WORLD'S CLASSICS

THOMAS AQUINAS	**Selected Philosophical Writings**
FRANCIS BACON	**The Essays**
WALTER BAGEHOT	**The English Constitution**
GEORGE BERKELEY	**Principles of Human Knowledge** and **Three Dialogues**
EDMUND BURKE	**A Philosophical Enquiry into the Origin of Our Ideas of the Sublime and Beautiful** **Reflections on the Revolution in France**
CONFUCIUS	**The Analects**
DESCARTES	**A Discourse on the Method**
ÉMILE DURKHEIM	**The Elementary Forms of Religious Life**
FRIEDRICH ENGELS	**The Condition of the Working Class in England**
JAMES GEORGE FRAZER	**The Golden Bough**
SIGMUND FREUD	**The Interpretation of Dreams**
THOMAS HOBBES	**Human Nature** and **De Corpore Politico** **Leviathan**
DAVID HUME	**Selected Essays**
NICCOLÒ MACHIAVELLI	**The Prince**
THOMAS MALTHUS	**An Essay on the Principle of Population**
KARL MARX	**Capital** **The Communist Manifesto**
J. S. MILL	**On Liberty and Other Essays** **Principles of Political Economy** and **Chapters on Socialism**
FRIEDRICH NIETZSCHE	**Beyond Good and Evil** **The Birth of Tragedy** **On the Genealogy of Morals** **Thus Spoke Zarathustra** **Twilight of the Idols**

A SELECTION OF **OXFORD WORLD'S CLASSICS**

	Bhagavad Gita
	The Bible Authorized King James Version *With Apocrypha*
	Dhammapada
	Dharmasūtras
	The Koran
	The Pañcatantra
	The Sauptikaparvan (from the Mahabharata)
	The Tale of Sinuhe and Other Ancient Egyptian Poems
	The Qur'an
	Upaniṣads
ANSELM OF CANTERBURY	**The Major Works**
THOMAS AQUINAS	**Selected Philosophical Writings**
AUGUSTINE	**The Confessions** **On Christian Teaching**
BEDE	**The Ecclesiastical History**
HEMACANDRA	**The Lives of the Jain Elders**
KĀLIDĀSA	**The Recognition of Śakuntalā**
MANJHAN	**Madhumalati**
ŚĀNTIDEVA	**The Bodhicaryȧvatȧra**

A SELECTION OF **OXFORD WORLD'S CLASSICS**

	The Anglo-Saxon World
	Beowulf
	Lancelot of the Lake
	The Paston Letters
	Sir Gawain and the Green Knight
	Tales of the Elders of Ireland
	York Mystery Plays
GEOFFREY CHAUCER	The Canterbury Tales Troilus and Criseyde
HENRY OF HUNTINGDON	The History of the English People 1000–1154
JOCELIN OF BRAKELOND	Chronicle of the Abbey of Bury St Edmunds
GUILLAUME DE LORRIS and JEAN DE MEUN	The Romance of the Rose
WILLIAM LANGLAND	Piers Plowman
SIR THOMAS MALORY	Le Morte Darthur

A SELECTION OF OXFORD WORLD'S CLASSICS

A SELECTION OF **OXFORD WORLD'S CLASSICS**

	Travel Writing 1700–1830
	Women's Writing 1778–1838
William Beckford	Vathek
James Boswell	Life of Johnson
Frances Burney	Camilla Cecilia Evelina The Wanderer
Lord Chesterfield	Lord Chesterfield's Letters
John Cleland	Memoirs of a Woman of Pleasure
Daniel Defoe	A Journal of the Plague Year Moll Flanders Robinson Crusoe Roxana
Henry Fielding	Jonathan Wild Joseph Andrews and Shamela Tom Jones
William Godwin	Caleb Williams
Oliver Goldsmith	The Vicar of Wakefield
Mary Hays	Memoirs of Emma Courtney
Elizabeth Inchbald	A Simple Story
Samuel Johnson	The History of Rasselas The Major Works
Charlotte Lennox	The Female Quixote
Matthew Lewis	Journal of a West India Proprietor The Monk
Henry Mackenzie	The Man of Feeling

A SELECTION OF **OXFORD WORLD'S CLASSICS**

JANE AUSTEN	**Emma** **Persuasion** **Pride and Prejudice** **Sense and Sensibility**
MRS BEETON	**Book of Household Management**
ANNE BRONTË	**The Tenant of Wildfell Hall**
CHARLOTTE BRONTË	**Jane Eyre**
EMILY BRONTË	**Wuthering Heights**
WILKIE COLLINS	**The Moonstone** **The Woman in White**
JOSEPH CONRAD	**Heart of Darkness and Other Tales** **The Secret Agent**
CHARLES DARWIN	**The Origin of Species**
CHARLES DICKENS	**Bleak House** **David Copperfield** **Great Expectations** **Hard Times**
GEORGE ELIOT	**Middlemarch** **The Mill on the Floss**
ELIZABETH GASKELL	**North and South**
THOMAS HARDY	**Jude the Obscure** **Tess of the d'Urbervilles**
WALTER SCOTT	**Ivanhoe**
MARY SHELLEY	**Frankenstein**
ROBERT LOUIS STEVENSON	**Strange Case of Dr Jekyll and Mr Hyde and Other Tales**
BRAM STOKER	**Dracula**
WILLIAM MAKEPEACE THACKERAY	**Vanity Fair**
OSCAR WILDE	**The Picture of Dorian Gray**

The Oxford World's Classics Website

www.oup.com/uk/worldsclassics

- Information about new titles
- Explore the full range of Oxford World's Classics
- Links to other literary sites and the main OUP webpage
- Imaginative competitions, with bookish prizes
- Articles by editors
- Extracts from Introductions
- Special information for teachers and lecturers

www.oup.com/uk/worldsclassics

Margaret 2432100